The Man Who Made
Wall Street

Drexel University
Book Award

Presented to
Carolyn Schoen

THE MAN WHO
MADE WALL STREET

ANTHONY J. DREXEL
AND THE RISE OF MODERN FINANCE

Dan Rottenberg

PENN

University of Pennsylvania Press

PHILADELPHIA

10 9 8 7 6 5 4 3 2 1

First paperback edition 2006

Published by

University of Pennsylvania Press

Philadelphia, Pennsylvania 19104-4112

Library of Congress Cataloging-in-Publication Data

Rottenberg, Dan
    The man who made Wall Street : Anthony J. Drexel and the rise
of modern finance / by Dan Rottenberg.
        p. cm.
    ISBN-13: 978-0-8122-1966-1 (pbk. : alk. paper)
    ISBN-10: 0-8122-1966-X
    Includes bibliographical references and index.
    1. Drexel, Anthony J. (Anthony Joseph), 1826 – 1893. 2. Bankers
— United States — Biography. 3. Capitalists and financiers —
United States — Biography. 4. Bankers — Biography. I. Title.
HG2463.D66 R67   2001
332.1'092 B —dc21   2001027621

Text design by Dean Bornstein

To my mentors of years ago:

Joel Sayre, Nancy Sweeten, Digby Baltzell,
and especially Hugh Ronald

Contents

Introduction: History's Hero, Posterity's Orphan · XI

Prologue: The Day the World Changed · 1

PART I: SURVIVAL

1. The Artist as Fugitive · 9

2. The Making of a Currency Broker · 20

PART II: SUCCESS

3. "As Good a Bargain as Possible" · 33

4. "A Wild and Reckless People" · 45

PART III: STRUGGLE

5. "The Yankees Did Not Whip Us in the Field" · 59

6. The Rise of George Childs · 73

7. The Delusions of Jay Cooke · 79

PART IV: POWER

8. "A First-Class Businessman" · 91

9. Panic and Progress · 107

10. The Perils of Partnership · 120

11. Railroad Boom · 127

PART V: SALVATION

12. Reluctant Titan · 139
13. Two Social Revolutionaries · 149
14. The Burden of Conscience · 162

Epilogue: The Death and Rebirth of
the House of Drexel · 172

Appendix I: Simplified Genealogy · 185
Appendix II: Principal Characters · 186
List of Abbreviations · 192
Notes · 193
Bibliography · 233
Acknowledgments · 243
Index · 247

The blossom cannot tell what becomes of its aroma, and no man can tell what becomes of his influence.

—HENRY WARD BEECHER

The more you are talked about, the less powerful you are.

—BENJAMIN DISRAELI

Introduction:
History's Hero, Posterity's Orphan

THE SEEDS OF THIS BOOK were planted in the mid-1970s, when, in the course of reading Edwin Hoyt's 1966 history *The House of Morgan*, I encountered this sentence: "By the time his father died, Pierpont was not used to yielding to anyone, save Anthony Drexel, senior partner in Drexel, Morgan & Co."

This offhand remark puzzled me. When J. Pierpont Morgan's father died in 1890, Morgan himself was 52, respected and feared on two continents. He was said to control the fate of railroads, corporations, and governments. Strong men trembled before his blinding intellect, his brusque manner, his intimidating glare. The notion that such a titan would defer to anyone seemed inconceivable on its face. Was it possible that this mighty financier was still a junior partner in someone else's firm? Who on earth was Anthony Drexel that he could command such esteem from the world's most powerful man?

Hoyt's book provided no explanation. Nor did the dozen or so other Morgan biographies I scoured. Those that mentioned Anthony Drexel did so only in passing and seemed reluctant to explore his relationship with Morgan. More often than not their oblique references to Drexel, like Hoyt's, raised more questions than they answered.

My initial curiosity about Drexel evolved into an obsession that has consumed more than twenty years. Early in this hunt I reasoned that Drexel was a pivotal figure of modern history whose financial and moral support were largely responsible for transforming Pierpont Morgan from a bewildered underachiever into the confident overachiever who, more than any other individual, ushered America into the industrial age. The great banking house that came to be known as J. P. Morgan & Co. was in fact founded not by Morgan but by Anthony Drexel. And although the world subsequently perceived Pierpont Morgan as a one-man financial dynamo, my investigation suggested that Pierpont was in fact the most visible member of a troika consisting, in roughly equal parts, of Pierpont in New York, his father Junius Morgan in London, and Anthony Drexel in Philadelphia.

I presumed that some Morgan scholar would splash cold water on my thesis by demonstrating that Drexel wasn't as significant as I thought. But when I contacted three of the world's leading authorities on Pierpont Morgan, all readily agreed that Drexel's role in Morgan's success, not to mention global financial history, had been slighted by historians.

"Anthony Drexel was the best thing that happened to both J. P. Morgan and Junius," Morgan biographer Jean Strouse told me the first time I met her. The late New York University history professor Vincent Carosso, author of the definitive work on the Morgan banks, produced the manuscript of an extensive paper he had written—but never published—on "The House of Drexel." D. W. Wright, historian/archivist at J. P. Morgan & Co. and before that registrar and archivist of the Pierpont Morgan Library for twenty years, directed me to *his* unpublished internal manuscript on the Drexel banks, "Another Philadelphia Story." It contains this unequivocal judgment:

> The Morgan firm's involvements with government financing, foreign exchange, commercial credits, railroad reorganization, and even the first investments in Edison's electric light are all Drexel-Morgan accomplishments. History has often in retrospect been too quick to credit these activities to Pierpont Morgan alone. In fact . . . the Morgan firm would not have become what it did in the 20th Century without the Drexel partnership during the 19th Century. *More than any other American of the 19th Century, Anthony J. Drexel altered the course of American finance.* (italics mine)

These testimonials shared two characteristics: All attested to Drexel's importance, and all had been expressed privately. With a few exceptions—most notably Carosso's scholarly *The Morgans*—these views had never surfaced for public consumption.

Jean Strouse's otherwise excellent *Morgan: American Financier* is a case in point. In that book Strouse does not dispute Drexel's critical role in Morgan's career; she simply minimizes it. Her book devotes less attention to Anthony Drexel than to the writer Henry James (who never met Morgan). At one point she describes Drexel as one of "the men assigned to work with" Morgan; at another she lists Drexel among the "men of integrity and skill" with whom Morgan "was surrounding himself."

In due course I found that Drexel's mentoring exploits were not limited to Pierpont Morgan. With Anthony Drexel's patronage, Jay Cooke financed the Union cause during the Civil War; George Childs developed the *Philadelphia Public Ledger*, the first major American newspaper to achieve political independence and commercial success simultaneously; Drexel's former office boy Henry Codman Potter became Episcopal bishop of New York and launched the Cathedral of St. John the Divine, the nation's largest church; and Drexel's niece

Katharine Drexel created a revolutionary nationwide network of schools for blacks and Native Americans and ultimately achieved sainthood. These and other Drexel protégés played major roles in fostering America's emergence into the modern world.

In many of his visionary business practices Drexel was generations ahead of his time. His policy of giving annual New Year's Day pay raises or dismissals can be seen as a forerunner of modern corporate year-end evaluations. He was one of the first businessmen to offer "sweat equity" to deserving employees who could not afford to buy shares in the company. His refusal to side with relatives when he considered them mistaken anticipated the modern business practice of basing decisions on merit rather than bloodlines. In his spare time Drexel founded an innovative university that flourishes to this day.

In a sense, Drexel was a real life version of George Bailey, the fictional protagonist in Frank Capra's 1946 film It's a Wonderful Life—a self-effacing banker who touched far more lives than he or anyone else appreciated and consequently shaped his world. Capra's film fantasy rested, of course, on a flimsy thesis: the notion that Bailey's town without Bailey would have been a charnel house. In the real world, in most cases, if Bailey hadn't been on hand to rise to a crisis, someone else would have solved the problem in his place. By the same token, if Anthony Drexel hadn't awakened Pierpont Morgan, Jay Cooke, George Childs, and Katharine Drexel to their potential, perhaps someone else would have done so—or perhaps someone else would have financed American industry, funded the Union's Civil War efforts, demonstrated the commercial virtues of independent journalism, and educated blacks and native Americans.

Sidney Hook observes in The Hero in History that only a handful of historical figures—Caesar, Cromwell, Napoleon, Lenin, for example—can truly be said to have "redetermined the course of history" by their having existed. The rest merely rendered a service that someone else probably would have performed in their absence. But certainly the message of It's a Wonderful Life—that each of us influences more lives more profoundly than we realize—is valid. Anthony Drexel's life epitomized this concept.

Why, then, has Anthony Drexel been virtually ignored by historians and even by Morgan biographers?

To Wright, the J. P. Morgan & Co. historian, the explanation lies at least partly in what he calls an accident of history: "Whereas the Morgan firm's records largely survive, comparatively few of the Drexel & Co. financial records are preserved." Most historians, understandably, prefer to work from a wealth of available records rather than a scarcity, and not just for the sake of convenience: Fragmentary or incomplete records can yield false impressions. Anthony Drexel was an intensely private man who worked assiduously to avoid the limelight. He granted no interviews, kept no diaries, held no public offices and destroyed his personal papers. (His company compounded the problem in the 1950s by destroying nearly all its nineteenth-century records.) Moreover, Drexel's straitlaced life was unsullied by financial or sexual scandal, unlike, say, the lives of his more colorful Wall Street contemporaries Jay Gould and Jim Fisk.

For both these reasons, historians and biographers have taken the path of least resistance and focused their energies elsewhere. As a further consequence, Anthony Drexel appears frequently as a peripheral character in other people's stories but never receives the three-dimensional treatment that would throw him into proper—and accurate—focus. He has always been portrayed as Rosencrantz or Guildenstern to someone else's Hamlet, and his stature has suffered accordingly.

In *The House of Morgan*, for example, Ron Chernow flatly asserts, "From a personal standpoint, the Drexel-Morgan match wasn't smooth." Chernow appears to have based this erroneous conclusion on a single piece of evidence: the banker Joseph Seligman's description of Pierpont Morgan as "a rough, uncouth fellow, continually quarreling with Drexel in the office." Apparently Chernow was unaware that the "Drexel" to whom Seligman referred was not Anthony (whom Morgan revered) but Anthony's younger brother Joseph (whom Morgan despised). Presumably Chernow failed to investigate this point adequately because, after all, Chernow's first priority was not Drexel but Morgan. In this manner are errors concerning the Guildensterns of history repeated and compounded.

But posterity's neglect of Anthony Drexel, I think, reflects deeper and more inherent flaws in the process by which history and biography are pursued and promulgated. Biographers inevitably become, at least subconsciously, advocates for their subjects, if only to justify their efforts and promote their work. Moreover, some of society's most important activities—banking and finance, for example—tend to be complicated and prosaic to everyone but their practitioners. Even such a celebrated financier as Pierpont Morgan did not become a salable commodity for biographers until the 1940s. Any subtle nuancing of Morgan's Olympian image—any suggestion that the credit for Morgan's achievements should be shared with someone else—runs the risk of confusing and therefore alienating a reading public (and even an academic community) whose attention span for financial history is tenuous to begin with.

Likewise, any suggestion that a leading mover and shaker from a world-beating masculine city like New York may have actually looked up to an allegedly stodgy and effete place like Philadelphia is likely to confuse the reading public even further. Nathaniel Burt, in *The Perennial Philadelphians*, was on to something when he referred to the Drexel-Morgan alliance as "this subservience of New York to Philadelphia" which "has been, it would seem, easily forgotten by all New Yorkers and biographers of the great J. P."

One other biographical convention has worked against Anthony Drexel, especially in biographies of Pierpont Morgan. Most biographies typically focus on the manner in which characteristics are transmitted from parents to children—or, conversely, the manner in which children reject or cast off their parents' traits. Parental influence is presumed to be critical to the subject's ultimate development and success or notoriety. Certainly a parent's blessing or curse is vital in determining a child's future direction, but the blessing of an outside patron or mentor—uncluttered by familial or Freudian issues—is equally essential. Anne Sullivan, not Helen Keller's parents, was Keller's "miracle worker." Junius Morgan was unable to endow his son Pierpont with self-confidence—but Anthony Drexel did. Indeed, Anthony Drexel bolstered Pierpont Morgan's confidence in much the same way that, a generation earlier, London banker George Peabody had reinforced Junius Morgan's confidence. Yet most Morgan scholarship to date, like most biographical scholarship, has assumed that wisdom and ability are primarily acquired from parents. A patron like Drexel disturbs this thesis and so is most conveniently downplayed, if not ignored.

This book seeks to correct some of these injustices. It seeks to rescue an important historical figure from obscurity. It attempts the paradoxical challenge of bestowing credit upon a man who instinctively recoiled from taking credit. It seeks to explain to twenty-first-century audiences the complexities of nineteenth-century finance in plain English and with minimal jargon. Above all, it addresses two fascinating questions. How could an honest man triumph against Wall Street's sharks in the age of the robber barons? And how could such an influential figure have eluded public attention, both during his lifetime and after it?

By extension, this second issue raises another intriguing question. How many other significant figures, past and present, have escaped public attention even for Andy Warhol's allotted fifteen minutes of fame?

Unlike that of most biographers, my research began not with Anthony Drexel's papers—since most historians had already concluded that no such papers existed—but with the conviction that his career merited investigation. I tried to reconstruct his persona through the papers of others who had dealt with him. This task involved endless hours scouring the preserved correspondence of Pierpont Morgan, Junius Morgan, George Childs, Jay Cooke, Katharine Drexel, and others in archives, libraries, banks, investment houses, and cardboard storage boxes in Philadelphia, New York, London, and elsewhere. I tried to immerse myself not only in Anthony Drexel but in his profession, his community, his family, his friends and rivals, his church, and the age in which he functioned.

The results confirm what the best historians know instinctively: that there is always more material out there than we think, if we're willing to search for it. All told, I found roughly 150 letters and cables from Anthony Drexel's own hand —no vast haul for twenty-three years' work, but far more than had been thought to exist.

The picture of Anthony Drexel that emerges from this research, while clearer than anything previously assembled, may nevertheless be skewed by the limitations of the available material. All the Drexel letters I found were written during the last twenty-four years of his life—the earliest is dated 1869, when he was already forty-two—so I have little first-hand sense of what Drexel was like as a young man. I found extensive letters from Drexel to his nieces but none to his children, which doesn't necessarily mean that he cared more for his nieces than for his children (although I have reason to believe that was the case). Historians tend to emphasize that which is documented, but Anthony Drexel's most important relationships—with his family, with Pierpont Morgan, and with his best friend George Childs—were mostly verbal and so have barely survived on paper. His transatlantic correspondence with Junius Morgan, on the other hand, survives in abundance and testifies to the closeness of that relationship.

Because this is the first biography of Anthony Drexel, I have chosen in some cases to quote at length from the long buried manuscripts I have unearthed. If we cannot hear Anthony Drexel's voice speaking directly to us, these excerpts strike me as the next best thing. Similarly, my notes provide not merely citations but, wherever possible, discussions as to how I reached my conclusions when the evidence conflicted (as historical evidence often does). My purpose has been not merely to tell a fascinating story and stimulate interest in my subject, but to provide future researchers with the tools to pick up where my efforts have left off.

Readers may criticize me for raising the question of who outranked whom within the Drexel-Morgan troika, and for seizing upon any evidence I found that the two Morgans deferred to Drexel. Throughout their long relationship, the Morgans and Drexel themselves never raised this question, so it is perhaps unseemly for me to do so now. Indeed, the success of their relationship stems from the remarkable personal chemistry among the three men, which rendered any hierarchical structure superfluous. In my defense I can only point out that setting the historical record straight necessarily involves stressing Drexel's importance to the Morgans, since previous works on the subject have largely overlooked his role.

Anthony Drexel exemplified the old adage that there is no limit to what a man can accomplish if he doesn't mind who gets the credit. His great success stemmed from his willingness—his eagerness, even—to let the Morgans and others take full credit for his contributions. Presumably his approach to his life and work offers valuable lessons for the rest of us. For that reason I am exposing Drexel's life to public scrutiny over what would surely be his strenuous objections. What Arthur Miller said of Willy Loman applies even more appropriately to Anthony Drexel: Attention must be paid.

D. R.

Prologue: The Day the World Changed

NOBODY NOTICED J. PIERPONT Morgan as he boarded the five o'clock ferry at the foot of Liberty Street. His name and his face, with its inflamed and bulbous nose, were not yet famous. On this eighth day of March in 1871 he was simply a preoccupied young banker swept up among a Wednesday afternoon crowd of New Yorkers sampling the transportation wonder of the age: the Pennsylvania Railroad's new connection to Philadelphia.

This greatest of American corporations had invaded New York just four years earlier boasting of a system so extensive and comfortable "that travel has been changed from tedious labor to pleasant recreation." Any passenger on its lines, the railroad claimed with only slight exaggeration, "can procure a ticket which will carry him almost anywhere; can have his baggage called for and checked at his home; can provide for a comfortable carriage to be in readiness at his door when the time for departure arrives; and can arrange the details of personal comfort for his journey to the extent of a berth, a state-room or a parlor car, as his taste or inclination may require."

After a day's work, Pierpont Morgan could emerge from his office at 53 Exchange Place and arrive within minutes at the Pennsylvania's ferry slip, just a few blocks from Manhattan's financial district. From here a steam ferry would carry Morgan and his fellow passengers across the Hudson to the railroad's immense Jersey City depot, bustling with ticket offices, waiting rooms, restaurants, and twelve tracks headed for points north, south, and west.

Once they boarded the Philadelphia train, no further transfer would be necessary. The Pennsylvania's Connecting Railroad, built four years earlier across Philadelphia, now linked the Pennsylvania's New Jersey Division with its Main Line to the west. As a result, a traveler could relax in upholstered comfort until his train arrived at the Pennsylvania's seven-year-old depot in West Philadelphia, where Morgan's host Anthony J. Drexel awaited him, just a few minutes' carriage ride from Drexel's own home.

Less than ten years earlier this same journey between America's two largest cities had required two ferries—one across the Hudson and a second across the

Delaware from Camden to Philadelphia. New Yorkers and Philadelphians still in their prime could recall a time when travelers from New York took a steamboat for twenty-seven miles to South Amboy, New Jersey, and proceeded from there by horse-drawn rail car; and *their* elders could still remember when the trip required twenty-two hours, by steamboat and stagecoach, with an overnight stop at New Brunswick. Yet tonight Pierpont Morgan would dine at Anthony Drexel's mansion in West Philadelphia barely three and a half hours after boarding the ferry from lower Manhattan. As Drexel explained in his invitation, Morgan could return to New York as early as 7:30 the following morning on a train arriving at 10:45, or take a 9:45 train arriving at 1 P.M. That way, Drexel wrote, "We would then have ample time to compare views without your losing any business time."

Drexel himself seemed as accommodating as the railroad. "Any day you will telegraph or write to me which train you will leave by," the great banker had wired Morgan four days earlier, "I will be on hand to meet you."

Yet Pierpont Morgan probably felt neither pleased nor reassured by these arrangements. More likely he felt bewildered. He and Anthony Drexel were strangers to each other, and Drexel's invitation, while unfailingly polite, contained not one word to explain its purpose. "Some time since I received a communication from your father," Drexel had written in his first correspondence six days earlier, "the nature of which and my reply thereto he has no doubt written to you about." But in fact Morgan's father, the London banker Junius S. Morgan, had provided no explanation to his son whatsoever.

"I have had a visit from Mr. A. J. Drexel, of Drexel & Co., Philadelphia," Junius had written to Pierpont in January. "It is possible he may want to see you about a certain matter, and if he does I hope you will go to see him." That was all Junius Morgan had said. Nor had he mentioned the subject again.

Pierpont Morgan doubtless knew that Drexel, at age forty-four, had built a family currency brokerage into an influential private bank of great reputed wealth, with branches in New York and Paris. But at this stage Morgan had reason to doubt the power of human institutions, even impressive ones like the Drexel bank and the Pennsylvania Railroad. At the age of thirty-three the foundations of Morgan's life—his health and his business—seemed to be crumbling.

His banking partnership was about to expire and was unlikely to be renewed. Wall Street, where Morgan earned his living, was a noisy racket of grasping speculators, pushy foreigners, and clattering tickertapes that mocked his need for order and control. Instead of being esteemed as a descendant of Yankee merchant princes, he was widely perceived, as a confidential report by R. G. Dun's credit agency had put it, as "considered of excellent char., extra ability, shrewd, quick of perception, but oftentimes close & sometimes erratic in minor details which with his peculiar brusqueness of manner has made him & his house unpopular with many."

Morgan himself had made several hundred thousand dollars as a gold speculator during the Civil War, but in his youthful impetuousness he had been stained with scandal just like the profiteers he despised. He was plagued by severe headaches, perpetual fatigue, insomnia, and fainting spells, as well as skin eruptions that inflamed his face and enlarged his nose. By mail from London, Morgan's domineering father regularly lectured him about everything from his lapses of character to his irregular bowel movements. Morgan had no further need for money—he was earning $50,000 a year at a time when 80 percent of American families earned less than $500—and no desire to continue in business, and he had said as much in letters to his father. Instead he vaguely proposed to settle down to live like an English squire, perhaps raising prize dogs or a herd of pedigreed cattle.

Yet Pierpont Morgan also knew that at this critical moment his father in London was in trouble and might need his help. Six months earlier Junius had underwritten a risky bond issue to lend the infant French Republic 250 million francs—50 million dollars—with which to raise an army and govern the country while the Republic fought to end the Prussian army's siege of Paris. But in January Paris had capitulated to the Prussians, and now the Parisians were about to revolt against the French Republic itself. If Junius Morgan hoped to dispose of his unsold bonds and salvage his reputation among investors, the French Republic must be restored. That would require more capital than the Morgans alone could raise. Junius needed an ally with resources, experience, and international connections. He also needed a mentor to keep an eye on Pierpont. That was why the unwitting Pierpont had been dispatched to meet Anthony Drexel.

But who was Anthony Drexel? This stranger to Morgan was a familiar figure to ordinary Philadelphians, although few people knew him intimately. On any fair morning, businessmen on Chestnut Street were said to set their clocks by the hour when Anthony Drexel strode past en route from his West Philadelphia mansion to his office in Third Street, in lock step with his closest friend, the newspaper publisher George W. Childs. With his face aglow from his three-mile walk, Drexel politely acknowledged greetings left and right until he finally disappeared beneath the modest inscription "Drexel & Co., Bankers" above his office door.

Or Philadelphians would see him on fall afternoons, mounted on a bay horse, riding not with an equestrian's grace but with the loose rein and careless ease of a man simply enjoying the season's changing colors. At the opera he was conspicuous for the simplicity of his clothes, the absence of flowers in his lapel, his unwillingness to burst his gloves in frantic applause for favored prima donnas, and for his earnest and unaffected attention to the music. In middle life he was a bald, stout man of medium height, with ruddy complexion, a handsome nose with delicately chiseled nostrils, a kindly but firm mouth shaded by a heavy brown moustache, and a decidedly double chin. His manner and the rigid lines of his mouth seemed grave, but one observer saw something very different in his keen, dark, expressive eyes: the geniality of Robin Hood's merry friar.

Pierpont Morgan may have been dimly aware of Anthony Drexel's reputation as a decent man who had somehow managed to thrive among Wall Street's sharks. He probably knew that Drexel was a friend of President Grant as well as one of the few businessmen Grant was said to trust implicitly. Good things seemed to happen to people who crossed Tony Drexel's path. With Drexel's support, an obscure banker named Jay Cooke had become the nation's financial savior during the Civil War. A Dutch immigrant neighbor of Drexel's youth, John H. Harjes, was now managing the Drexel family's branch bank in Paris. Drexel's closest friend, George W. Childs, had evolved from a penniless clerk into the celebrated proprietor of one of America's most respected newspapers, the *Philadelphia Public Ledger*. Drexel's former office boy, Henry Potter, had become a prominent Episcopal clergyman in New York.

It could not have occurred to Morgan at this low point in his life that Anthony Drexel was about to engineer an even more dramatic transformation within Pierpont Morgan himself. Morgan was about to meet the first businessman, other than his father, whom he could admire and respect, and the chemistry generated by that relationship would reshape the future of international finance.

Within three years of this night Morgan would be unable to travel anywhere without influencing stock and bond prices. Instead of retiring to a life of books, art collecting, and grand tours of Europe, over the next forty years Morgan would play a major role in stabilizing the chaotic U.S. economy. He would build and expand the great railroads, create the world's first modern corporations, and impose order upon the market's destructive forces. For better or worse, from this moment Morgan's name would become synonymous with America's transformation from a rural agricultural society into a modern industrial state. Yet a century later Anthony Drexel would remain as distant and unknown to most Americans as he seemed to Morgan this evening on the train to Philadelphia.

That conundrum was no accident. As Morgan would come to discover, Anthony Drexel was a rich and powerful man who seemed to actively avoid fame, fortune, and power, and to seek instead the obscurity and serenity that had eluded his father. What Anthony Drexel did not shrink from was the future. Drexel had witnessed his father's struggles with the old pastoral world now receding into pleasant memory, and so he felt no qualms about discarding that world for the new and unknown world to come. That was why Anthony Drexel was waiting tonight for Pierpont Morgan at the West Philadelphia depot. Anthony Drexel was about to change Pierpont Morgan, and Morgan was about to change the world.

PART I

SURVIVAL

CHAPTER ONE

The Artist as Fugitive

SIXTY-ONE YEARS BEFORE Pierpont Morgan's appointment with Anthony Drexel, an Austrian youth awaited a far more frightening nighttime rendezvous along a desolate bank of the Rhine. It was the ninth of August in 1809, and the apprehensive young man was a painter's apprentice named Francis Martin Drexel who would one day become Anthony Drexel's father.

Francis had been born just a few miles from this spot seventeen years earlier, on Easter Sunday 1792. Dornbirn, his birthplace, was a bucolic Austrian town of some five thousand souls nestled in a fertile valley surrounded by the Bregenzer Forest. From the snow-capped Apenzell Mountains above their town the burghers of Dornbirn could easily see the Rhine as it cut through their valley and flowed into Lake Constance, but otherwise they were effectively insulated from the outside world. In this picturesque and self-contained western end of the Tyrol, Francis M. Drexel's solid, simple, devoutly Catholic ancestors had worked the soil at least as far back as the early seventeenth century and possibly for centuries before that.

His father, Francis Joseph Drexel, was the first Drexel to leave the land, becoming one of Dornbirn's most prosperous merchants. In the process Francis Joseph inevitably developed the family's first connections across the nearby national borders of Switzerland, Bavaria, and Liechtenstein. This experience stimulated his greater ambitions for Francis Martin, the elder son among his three children. Old Francis resolved to give his son a thorough grounding in languages, which the lad could use to help expand his father's trading business.

This plan suffered from a single (albeit not insurmountable) flaw. By forsaking farming in order to follow his inclination for trade, old Francis had introduced, however subliminally, the notion of free choice into a family that had previously assumed that its fate was predetermined. But young Francis, whose future the father now proposed to mold in his own image, felt no interest in either farming or his father's business; *his* natural inclination, he had sensed from his earliest years, favored painting.

Nevertheless, an eleven-year-old boy was in no position to question his father. So late in 1803 Francis Martin Drexel was sent to study languages at the celebrated school of the Convent della Madonna at Saronno, near Milan, some two hundred miles away. He thus became the first member of his family to venture for any lengthy period beyond the tranquil valleys of the western Tyrol.

Young Francis remained at the convent for thirteen months, learning to speak Italian like a native and picking up some French as well. His father next intended him to continue his studies in France. But at this point the outside world intruded upon the inhabitants of the Tyrol. Napoleon's invasion of Austria in 1805 destroyed lives and property, disrupted trade, and altered commercial regulations, causing the failure of the elder Drexel's business partnership. By the end of 1805 the Tyrol had been ceded to the Napoleonic state of Bavaria, young Francis was back home, and his father was now so impoverished that he had no choice but to abandon his plans for his son's education and let the boy follow his own desires. On the first of January 1806, when he was not yet fourteen, young Francis was apprenticed to a painter in the village of Wohlfurt, five miles north of Dornbirn.

Here he stayed for three and a half years and might have remained for the rest of his life but for a second and far graver crisis. Goaded by the tyranny and oppressive taxation of the occupying French and Bavarians, the Tyrolese mountaineers revolted in 1809. That April, led by a patriotic innkeeper named Andreas Hofer, these remarkable peasants-turned-warriors overwhelmed a Bavarian army at Sterzing; in early May they took Innsbruck, the provincial capital; and on May 29 they forced Napoleon's troops to withdraw from Hohenems, just eight miles from the Drexel home in Dornbirn.

Even after the French and Austrian armies signed an armistice in July, following the French victory in the battle of Wagram, the Tyrolese under Hofer refused to recognize the truce and continued to fight. The elder Francis Drexel appears to have been an officer among these insurgents, and young Francis may have joined the uprising as well. (For the rest of his life young Francis carried with him a watercolor of Hofer and a Tyrolese pewter coin minted under Hofer's short-lived government, both of which suggest his devotion to the Tyrolese cause.)

The revolt lasted into December 1809, with Hofer slipping past the enemy and keeping resistance alive until he fell into French hands and was executed in Mantua, Italy, in February 1810. But in the province of Vorarlberg, where the Drexels lived, the uprising ended abruptly months earlier, on the fourth of August, when a French army struck through the valley, attacked the local guerrilla bands from the rear and cut them off from the rest of the Tyrol, forcing them to surrender without a battle.

Almost immediately, the French announced the price they would exact from the Vorarlbergers: All able-bodied men and boys from sixteen to forty-five would be liable for service in Napoleon's regiments, possibly to fight against their own fellow Austrians. The elder Francis Drexel was forty-seven and thus exempt from this draft, but his son was seventeen. The father quickly made a hard decision: His son would be better off adrift and alone among strangers in the outside world than as cannon fodder in Napoleon's army. Perhaps the boy would find a living across the Rhine in neutral Switzerland; perhaps he would wind up elsewhere. There simply was no time to plan anything but his son's immediate escape.

Thus on the morning of August 9, 1809, barely four days after Vorarlberg capitulated to the French, the well-connected Drexel father made arrangements with a Swiss ferryman to conduct his son across the Rhine. That night at six o'-clock, father and son, along with another draft-prone neighbor named Caspar Thurnher, set out from Dornbirn for Lustenau, an Austrian village on the Rhine some five miles to the west. Here, as the elder Drexel had prearranged, they met the ferryman. At ten o'clock, on a night young Francis later called, in his awkward English, "as dark as there probably any ever had been," he separated from his father. They would not meet again for more than two years, and only once more after that for the rest of both men's lives.

Because the Rhine was guarded by the French on the east side and by the Swiss on the west, the ferryman crossed at the river's most dangerous (and therefore least guarded) point. Their boat reached the opposite shore only after what Francis later described in his memoirs as "great toil." Here the ferryman explained to the two young men how and where to proceed to avoid the guard posts, and then left them on their own.

For three quarters of an hour young Francis and Thurnher waded through marshes, ditches, and bushes. When they finally spotted a light in the distance they resolved to head toward it. A half hour's walk brought them, at midnight, to the village of Diepoldsau. It was Saturday night, the entire village was asleep, and that single light had been left burning by the inhabitants, in keeping with Catholic tradition, for the sake of departed souls. After knocking on several doors, the two fugitives finally roused one household. Thurnher concocted a long tale as to how they had come from another town in Switzerland, lost their way, and now needed directions to a public house. But the ruse failed almost immediately: The family, it turned out, knew Drexel's father and noticed how

Francis resembled him. Nevertheless, they directed the two fugitives to a public house and wished them well.

The next day the two friends parted—Thurnher to seek work, Drexel to find the village priest, who was another acquaintance of his father. Francis stayed with the priest in Diepoldsau for the next five nights before setting out to seek work. His father had given him letters of introduction to a man in Altstatten, but for some unexplained reason Francis passed through that town without presenting his papers. Instead he continued some fifteen miles southwest to Appenzell, where he was advised to look for work in Trogen, some fifteen miles north and just a few miles from Altstatten whence he had come. Here he found his first job: assisting a house painter named John Meyer for six weeks. His compensation was board plus the equivalent of forty American cents per week.

Francis Drexel's first week on his own established his pattern for the next five years: The former art student would become a fugitive, wandering through Switzerland, France, and Italy, living by his wits and his impulses, always poor, often penniless, sometimes in rags, repeatedly suffering for his naïve faith in his fellow man. Yet his later memoir of these travels suggests that his loneliness and desperation during those years were transcended by his intoxication with a life of freedom, adventure, and intensity. Francis was experiencing first hand what Mary Wollstonecraft had observed less than thirty years earlier: "Nothing, I am sure, calls forth the faculties so much as the being obliged to struggle with the world."

His presumed (if unspoken) goal was to survive the Napoleonic wars until he could return home to Dornbirn. But at some point his fascination with the novelty of his vagabond life seems to have become an end in itself. However terrifying the next five years may have been, for the rest of his life Francis Martin Drexel would repeatedly seek out risk and reject security, often when there seemed no logical reason to do so.

By October he was on his way across the Splügen Pass into Italy, apparently intending to return to the neighborhood of the convent he had attended as an eleven-year-old. The fact that he was once again within Napoleon's jurisdiction does not seem to have occurred to him. In Chiavenna, just over the border from Switzerland, he found temporary work painting two coaches, which took him six weeks. From there he proceeded to Milan, hoping he might be admitted to the Academy of Fine Arts, but in that city he found neither a vacancy nor work of any kind. At Saronno, however, he was warmly received by the Morandi family, whom he had come to know as a schoolboy at the convent. They urged him to stay with them at least through the winter, but he refused. "I had too much bashfulness and honor to accept the offer," he explained in his memoirs. So with a cane in his hand and all his personal effects in a bundle covered with oil cloth on his back, Francis tramped on foot back across the Splügen and into Switzerland amid the December snows.

Near the Swiss town of Chur he fell in with two other pedestrians: one a boy of about fifteen, the other a man of about thirty who said he had just been discharged after eight years' service in a Swiss regiment allied with the French and was now on his way home to Glarus, about thirty miles to the northwest. Amid rain and snow they proceeded together to Wallenstadt, by Lake Wallensee, where they found a fair in progress and the inns so full that the three travelers had to share a single bed. Francis slept like a log and was thunderstruck to discover upon awakening the next morning that all his money was gone.

"My father, at parting, had advised me always to put my money in my vestcoat and that under my bed pillow," he noted in his memoirs, "that by those means I might not get robbed without at least awaking; which advice I punctually always followed." But on this night he had slept so soundly that the precaution had been useless.

The room contained three other beds, each of which slept two men. Francis was one of the first up and immediately announced his loss. His soldier companion helped him strip the beds in search, but they found nothing. Francis was convinced that the soldier had the money in his pocket and accused him on the spot. He also complained to the landlord, who replied that he did indeed have such money as Francis described but asked if Francis had marked the coins to prove that they belonged to him. Lacking such proof, Francis never saw another penny. It was a vivid lesson in the importance of portable credit—the challenge he would confront as a banker more than a quarter-century later.

Francis now found himself utterly without money or friends, "a hopeless stranger" in a strange country, with no prospect of work and with winter fast approaching. Near the lakeside, overcome by his situation, he burst into tears. A woman who observed his distress comforted him and gave him half her wine in exchange for his help in carrying her bundles. She also gave him a valuable piece of advice: If he boarded the lake boat without mentioning his poverty, the boat would take him the length of the lake—fifteen miles west—at no cost, because the fare would not be collected until the passengers got off. Sure enough, when Francis disembarked at Weesen and payment was demanded, he told the collector that he had no money and was let go with no more penalty than a severe reprimand.

On this boat his luck took a turn for the better: He met a twenty-eight-year-old merchant named Herburger who had served with Francis's father in the Tyrolese revolt and, like Francis, had fled the Tyrol to avoid the French draft. Herburger treated Francis to a square meal and continued to pay his expenses for the next three days until they reached Einsiedeln, a Swiss monastery famous as the site of miracles. Here they parted company, Drexel heading for Luzern some thirty miles away to seek work. On Herburger's advice, he followed the custom of German journeymen by going from house to house begging for food and shelter, which sustained him until he reached Luzern.

In Luzern he finally found work—apparently as a house painter—but no end to his troubles. The pay was equivalent to only thirty-two cents a week (plus his board), and his boarding-house companions enticed him into gambling with them at cards, with the result that "I generally lost my wages one to two weeks before I had earned them." In practical terms, this meant that in the depths of an Alpine winter Francis had no money to buy stockings and had to bind rags around his feet.

By Easter of 1810 he had resolved to turn over a new leaf. He asked his employer for a pay raise and, to his astonishment, had his wages doubled. This increase enabled him to find new lodging, repair his clothes, and put some money aside. "I from henceforth became very economical," he wrote later. Yet in Luzern he became restless again. Hoping to improve his fortune, he left—on foot, as usual—in late July for Basel. After a sleepless night in a village inn at Durnen, where he found bloodstains on the sheets and all over the floor of his room, he arose early, slept for several hours in a field, and reached Basel that afternoon. Here he found work with one Peter Biermann for two French crowns a week—his highest wages yet—until the end of October, when he was laid off with a promise of more work the following spring.

Consistent with his restless nature, Francis did not hang around Basel. In Biel, forty miles south, he was hired to paint coaches for the local postmaster. But he was outraged to find himself paid the equivalent of only eighty cents a week to do virtually all the work, while the foreman who hired him—a German from Hamburg named Ludwig Krone—received $10 for doing virtually nothing but took all the credit. "Without me," Francis later wrote indignantly, "he would absolutely not have been able to finish what he began."

Of this and other apparent wrongs suffered by Francis during his travels, of course, we have only his side of the story to go on. It is possible, for example, that the foreman shouldered other responsibilities of which the naïve Francis was unaware. And it is certainly likely that Francis's expectations of his fellow men were hopelessly unrealistic. But in any case Francis in this period was clearly developing strongly held opinions and a keen sensitivity to injustice—real or perceived.

He was less successful in his choice of companions and in his ability to protect himself from swindlers. Notwithstanding his resentments against his foreman Krone or his gratitude for steady employment through the winter, in March 1811 Francis decided to leave with Krone and head for Paris. After passing through Besançon, Dôle, and Dijon, they encountered what more sophisticated travelers would recognize as a classic scam. While they walked along the canal running northward toward Auxerre, they were joined by a distinguished-looking French gentleman who struck up a conversation with them. As they conversed they were passed by an oddly dressed man who, after questioning by the Frenchman, explained that he was a Spanish officer recently imprisoned in Dijon. The Spaniard said he had just been taught to play cards the night before and offered to sell them a deck he had been given. When the Frenchman asked him to demonstrate, the Spaniard sat down by the roadside, using his hat as a table and setting up a guess-the-card game, clearly a nineteenth-century variation of three-card monte.

"The Frenchman immediately pulled out his watch against a French guinea that he would guess it, and won the guinea," Francis later related. "So easy seemed to be gain here, and apparently so plain, that the Frenchman, my companion, and myself were disputing who should play first." With feigned reluctance, the Frenchman deferred to Krone, who in a matter of five minutes lost every penny he had—eighteen guineas—then his watch, and finally his gold seals. Drexel, finally realizing what was afoot, declined to play further and urged Krone to join him in attacking the two swindlers, but "his courage failed him, he was stupefied, overcome."

Although Francis had apparently lost nothing to the swindlers, he now felt responsible for his impoverished companion. He assured Krone that the two of them were committed to each other and lent Krone three guineas—and Krone, thus rescued from poverty, promptly resolved to walk no more but to proceed toward Paris by coach. "I had much against my will to follow suit or run the chance to see my companion no more," Francis recalled. Given the dubious value of Krone's companionship—at least as Francis described it—the passage offers poignant insight into young Drexel's loneliness and his desperation to build lasting relationships.

They reached Paris in April 1811 on a large packet on the River Seine and found work in the Faubourg St. Antoine. Francis appears to have arrived with every intention of remaining; he visited the principal sights and even saw

Napoleon at a distance. But after three weeks his work ended, and after five weeks he had tired of the City of Light and was on his way back to Switzerland. Even Francis, in retrospect, acknowledged this decision as inexplicable: "I got (unfortunately) tired of Paris (at which place I ought to have stayed)," he wrote some twenty years later.

In May he was back in Basel, but lack of work there drove him to Mulhouse in Alsace, where he stayed three weeks painting coaches. But Mulhouse didn't suit him either, so he returned to Basel and found work with his old boss Biermann. Here he was placed in charge of thirteen journeymen and paid the very high wage of four French crowns a week, the most he had ever received. At the age of nineteen, Francis for the first time had enough money to live comfortably, and he even indulged in the luxury of fine clothes. But again this situation was too good to last. His fellow workmen, jealous of his success, conspired against him and made his life so disagreeable that after about six months Francis left Basel again on yet another risky venture: a visit to his parents at their home in Dornbirn.

Near the end of January 1812 Francis set out for Austria in his best clothes, with money in his pocket. Proceeding across the northern edge of Switzerland, with a brief foray into Bavaria, he reached Dornbirn after an absence of two and a half years. As he had planned, he arrived during the local carnival, but he chose not to appear until nighttime—a wise precaution, as he quickly discovered. Napoleon had just begun to recruit a huge army for his Russian campaign. To avoid exposing himself, Francis went first to the house of an uncle named Luger, who advised him that a conscription was expected soon. Luger sent for Francis's sister, and in the darkness she escorted him home, where she had left her fiancée. According to Francis, his sister entered the house first and brought out his mother, who gave him a warm embrace. Then his sister removed the candle and, in the darkness, introduced her lover to Francis, calling Francis "a friend of hers from some miles off."

Learning that his father, at that moment, was attending a masked ball at the local hotel, Francis proceeded there with his sister, both of them covering their faces with black handkerchiefs. No one recognized Francis, although from his size and fashionable dress many guests thought him to be the governor, "for which my sister got rather wrongfully suspected by bad tongues and equal base minds, and furnished such persons talk for sometime afterwards."

The next morning, while Francis lurked secretly in his parents' house, an order went out for all young men to appear at the government house for physical examination for military service. His father too had received a notice ordering him to make young Francis appear. Father and son quickly concluded that young Francis must flee the country again, and without delay.

This time the frontiers had been sealed as soon as the conscription order had gone out; even the ferryman at Buren, on the Rhine west of Dornbirn, had strict orders not to let any young men across. The elder Drexel tried to bribe the ferryman as well as the corporal of the guard, without success. There seemed no alternative for young Francis but to sign up and fight—and most likely die—for Napoleon on the steppes of Russia. But at last the ferryman was persuaded to leave the boat unlocked; when he and the guard went to supper, the two Drexels climbed into the boat and rowed across to Switzerland. Here they parted once more—young Francis for Zurich, and his father back to Dornbirn by another ferry to avoid suspicion.

What happened to the ferryman for this transgression is not recorded. But a year later, in St. Gallen—only some twenty-five miles from Dornbirn—young Francis ran into an acquaintance from home who told him the consequences to his father. In the conscription, the elder Francis Drexel had been forced to draw a lot for his son—and when his number was called, the father was arrested and heavily fined for his son's failure to appear. Young Francis was also stripped of his citizenship as well as any patrimony he might inherit.

Francis was in Lausanne, working and taking art lessons, in October 1814 when he learned that Napoleon's downfall had restored the Tyrol to Austrian sovereignty. A general amnesty had been granted that made it safe for him to return home, which he did right away. But he spent only three months in his parents' house. This time the catalyst for his departure was a chance encounter in church one Sunday with Dornbirn's richest man, who told him that the Emperor Francis was expected to pass through Dornbirn the next day and that the local authorities needed a commemorative painting for the occasion. Young Francis agreed to do the job.

He went straight home and, working continuously from noon Sunday to six o'clock Monday morning, produced a huge life-size watercolor portraying the Emperor Francis, Tsar Alexander of Russia, and the King of Prussia kneeling together in thanksgiving after the Battle of Leipzig. This work was quickly incorporated into a triumphal arch, and after the Emperor passed through it young Francis was presented to him. The Emperor expressed interest in Francis's talent and directed his secretary to make note of Francis's name.

This interview encouraged Francis and his friends to believe that the Emperor might send him to a good art academy, but of course no such luck followed. The Emperor departed at noon, never to contact Francis again. By the end of February 1815, the disillusioned young Francis—having tasted the wider world and outgrown his native town—left Dornbirn and his family again. When he next returned, more than forty years later, he would do so as an old and successful American capitalist.

Francis now took to the road in Switzerland and Bavaria as an itinerant portrait painter, a role that fulfilled both his artistic ambition and his apparent need to keep moving and exploring new horizons. While working in Basel in April 1817 he learned of passenger ships that regularly sailed down the Rhine to Amsterdam and from there to America. Having nothing to tie him down, he decided to go along. "The prospect being a novel one to go to such a distant place," he later explained with dubious logic, "several whose acquaintance I made went also, and above all one fool makes many, I resolved to go too and see that other half of the world or at least a portion of it. I reasoned to myself since my native place having but five thousand inhabitants would never employ me professionally, and being obliged to be from home it would be of no matter whether I was one hundred or ten thousand miles off."

This voyage, like most of Francis Drexel's experiences, did not pass smoothly. En route to Amsterdam the passengers were summarily ordered to leave the boat, causing them costly delays while they waited for replacement boats. Francis, demonstrating entrepreneurial instincts, urged the passengers to pool their resources so as to collectively charter a ship of their preference when they reached Amsterdam. To his astonishment, his proposal was greeted with threats and insults, so that he wound up leaving the group altogether and proceeding to Utrecht in a small craft with two Frenchmen and a weaver.

Once aboard the *John of Baltimore,* the ship that was to take him from Amsterdam to Philadelphia, Francis found himself assigned to a steerage berth, even though he had paid for a room, but "to my remonstrations I was laughed at." After two weeks at sea the passengers' rations were cut in half and Francis was delegated by several passengers to complain to one of the owners, who "without further ceremony seized me by the throat, threatening me at the same time with putting me in iron" while "those who instigated me to speak stood alongside of me motionless." Nevertheless, on July 28, 1817, after seventy-two days at sea, Francis stepped off the *John of Baltimore* and onto Callowhill Street in Philadelphia.

Francis promised himself that if he fared poorly in America he would return to Europe after six months; if he did well he would stay for six years; but by no means would he settle permanently. When he wrote this years later he clearly intended it ironically: Francis did indeed become an American and a Philadelphian. Yet he remained a rolling stone, subsequently traveling thousands of miles instead of hundreds and often spending years away from home. All that had really changed was his base of operations. The former provincial hayseed was about to take his place in a great cosmopolitan city.

CHAPTER TWO

The Making of a Currency Broker

PHILADELPHIA IN 1817 was America's second largest city—with a population of some 67,000, just behind New York—and the third largest in the English-speaking world, after London. Its Quaker founder, William Penn, had designed it in 1681 as the world's first planned community, a "greene country towne" of parallel streets interspersed with gardens, trees, and public parks. Nearly a century and a half later that dream had largely worn thin. The charm of the Colonial era was past, poor people lived in alleys, and an utterly new phenomenon—urban violence—was beginning to manifest itself. But to a visitor who kept to the main streets, Philadelphia largely maintained the utopian facade of neat red-brick houses Penn had envisioned in 1681.

After serving as the capital of the colonies during the Revolution and of the United States from 1790 to 1800, Philadelphia had evolved into the new nation's financial and intellectual center: "the Athens of America," the great portrait painter Gilbert Stuart called it. Within a few blocks of the Delaware River flourished the federally chartered Second Bank of the United States as well as the Bank of North America and the bank of America's wealthiest man, Stephen Girard. Merchants, ship owners, ship builders, wheelwrights, weavers, and glass blowers prospered here as in no other American city.

But Philadelphia was also home to great painters like Thomas Sully and Rembrandt Peale, architects like Benjamin Latrobe and William Strickland, cerebral publications like Nicholas Biddle's *Port Folio* and Washington Irving's *Analectic*, and innovative museums and institutions like the Pennsylvania Academy of the Fine Arts, the American Philosophical Society, the Academy of Natural Sciences, and the Athenaeum.

As the world's only city founded and profoundly influenced by Quakers, Philadelphia radiated a tolerant spirit that attracted refugees from Napoleonic France and other lands. Many of these immigrants would subsequently blend into the city's leadership by anglicizing their names: the Germans as Pepper, Wistar, Wister, Lewis, Rittenhouse, and Pennypacker; the French as Markoe,

Borie, Geyelin, Vauclain, and Nalle. But the opportunities Philadelphia offered for economic advancement appeared to be offset by a rigid social order in which wealth and standing were closely guarded by a small circle of old families.

If Francis Drexel had seemed in Europe like Voltaire's vagabond *Candide* come to life, his entrance into Philadelphia bore uncanny echoes of Benjamin Franklin's arrival there nearly a century earlier. Like Franklin in 1723, Francis was a young man (twenty-six years old, whereas Franklin was seventeen) and a complete stranger; and like Franklin he had just a few dollars in his pocket but the whole world before him.

He had brought a single letter of introduction, to an artist named Rieder who lived at Seventh and Spruce Streets, and he headed there immediately upon debarking. Rieder was sick and sent Francis to the family of Gottlieb Grundloch, an innkeeper on Bread Street near the river, who boarded Francis for six weeks. Within a month of his landing Francis had painted portraits of Mrs. Grundloch and her daughters; soon he moved into his own studio at 131 South Front Street, facing the Delaware River. His combination of energy and passable talent seems to have carved a modest niche for him as a portrait painter—not in a class with Sully or Peale, but adequate for clients who couldn't afford the masters.

Contrary to Philadelphia's traditional reputation for frostiness toward outsiders, Drexel seems to have achieved almost instant social and professional acceptance. Within a year of his arrival he exhibited nine oil paintings and two drawings at the 1818 exhibition of the Pennsylvania Academy of the Fine Arts. In 1820 he was elected to the Musical Fund Society, site of the city's best concerts, plays, and operas; that same year he was teaching piano and drawing to the Newbold family's children, one of whom later founded the brokerage house of W. H. Newbold's Son. By 1822 Francis was sufficiently well known to be listed in newspaper advertisements as one of five references for a local boarding and day school. That same year he was elected to membership in the German Society of Philadelphia.

For more than eight years Drexel worked industriously at his chosen profession in Philadelphia, neither starving in a garret like Van Gogh nor making a fortune like Sir Joshua Reynolds; in his own words, he "continued to do middle well." He augmented his portrait commissions by teaching art at a girls' seminary for a salary of $72 per quarter. He also applied himself assiduously to mastering the English language. As a grammatical exercise he copied specimens of prose and poetry and concocted epigrams in the style of his hero, Benjamin Franklin. (For example, "There is but one way of doing business, and that is the right way" and "Men are subject to various inconveniences merely through lack of a small share of courage, which is a quality very necessary in the common occurrences of life, like in battle.")

Drexel appears to have made a number of friends soon after establishing himself. The closest was one Martin Fisher, to whose daughter Mary he became engaged. But Mary died suddenly shortly before the marriage, and this tragedy also inexplicably ended the friendship. "The family before her death treated me like a son of theirs," Francis later wrote, "but after that sad catastrophe Mrs. Fisher did me the honor to detract from my conduct and honor, as she had admired and praised before."

Shortly afterward, on April 23, 1821, Francis married twenty-six-year-old Catherine Hookey, whose father Anthony operated a grocery store at Third and Green Streets and was one of the founders (in 1787) of Holy Trinity, the Roman Catholic Church for German-speaking Philadelphians. The Hookeys seem to have sprung largely from English Quaker stock, perhaps mixed with some Pennsylvania Dutch blood. Catherine's great-uncle Nicholas Buck was a founder of Bucks County, north of Philadelphia; another great-uncle, Simon Snyder, had been governor of Pennsylvania from 1808 to 1817. Francis and Catherine settled into a house at 40 South Sixth Street, near Chestnut, then a muddy and forlorn outpost a block west of a city that essentially ended at Fifth Street. Here the Drexels had the first two of their six children, Mary Johanna in 1822 and Francis Anthony two years later.

Unfortunately, or perhaps inevitably, the marriage also confronted Francis with perhaps the most obnoxious of his long list of tormentors. Catherine's eldest sister had eloped with an Irish adventurer named Bernard Gallagher, who had returned to work at a grocery near Sixth and Chestnut Streets. Gallagher made a habit of spreading rumors about any young man who visited the Hookey household, and he and Francis apparently took an instant dislike to each other. According to Francis, Gallagher sent numerous anonymous letters to Catherine, to the two girls' seminaries where Francis now taught drawing, and to their neighbors, accusing Francis of seducing students at the seminary. Francis responded by filing a suit for damages, which Gallagher settled in April 1824 for $2,100—an extraordinary amount at a time when most Americans earned only a few hundred dollars a year. Despite this apparent vindication, the incident cost Francis both his teaching positions and what he called "considerable" business as a painter. And of course the lawsuit further fed the rumors Francis had hoped to silence. He seems, again naively, not to have appreciated the unanticipated side consequences of going public with a private dispute.

(Even today, it is impossible to say with certainty that the rumors spread by Gallagher were false.)

Eager to escape from an unpleasant situation, Francis now seized on a plan that would also satisfy the hunger for adventure that had lain dormant for eight years. He noticed that the great painter Gilbert Stuart, now well past his prime, continued to enjoy fame and prosperity through his portraits of George Washington, even as Stuart turned seventy in 1826. He also noticed that a South American hero equivalent to Washington had arisen in the person of Simon Bolivar, who had liberated Venezuela, Colombia, Bolivia, and Peru from Spain. In the wake of his dispute with Bernard Gallagher, Francis Drexel determined to do for Bolivar and his new nations what Gilbert Stuart had done for Washington and America: He would produce portraits of Bolivar large and small and sell them to patriotic South Americans at a large profit.

The scheme required Francis to abandon Catherine for years at a difficult time for her. When he departed for South America in the brig *Navarre* on May 15, 1826, she had two small children at home and was five months pregnant with a third. Anthony Joseph Drexel, the most accomplished of Francis M. Drexel's six children, would not meet his father until he was more than three and a half years old.

On the day Anthony J. Drexel was born in Philadelphia—September 13, 1826—his father had just arrived at the port of Guayaquil in Colombia (later Ecuador). His luggage included a trunk filled with uncolored aquatint 9 1/2-by-11 1/2-inch portraits of General Bolivar, presumably painted by Francis and reproduced by a Philadelphia engraver at a cost to Francis of $2,500. Bolivar—then the simultaneous president of Colombia, Peru, and Bolivia—had reached the height of his popularity, and Francis also hoped to paint full-size portraits from the engraving as a way to promote himself throughout South America as a commission portrait painter.

Yet even as Francis uncrated his engravings in Guayaquil, Bolivar himself was hastening by boat from his capital in Lima, Peru to confront a revolt against him in Colombia. It was the beginning of the end for the great liberator, who would hereafter increasingly be perceived as a dictator in the countries he had freed. With Bolivar's popularity in decline, Francis Drexel found himself stuck with a cargo of depreciated goods. For his portraits of Bolivar he was able to take in only $400—a net loss of $2,100. "Eight months sooner would have realized me double the amount of cost," he noted ruefully in his memoirs.

But Francis was scarcely discouraged by this failure of his grand scheme. As in Napoleonic Europe fifteen years earlier, he seems to have relished one more opportunity to test his survival skills in a strange environment. He also seems to have quickly grasped the old adage that in the land of the blind the one-eyed man is king. In Philadelphia he had been a competent but decidedly second rate artist; in South America, on the other hand, he offered a unique service to a continent eager to celebrate its newfound independence and prosperity. The mere fact that Francis came from such a sophisticated city as Philadelphia was sufficient to attract the patronage of Ecuador's leading citizens. During his two and a half months in Guayaquil Francis painted at least sixteen oil portraits (at $100 each) and seven miniatures (at $50 each), among them a portrait of Bernardo Roca, later president of Ecuador. Francis took in more than $2,000 during this period, so that even after paying off the heavy expenses for his passage he was able to send $700 home to his wife.

This initial success emboldened Francis to spend the next three and a half years traveling four thousand miles through South America, a backward and dangerous continent where malaria and yellow fever were ubiquitous, sanitation was primitive, and revolutions and earthquakes were common. The soldiers the new South American governments employed to maintain order and justice were mostly convicts sentenced to the army in lieu of prison, or Indians drafted from their homes by force. Yet the journal of Francis Drexel's journeys up and down the Pacific coast contains not a single expression of concern for his physical safety, even as he blithely noted (in describing the Prieto rebellion in Chile) that more than two hundred people were annually stabbed or knocked on the head by footpads in Santiago. His only recorded annoyance concerned the theft of his pencils, paint box, and boots and the rifling of his trunk by Indian soldiers on the road to Puno, and his difficulties in collecting fees from some of his clients.

As was the case for Francis in Europe, much of this traveling seems to have been motivated solely by a thirst for adventure. In 1828, for example, he traveled by donkey through the Bolivian jungle to the primitive Indian capital of La Paz, causing his historian great-grandson Boies Penrose to observe, more than a century later, "Why Drexel ever imagined he would make any money in that half-savage region is a mystery."

Why a man who was the sole support of his wife and family would risk his life this way is a good question as well. But in fact Francis Drexel's experience was not unlike that of the nineteenth-century immigrant Jewish peddlers who rode pack mules and wagons to remote Southern and Western U.S. towns before ultimately founding major department stores and investment houses, or the late twentieth-century laborers from, say, Pakistan, Turkey, and Italy who were forced by economic necessity to spend years separated from their families while laboring in Britain, Germany, or Switzerland. And in fact throughout his South American odyssey Francis Drexel did send money home periodically to Catherine in Philadelphia—more money, apparently, than he had ever earned before at home in the "Athens of America." During his four-year absence Drexel made (on paper) a grand total of $22,610. Of this amount he sent $12,545 home to Catherine, $3,260 went for expenses, and another $6,768 remained uncollected.

But Francis acquired something else in South America that was even more useful: an appreciation for the value of currency movements and fluctuations. When he sailed from Peru to Valparaiso, Chile, in June 1829, for example, all his money was in gold—a commodity whose value was unquestioned but which was not easily transported or concealed. He had trouble getting his gold out of Peru but managed to smuggle $1,500 worth on board the vessel when he left. Upon his arrival at Valparaiso on July 14 he sold his gold at a discount for a more portable bill of exchange payable to him in Philadelphia. That experience may have provided his first perception that profits could be made by assuming credit risks—a business which, after all, could hardly be more risky than fleeing from Napoleon or traipsing through the Bolivian jungle.

Details of his homecoming to Philadelphia on April 10, 1830 are not known, but it must have been a relief for Catherine and their three children, for while Francis was away his slanderous brother-in-law Captain Gallagher had repeatedly told the Hookey family that they would never see "that damned Dutchman" again. One clue to the welcome Francis received from his wife is the birth of their fourth child, Joseph Wilhelm, on January 24, 1831, just nine and a half months after Francis returned.

Once back in Philadelphia, Francis resumed his painting but increasingly pursued other sources of income. From September 1830 to July 1831 he attempted a career as a brewer in partnership with a man named Partenheimer; their staff consisted of four Irish immigrants and a blind horse. Francis also sold trimmings and small wares from his house on Sixth Street. The estate records of Stephen Girard record a payment of $119.24 to Francis Drexel for funerary crêpe used at the millionaire merchant/banker's funeral in 1831. In 1834 Francis apparently spent some time painting portraits in Princeton, New Jersey.

Sometime in the early 1830s Francis put pen to paper in order to preserve for posterity his years as a struggling vagabond artist in Europe and South America. "Having conversed with children born in America from German parents," he explained, "who were not able to say where their father or mother were from except from Germany, an ignorance which could do no honor to them nor their parents, has made me anxious to leave this to my children." Yet neither Francis nor his children left posterity any discussion of the family's more significant and lucrative (if less colorful) history after 1830. So his son Anthony Drexel's early life must be pieced together from the slender scraps left by others and without help from the Drexels themselves.

When he was in Philadelphia, Francis Martin played the classic *paterfamilias* who rigorously but lovingly supervised his children's training in music, languages, and art. On the other hand, Francis was away in South America for the first four years of Anthony's life, and away again for long stretches between Anthony's ninth and twelfth birthdays. So it is possible that the greatest influence on Anthony's life was not his father but his mother—and of her almost nothing has been written.

Anthony's formal education apparently began at the age of seven, in 1833, when he and his siblings were enrolled in a new French and English boarding and day school for girls and small boys operated by Madame Athenaide Buchey in her house on what is now the 600 block of Spruce Street. (Francis Martin Drexel is said to have painted portraits of Madame Buchey's three daughters in lieu of tuition payment.) The school offered instruction in subjects ranging from writing, arithmetic, chemistry, and foreign languages to painting, singing, piano, and guitar.

Madame Buchey, who operated the school until 1853, appears to have been a progressive educator. She took children at very young ages because, she contended, "Infancy is the proper time for acquiring the true accent of a foreign language"—a notion embraced more than a century later by most modern educators. The school's instruction, she said, "is adapted to the capacity of the learner, and conveyed in the manner best calculated to develope [sic] the powers of the understanding." In her approach to discipline, Mme. Buchey said, "Mildness is united with as much strictness as it is deemed indispensable for inspiring the youthful mind with a due regard to propriety, and a clear discrimination of right and wrong."

In 1835 Francis was off on his wanderings again, this time to Mexico and Central America. A handbill from Mexico City dated August 5, 1835 announced his availability to paint portraits and miniatures, but little other evidence of his journey exists. Francis could not have stayed much more than a year in Mexico, because an ad in the Princeton, New Jersey *Whig* of August 19, 1836 announced his presence there for a short stay, during which he offered to provide "good likenesses" to "the ladies and gentlemen of Princeton and vicinity." The last two of his six children—daughters Heloise and Caroline—were born in Philadelphia in 1837 and in 1838 respectively. But in 1837 Francis Drexel briefly moved again, this time with his wife and family. He had found another trade— and this one, finally, persuaded him, at the age of 45, to abandon his artistic career once and for all.

Trading in currencies—"money shaving," as it was then called—was a risky occupation in the best of times, but it was far more perilous when Francis Drexel first got into it. Since the founding of the Republic in 1776, paper currency had been issued not by the federal government but by individual chartered banks. In effect these banks were legally empowered to issue their own notes—a privilege that required the issuing bank to redeem those notes in specie (gold or silver or some equivalent) on demand. Just as banks today issue credit cards to save customers the inconvenience of carrying cash, so the early American banks issued notes to spare customers the need to carry gold or silver.

Then as now, bankers served their customers and society by putting idle monetary assets to use in greasing the wheels of commerce. Today that service usually involves lending money or investing capital. But in an age of bad roads and primitive communications these bank notes, with their assurance of portable credit, were much more vital to merchants and travelers engaged in moving goods (or themselves) from one place to another. The notion of debt financing was then in its infancy; businesses and governments alike usually financed themselves from their own revenues. Investments, loans, and the sale or mortgage of real estate were largely direct transactions between individuals. So banks were rarely called upon to lend or invest large quantities of capital.

All but one of these early note-issuing banks operated under state charters, and their notes invariably declined in value as they crossed state lines (just as, say, Canadian dollars today circulate with less alacrity in Boston than in Toronto). The only national bank was the Bank of the United States (1791–1811) and its successor, the Second Bank of the United States (1816–36), both headquartered in Philadelphia. This bank, a joint partnership of the federal government and private stockholders, was created to handle government transactions, hold federal deposits and issue bank notes at its branch offices across the country. Under the leadership of the Renaissance Philadelphian Nicholas Biddle, this de facto central bank generally stabilized banking conditions and currency rates from one state to another. But to President Andrew Jackson the Second Bank of the United States represented a dangerous concentration of "money power" competing unfairly with the state-chartered banks. "I do not dislike your Bank, any more than all banks," Jackson naively informed Biddle. "But ever since I read the history of the South Sea bubble, I have been afraid of banks." (The bubble to which he referred was a speculative hoax that had ruined many English investors in 1720.) In 1832 Jackson vetoed the renewal of the Second Bank's national charter, causing it to expire in 1836. The Bank continued to function until 1841, but only under a state charter.

Thus after 1836 the only incorporated banks in the country—and consequently the only banks issuing notes—were those holding state charters. Yet Jackson and his advisers had grown suspicious not only of the Bank of the United States but of paper money per se, which they blamed for causing alternating cycles of inflation and depression. Unable to persuade Congress to restrict the circulation of bank notes, in July 1836 Jackson on his own authority issued the Specie Circular, requiring payment in gold or silver for all public lands. His aim was to bolster the soundness of currency, but he accomplished precisely the opposite; suddenly gold and silver virtually disappeared from circulation, to be replaced by paper notes of dubious value. Western banks, unable to meet the sudden demand for gold and silver, began to fail one after the other, and by the spring of 1837 the entire country was gripped in its first major financial depression.

Within ten weeks of Jackson's departure from office in March 1837, thousands of banks and businesses from New Orleans to Boston had closed their doors, credit had virtually vanished from the United States, some parts of the country had been reduced to the simple process of barter, and even the government (whose own resources had disappeared as well) was reduced to printing currency to pay its clerks.

The surviving state-chartered banks had a hard time meeting their legal requirement to come up with the necessary gold or silver to redeem notes on demand, so the value of their notes varied widely from place to place, generally falling more and more below their face value as the notes moved farther from their place of issue. As long as the United States lacked a uniform bank currency, a lively trade in buying and selling the rash of paper money in circulation persisted. Some dealers and newspapers published guides (which they updated regularly) reporting the value of the many bank notes in circulation. By maintaining a liquid secondary market for bank notes—that is, providing the assurance that a holder could always find a buyer for his note at some price— these currency brokers enhanced the value of the dubious paper currency then in circulation. In this respect they were just as important to the health of the nation's economy in the 1830s and 1840s as stock and bond brokers became in the twentieth century.

It took the country six years to recover from the Panic of 1837, probably the longest economic contraction in America's history. By the time it had run its course, the Bank of the United States had closed up altogether and Philadelphia had permanently surrendered its primacy as the nation's financial center. Not until 1863 would the United States have a uniform national bank currency; not until 1913, with the creation of the Federal Reserve Board, would it have a central banking system bearing any resemblance to what was in place before 1837.

Yet every disaster creates fresh opportunities for change. Unnoticed by the world at large, two other events occurred in 1837 that would play a major role in imposing order on American finance. The first was Francis Drexel's decision to open a currency brokerage in Louisville, Kentucky, in partnership with a broker there named James M. Franciscus. The other was the birth, in Hartford, Connecticut, of Pierpont Morgan, whose life span, with uncanny timing, would cover the exact seventy-six-year period during which the United States lacked a central bank, and who in partnership with Francis Drexel's son would eventually strive, with remarkable success, to fill that void unofficially by himself.

Francis Drexel chose Louisville for his currency brokerage apparently on the advice of friends he had met in Mexico. His reason for locating there is unknown, but an observer can hazard an educated guess. Louisville lay in the heart of the western states whose banks were most starved for gold and silver; it also lay on the Ohio River, along which Mexican gold and silver could be shipped by steamboat to or from a port city like New Orleans in just five days. For a broker hoping to transfer gold and silver between western banks and the rest of the world, Louisville may have been an ideal location.

In South America and again in Mexico, Francis Drexel had dealt sporadically in foreign money and had developed relationships with important government figures. When Francis launched his new career in 1837, Spanish money and bills of exchange on Germany and Ireland were in great demand. Presumably Francis expected to capitalize on his foreign contacts and his linguistic fluency in both German and Spanish. Instead, once in business he appears again to have adapted his skills to the need of the moment: to track down foreign gold and silver for redemption of the accumulated notes of state banks in the U.S. hinterlands. Within two years Francis would bring his son Anthony, then just thirteen years old, into the currency business; thirty-two years after that, Anthony would beckon Pierpont Morgan to his monumental mission in life. But on the day Francis Drexel set aside his palette and opened his currency brokerage along the Louisville waterfront, he had no thought of changing the world. He was simply struggling to survive, just as he had been doing instinctively for twenty-eight years.

PART II

SUCCESS

CHAPTER THREE

"As Good a Bargain as Possible"

ALTHOUGH FRANCIS DREXEL found success as a Louisville currency broker, his Philadelphia-born wife Catherine insisted that he return to her home town. So at the beginning of 1838, after less than a year in Louisville, Francis opened a currency office in a narrow fourteen-foot-wide building at 34 South Third Street, in the heart of Philadelphia's financial district and just around the corner from Nicholas Biddle's ill-fated Second Bank of the United States.

The city to which Francis Martin Drexel returned in 1838 was half again as large as it had been on his first arrival in 1817. By 1840 it would approach 100,000 inhabitants, all of them still packed into two square miles between the Delaware and Schuylkill Rivers. Yet its upper classes—who from 1776 onward had championed the fragile new principles of democracy and equal rights to a skeptical nation and world—had themselves been forced to surrender the nation's political leadership to Washington in 1800, its financial leadership to New York in 1836, and its intellectual leadership to Boston somewhere in between. Philadelphia's gentry had responded to this rejection in turn by rejecting the world outside their narrow circle. Consequently, Philadelphia was becoming a city where social mobility was increasingly difficult. "The exclusive feature of American society," the British traveler Alexander Mackay would observe in 1846, "is no where brought so broadly out as it is in the city of Philadelphia."

Philadelphia society now ossified into an elite that cherished bloodlines and local roots above merit or even wealth. "I always feel socially superior to a man who is not a gentleman by birth," explained Sidney George Fisher, the distinguished Philadelphia diarist, "and I never yet saw one who had risen to a higher position whose mind and character, as well as his manners, did not show the taint of his origins."

In Fisher's approving view, Philadelphia society was "unpretending, elegant and friendly, containing many persons not rich, but few whose families have not held the same station for many generations, which circumstance has produced an air of refinement, dignity and simplicity of manner, wanting in New York."

{ 33 }

By contrast, "In New York wealth is the only thing that admits, and it will admit a shoe-black, poverty the only thing that excludes it and it would exclude grace, wit and worth."

Because of this emphasis on background and tradition, ambitious newcomers even then tended to gravitate to New York rather than to Philadelphia, and Philadelphia became the one Northern metropolis in a nation of immigrants in which native-born Americans remained not only in the majority but in firm control of the city's political and economic life well into the twentieth century.

Yet the immigrants snubbed by Old Philadelphians represented some of the Western world's most advanced and enlightened cultures. Francis Drexel was hardly unique: Every European political upheaval from the Edict of Nantes through the French Revolution and the Napoleonic wars had brought streams of French and German refugees to Philadelphia's relative freedom and stability. If Philadelphia society would not accept them into its leadership network, they would create their own, through marriages as well as business alliances.

One such refugee was Michel Bouvier, an infantryman in Napoleon's army who had fled France after Waterloo. A striking common destiny drove Bouvier's friendship with Francis M. Drexel. Both men were born in Europe in 1792; both came from small European villages and modestly successful petit bourgeois families; both had been involved in Napoleon's wars, albeit on opposite sides; both had begun their careers as artisans; both had emigrated to Philadelphia within a two-year period; and both subsequently evolved from artists to successful businessmen.

To these new arrivals the social barriers erected by Philadelphia's elite seemed downright benign compared to the violent social upheavals of Robespierre or Napoleon. In their eyes Philadelphia's passive adversity was no curse at all, but the blade on which they would hone their skills and eventually overtake and intermarry with their supposed social betters.

Another such immigrant was Jacques Marie Rosét, who landed in Philadelphia in December 1792, when he was twenty-seven and Philadelphia was the nation's capital. Within an hour of his arrival, as he and several fellow Frenchmen made their way up Chestnut Street, they had the remarkable good fortune to run into President Washington himself, who, recalling America's debt to France, wished them "Bienvenue en Amerique" and subsequently appointed Rosét to the Foreign Department of the General Post Office. His son John Rosét married into wealth through the Laning and Hollenback families of Wilkes-Barre, Pennsylvania. His mother-in-law, the legendary Wilkes-Barre beauty "Pretty Polly"

Hollenback Laning, was herself descended from the equally wealthy Bicking family, paper-makers of Bucks County, Pennsylvania. By the 1840s John Rosét was a prominent dry goods merchant whose store on High Street (now Market) west of Fifth, just two blocks from Francis M. Drexel's studio, boasted of importing window glasses for prominent customers like Thomas Jefferson and Benjamin Rush. His home on Pine Street offered another attraction: four marriageable daughters.

One of the young men calling on these daughters in the mid-1840s was a quiet fellow who instinctively shrank from display or self-assertion. Even in his youth Anthony Drexel was always neatly attired but never inclined to extravagant dress, preferring a plain black suit with a black tie. He had grown up a cultivated youth, fluent in French and German, capable in Spanish and Italian, and well informed about art and music; yet he was no conversationalist at all in the ordinary meaning of the term. What most attracted people to him was his attentiveness as a listener.

Rosét's third daughter, the refined and attractive Ellen Rosét, was five years younger than Anthony Drexel and had probably known him since childhood. She shared his cosmopolitan upbringing as well as his quiet domestic tendencies. Like many another young woman in her position, her social consciousness exceeded his. Her friends included Julia Riggs and Elisa Swaim, who as the future Mrs. George H. Boker and Mrs. Oliver Hopkinson respectively would become leaders of Philadelphia's most exclusive social circles. (George Boker, the poet and diplomat, was a cousin of Hannah Langstroth, whom Tony Drexel's brother Frank would marry in 1854.)

Like the Drexels, the Roséts had been Catholics in Europe, but by the time of Tony's and Ellen's courtship they had left that faith far behind them. After arriving in Philadelphia, Ellen's grandfather Jacques Rosét had attended the Dutch Reformed Church; in the 1840s, upon moving to Germantown in his eightieth year, he joined the Lutheran Church there.

When Francis Drexel arrived there in 1838, Philadelphia's Third Street financial district was a jumble of narrow three- and four-story houses extending from Market Street south two blocks to the Merchants Exchange, where the Board of Brokers met to buy and sell stocks. The neighborhood teemed with brokerage offices, banks, and insurance companies, all huddled close together because proximity to each other was essential in a world devoid of telegraph or telephone. The stock brokers tended to cluster their offices at the southern end of Third Street, near the Merchants Exchange. But the currency brokers like Francis Drexel gravitated to the northern end, near Market Street, which was then the center of a large nationwide wholesale trade.

Late each winter merchants from the western and southern states journeyed to Market Street to purchase their goods for the coming year. They paid for this merchandise with the paper notes issued by their home banks—the "red dog" money of Michigan, the "wild cat" money of Mississippi, and the "canal scrip" of Indiana, for example—which were generally as despised as their names imply. These currencies were valid at the issuing bank but were considered "uncurrent"—that is, unredeemable—beyond a hundred miles from home. Thus issuing banks used every means to keep their notes in circulation as far from home as possible, and traveling merchants who received these notes were constantly devising schemes to get rid of them.

The quickest way to do so was to sell the notes to the currency brokers. So Philadelphia's brokers waited on Third Street to buy and sell this uncurrent money at a sizable discount, given the risks involved. Years later a former "counting house boy" for one of the Market Street wholesale houses described the process as it worked in late 1838:

> I would be given a package of money, consisting of notes of all denominations, and sometimes from all States of the Union; I would go into Third Street, and from one broker to another, and finally sell to the one whose bid was the highest.

Francis M. Drexel had been operating on Third Street for less than a year at this point but apparently left a favorable impression on the counting-house boy:

> I found in the office of Mr. Drexel a man of most courteous manner, who talked in a voice most musical in its tones, and singularly pleasant to hear. The office was most modest and unpretentious in all its furnishments. A boy of sixteen or seventeen would, on such errands as these, very soon have his likes and dislikes formed from the manner in which he was treated by the broker. I soon learned to like to go to Mr. Drexel's office, and especially so when, after repeated visits, I was recognized by him. He would quickly impress a boy on such errands as mine as a man who wanted to make as good a bargain as possible, and when the bargain was made a man of spotless integrity in carrying it out to the minutest detail. In this respect I early learned the difference between him and some others near him who occupied more pretentious offices. I have stood at his counter several minutes chaffering over a concession, entertained by his musical voice and his singular tact and shrewd replies, and it almost always ended in his carrying his point and his boy cus-

tomer having the satisfaction of knowing that even then the bargain was as good, if not better, than he had been offered elsewhere.

The author of this account, benefiting from 55 years' hindsight (and, what's more, writing in the *Philadelphia Public Ledger*, a newspaper owned by Anthony Drexel and published by Drexel's closest friend), can be excused for retrospectively varnishing his memories of a subsequently famous acquaintance. Another Philadelphia banker, also interviewed more than half a century later, similarly portrayed Francis Drexel as an accessible and unpretentious gentleman who "kept a barrel of soda crackers under the office counter and often munched his lunch while serving customers."

By contrast, a contemporary account from the *Public Ledger* (published long before Anthony Drexel and his friend George Childs took charge of it) suggests that, under the pressures of wild currency price fluctuations, Francis Drexel could be as petty and grasping as anyone else. One Friday afternoon in February 1841 a reporter in the *Public Ledger* office on the southwest corner of Third and Chestnut Streets heard a commotion on the opposite corner, just a few doors from Francis Drexel's office. On investigation the reporter discovered that a few weeks earlier Drexel had sold several hundred dollars' worth of New Brunswick Bank notes to a broker named Montgomery, who had paid for the notes with a check—that is, an IOU—payable at a future date. Montgomery subsequently failed to market the New Brunswick Bank notes and consequently failed to pay the check he had written to Drexel.

Drexel attempted to salvage the loss by passing this check off to Montgomery in the course of other business. When this tactic failed, Drexel tried a more devious tack. He gave the check to a Mr. Brooks, a clerk in a nearby coal brokerage, instructing him to leave an order asking Montgomery to buy $350 in United States Bank notes at 89 percent of the loan's face value—a potentially lucrative transaction for Montgomery. Montgomery, unaware of Drexel's involvement and lacking the necessary notes in his own inventory, sent for them from another Third Street broker named Manley, who sent his son to deliver $330 in notes together with $20 from Montgomery to the coal clerk Brooks.

Brooks promptly locked the notes in his desk and at the same time threw down as payment the original check that Montgomery had given to Drexel. The younger Manley refused to receive the worthless check, and Brooks just as stubbornly refused to give up the notes or anything else in exchange for them. When young Manley returned to his father and told him that he had been tricked, the father—assuming Montgomery had initiated the fraud—went to Montgomery's office and vented his spleen upon "that mild and amiable little gentleman." Before the day was over, Montgomery, Brooks, and Brooks's employer had been arrested for larceny and conspiracy to defraud, and a warrant had been issued to break into Brooks's desk and remove the notes.

"It is quite clear," the *Ledger* report concluded, "that Mr. Drexell [sic] had used Mr. Brooks as a means of collecting a debt that he found it difficult to obtain in a direct business way, or by a course of legal proceedings." Yet Francis Drexel apparently escaped the incident unharmed.

Such an environment placed high value on forms of expertise that have long since vanished from American banking. A denizen of Third Street once recalled one of the Drexels' most valued employees:

> They had a banknote clerk who was a great expert on counterfeits. He could tell a bad note ten feet away. It was amusing to see somebody come up to the desk with a rather bad specimen of a counterfeit shinplaster. Before he could reach the desk George would get a corner of his eye on it and, without stopping work, call out, "Counterfeit!"

Dealing in uncurrent money wasn't the Third Street brokers' only activity. Since the concept of borrowing to finance a business wasn't yet accepted, much business was conducted on credit— that is, businesses furnishing IOUs to their suppliers in lieu of cash. Like uncurrent bank notes, these so-called "country checks" and "notes of hand" were similarly bought and sold freely in Third Street.

This business of Francis M. Drexel's was barely two years old, and his sons Francis A. and Anthony were only fifteen and thirteen, when the boys' formal education ended and they went to work as clerks in their father's office in 1839. Unlike his own father, Anthony was never one to question his father's plans for his future. From that point on, Anthony's cultural and business education alike would be confined to his father's office and his home, under the direct supervision of his father.

The father harbored what even in the nineteenth century were called "old-fashioned" expectations for his sons. Both boys did the work of men from the day they started, and their status as the boss's sons merely increased their burdens. While Francis Drexel's other employees kept regular work hours, Anthony and his brother were expected to come early and stay late, to do everything they were asked and never complain. The brothers often ate a cold dinner from a basket kept under the counter, and one or the other sometimes served as night watchman, sleeping under the same counter. But their father was also liberal about bestowing responsibility on his sons, as when he dispatched Anthony by stagecoach to New Orleans to supervise the transfer of a large gold shipment. Within a few years their father was routinely leaving his sons in charge of the office while he traveled about the country to claim the gold and silver of interior banks by redeeming the bank notes he had accumulated. "From his boyhood on," one observer wrote of Anthony, "he never knew what it was to be idle."

The boys' training was unique in one respect. Most American businessmen of the time were narrow men preoccupied solely with making money. The Drexel brothers, by contrast, were the products of a broadly educated, disciplined, and affectionate family. In the tradition of the nineteenth-century European upper middle class, their father who ruled supreme at the office was the same figure who set and enforced the family's demanding cultural standards at home.

How Anthony felt about this apprenticeship is unrecorded. Like many of his contemporary businessmen he was not given to introspection. His sole known reference to those early days appears in a letter he wrote nearly half a century later, in September 1887, to the banker Caleb Cope. "I remember the post notes the Bank of the United States issued although I was only 13 years old at the time I was in my Father's office at work," it says in part. "I know Danl Webster was notorious for not paying his debts. I remember a President of a New York Bank once saying to me a certain individual did not care any more for a protest than Danl Webster did."

By 1844 the nation had finally recovered from the panic of 1837. Now the U.S. economy shifted into a new expansive era, stimulated by European demand for American cotton and grain and by the first boom in railroad construction. Francis M. Drexel had not only survived the depression; as he accumulated more capital, he slowly and cautiously expanded the firm's services. He began buying and selling not only bank notes but also domestic and foreign bills of exchange, the standard instruments then used to finance trade and commerce. A bill of exchange was a written commitment to pay a specified sum to the bearer at a fixed future date. Usually, the seller of some goods would draw a bill of exchange from the buyer in order to give him credit for a few months, thus allowing the buyer to delay payment until the goods had arrived and been sold in turn to a retailer or manufacturer. Brokers like Francis Drexel provided a secondary market for these bills, just as they did for bank notes.

Francis also began accepting deposits and making loans, in two methods. He financed merchants by extending them short term credits, and he financed governments and corporations by buying, marketing, and circulating their bonds — certificates of indebtedness that could either be held for the interest they paid or be traded among speculators, just like bank notes. Before the 1830s only governments had found it necessary to issue bonds, usually to finance the huge costs of their wars. But the railroads—America's first big businesses—expanded the appeal of this financial tool.

In 1830 the Baltimore & Ohio Railroad carried its first passengers on horse-drawn cars; in 1832 there were only 229 miles of railroad in the entire country. Yet by 1840 America's railroads operated some 2,300 miles of track, and their work had barely begun. The railroads' appetite for ever greater amounts of money to build, equip, and consolidate their systems could not be satisfied by mere credits or IOUs. Bonds were the answer, but they involved far greater complexity and risk over a far longer term than financiers had previously dared to handle. One day a competing broker walked into Drexel's office and noticed a sign on the wall offering up to $1 million in Louisville & Nashville Railroad bonds, bearing an interest rate of 7 percent. More than half a century later the visitor recalled:

> I felt sorry for Drexel's that they were going out of the legitimate brokerage business to sell railroad bonds. My idea of the legitimate business was to buy and sell uncurrent money, etc. They made a success of the railroad bond issue, however, and it strikes me that they have done something in that line since.

By 1847, when Francis took his two sons into partnership and changed the firm's name to Drexel & Co., his little brokerage was well on its way to becoming a full-fledged private bank. In this new persona Drexel & Co. also became a disproportionately important player in the U.S. economy. Banks chartered by states had increased and flourished after 1811, when they rushed in to fill the void created by the failure of the First Bank of the United States. Unlike these incorporated chartered banks, private banks lacked the ability to issue bank notes. On the other hand, because they used only their own capital as a base for their operations, they enjoyed the flexibility of operating free from government restrictions or scrutiny. Because the closing of the Second Bank of the United States in 1837 had made banking an unstable and unpredictable business, the most respectable chartered banks began limiting their business to customers they knew well—usually customers located in their own back yards. This cautiousness opened opportunities that private banks rushed to seize, such as the business of guaranteeing payments between distant places.

In effect, what had originally been a coveted asset—a state bank charter—became an impediment as the financial demands of both industrial expansion and warfare among nations heated up. In 1843 *Hunt's Merchants' Magazine* noted approvingly that "mercantile banking is concentrating in the hands of private houses of known integrity, wealth, and business habits, because of the superior facility they afford over associations of irresponsible men, doing businesses in palaces at enormous expense."

From the 1840s through the rest of the nineteenth century it was not the chartered but the private bankers who functioned as the cutting-edge entrepreneurs of American finance. As early as 1847 it was not the chartered banks but the fledgling Drexel & Co. to which the U.S. treasury turned for help in financing the Mexican War. Drexel & Co. successfully sold some $49.2 million of the Treasury's 6 percent ten- and twenty-year bonds. All these loans were placed with investors at par value or better, and one of the loans—for $18 million—was the first Treasury loan subscribed for in specie (that is, in gold or silver). That success helped to usher in a new financial phenomenon: the sale of war bonds by the government to retail investors, through intermediary bankers like the Drexels.

Perhaps buoyed by this success, that same year Francis Drexel bought the building at 34 South Third Street where he had rented office space for nine years, putting down $2,500 in cash toward the $7,500 purchase price. He had already moved his family, in 1841, all the way across Broad Street to a house in what were then Philadelphia's bucolic western outskirts, on Chestnut Street near what is now 17th Street.

Despite his success, Francis appears to have remained as insecure and combative as ever. Beginning in 1841 he pursued three lawsuits claiming ownership of forty disputed houses in the nearby village of Kensington which he had bought at a sheriff's sale in 1840. The case persisted until 1846, when the Pennsylvania Supreme Court resolved it by denying Francis's ownership claim but requiring the rightful owner to pay Francis $1,786 in rents and profits lost during a period between suits when Francis's claim had been ruled valid.

Anthony Drexel was just twenty-one when he and his brother Frank were made partners in 1847, but by that time both had been working at their father's office for eight years. Although Frank was two years older, the more energetic "Tony" became by mutual consent the dominant brother from the first time their father left them by themselves. Frank functioned as the firm's inside man,

CHAPTER THREE

attending to details in the style of an office manager, while Tony provided the bank's primary service to the outside world: the process of finding and attracting lenders, depositors and borrowers and filling their needs.

. . .

If Philadelphia in the 1840s was a good place to practice private banking, it was no longer a safe place to practice Catholicism. For a long time the tolerant Quaker principles laid down by William Penn at Philadelphia's birth in 1681 had assured Catholics of uniquely fair treatment in terms of owning land, operating businesses, and enjoying civil relations with their Protestant neighbors. At the time of the Revolution in 1776 Philadelphia had been the only place in the English-speaking world where Catholics could celebrate mass openly. But in the 1840s the sheer numbers of seemingly unwashed Irish Catholic immigrants, together with a rise in Protestant revivalism, transformed Philadelphia into a major operating base for a Protestant crusade against alleged Papist conspiracies. By 1842 anti-Catholic agitators had established a Protestant institute to distribute anti-Catholic literature. A reactionary paper called the *Protestant Banner* began publishing early in 1842 and continued for many years. The nationwide Native American Party, organized in the Philadelphia suburb of Germantown in 1837, campaigned to deny the right to vote to immigrants who had been in the United States for less than twenty-one years. This agitation culminated in the so-called "Awful Riots" of 1844, when nativists burned two Catholic churches.

These riots forced Philadelphia's respectable Catholics to make a choice they had long avoided: either to embrace or to repudiate the unruly Irish Catholic immigrant workers who were the targets of the nativists. The riots also occurred at a time when several Philadelphia Catholic parishes were consumed with their own long and bitter internal power struggles between the bishops and lay trustees. The schism had begun in April 1820 when a dapper young priest named William Hogan became assistant pastor at somnolent St. Mary's Church. Hogan's charisma roused the congregation from its lethargy and captivated the lay trustees. But his independent spirit alienated the Church hierarchy (among other things, Hogan refused to board with his fellow priests, preferring the company of Protestant gentlemen). When the authoritarian Henry Conwell became bishop of Philadelphia in December 1820 and sought to suspend Hogan, the rogue priest fought the suspension and refused to acknowledge Conwell's absolute authority on Church matters. The St. Mary's trustees supported Hogan and seized the church property, whereupon the bishop placed St. Mary's under an interdict and designated nearby St. Joseph's as the legitimate parish church.

As a result, two hostile congregations arose: those faithful to Bishop Conwell

{ 42 }

on one side and Hogan's rebellious supporters on the other. The more fashionable bourgeois (and presumably more independent minded) Catholics resented the authoritarian dictates of bishops and so tended to side with Hogan; one history describes some of the Hoganites as "Catholics so zealous that they had been and were then rearing Protestant families."

Bishop Conwell, for his part, astutely perceived that much more was at issue at St. Mary's than the fate of a single recalcitrant priest. The Hoganite rebellion was actually a microcosm of a much broader social rebellion pitting (in the words of the theologian Martin Marty) those who embraced "the new ethos of industrial enterprise, urbanization and nationalism, accompanied by locally varying programs or creeds like liberalism, evolutionism, socialism or historicism" against those who cherished the institutions, values and beliefs of the "inherited religion of the West."

A St. Mary's congregation meeting in April 1822 to elect trustees ended in a riot at which the railing and part of the church wall were torn away. Hogan, by then excommunicated by Conwell, finally departed in November 1823 to embark on a new career as an anti-Catholic lecturer and writer, and by 1825 the interdict on St. Mary's was lifted, although a similar revolt by St. Mary's trustees was suppressed again by a new bishop in 1831. But the bishops' victory cost the Church the loyalty of many prominent Catholic families, and the Drexels were connected to the two parishes that suffered most from this conflict. At St. Mary's, Charles Bazeley, whose seminary employed the senior Francis Drexel as an art teacher, was a Hoganite trustee and enemy of Bishop Conwell. At the German parish, Holy Trinity, where similar trustees' revolts erupted periodically well into the 1850s, Francis M. Drexel's father-in-law, Anthony Hookey, had been a founding trustee in 1787, and Francis himself served briefly as trustee and represented the parish in business matters.

So it was small wonder that Philadelphia Catholics learned to downplay their Catholicism. Frequently they married Protestants as a way of melting into the landscape without incurring disapproval from their families or fellow Catholics. And as they succeeded in business or civic affairs they became less inclined to blindly accept the word of bishops, cardinals, or the pope. Like some of Philadelphia's most fashionable Quaker families before them, these Philadelphia Catholic families like the Drexels, Bories, and Bullitts gravitated to the Episcopal Church, the Protestant denomination closest in doctrine and liturgy to Catholicism. The motivations of ex-Quakers and ex-Catholics, of course, were quite different, but for both groups, the Episcopal Church offered an acceptable middle ground.

Anthony Drexel was eighteen when the Awful Riots of 1844 took place. As a well-to-do young man of liberal and cosmopolitan background he fit the profile of disaffected Philadelphia Catholics in the 1840s who became Episcopalians. Throughout his life he remained a man who, like his parents and brothers, took religion seriously. For the moment he remained a Catholic, but powerful forces were pushing him in another direction.

The year 1847 had been a watershed for the Drexels; the following year was a watershed for all American banks. On January 24, 1848, some forty miles from present-day Sacramento, California, a young hydraulic carpenter digging a millrace channel at John Sutter's fort spotted some shiny yellow flecks on the ground. As a result of James Marshall's discovery that day, more than half a billion dollars in gold would be taken out of California over the next five years; over the next twenty-five years, more gold would be mined in the world than in the previous 350 years.

The same year that launched the California Gold Rush would also witness the toppling of governments in Austria, Italy, France and Prussia, along with the revolt against laissez-faire economics instigated by Karl Marx and Friedrich Engels in *The Communist Manifesto.* European royalists and capitalists alike found their basic assumptions in jeopardy in 1848. By comparison, the United States—invigorated by its gold infusion and seemingly safe from invasion as well as from radical threats to property—suddenly appeared more attractive to European investors. Opportunity beckoned to any American banker willing to travel, and Tony Drexel's peripatetic father, now in his mid-fifties, was happy to oblige.

In 1839 Francis M. Drexel had dispatched young Tony to New Orleans for a gold shipment, but now the roles of father and son were reversed: From the age of twenty-one, Tony was for all practical purposes running an increasingly important bank while his father functioned as its field representative. At the same time, Tony and his family remained members of a religious minority operating in a hostile environment. The opportunities presented by the upheavals around them were great, but so were the risks.

Tony was prepared to seize the possibilities that few other financiers perceived. But unlike his father he would not move emotionally or impulsively. The first order of business was to build the kind of secure family life that Tony himself had never known.

CHAPTER FOUR

"A Wild and Reckless People"

ANTHONY DREXEL AND ELLEN ROSÉT were married on August 13, 1850, and one month later the 1850 census found them living near Seventh and Mulberry (now Arch) Streets with two Irish servants, twenty-year-old Matilda Brown and seventeen-year-old Ellen Fee. Although Anthony was not yet twenty-four and Ellen barely eighteen when they married, the pattern of their future life—as self-effacing pillars of their family, business and community— was already well established. By that time Anthony had spent eleven years at Drexel & Co., three as a partner. His older brother Frank was still single (he didn't marry until 1854, when he was thirty); their father and their younger brother Joseph (who joined the firm in the late 1840s) were available for travel; but Anthony remained in Philadelphia, ran the company, got married, and raised a family. Even in his twenties he was in many respects his family's senior member.

This seniority was a critical point in the 1850s, when private banking partnerships like Drexel & Co. were becoming important forces in American finance. Like Europe's great merchant banks, America's private bankers mostly served wealthy individual investors, businesses, and governments that turned to these houses not for their capital resources (which generally were modest) but for their services—especially their ability to recruit capital on terms acceptable to lenders and borrowers alike. Contrary to popular perception, financiers then and now were not necessarily wealthy themselves; they were middlemen whose primary asset was their ability to attract funds from depositors or investors for the use of borrowers.

These fund-raising talents in turn depended heavily on the partners' reputations within the business community. And no partner set a firm's tone and direction as much as the head of the house, usually called "the senior." Many private banks, in both Europe and America, were headed by a member of the founder's family. The Rothschilds, Warburgs, Hambros, Barings, and Browns all followed this pattern. And so did the Drexels, with one difference—beginning in the early 1850s the role of "senior" was effectively assumed not by its eldest member, Francis Drexel, but by his second son Anthony.

Anthony Drexel's 1850 marriage record is the earliest suggestion that he was no longer a practicing Catholic. The marriage was performed by the Reverend Dr. John Ludlow, a Dutch Reformed clergyman who had been provost at the University of Pennsylvania since 1834; he was also the father-in-law of Ellen Drexel's oldest sister, Mary Ann Rosét Ludlow. When Anthony's and Ellen's first child, Emilie, was born barely a year later, the baptism took place at Philadelphia's Third Reformed Dutch Church.

In 1839 the English heiress Hannah Mayer Rothschild had been ostracized by her famous Jewish banking family for marrying outside the faith. And from the mid-1830s onward, the five European Rothschild brothers repeatedly found themselves searching in vain for a son or nephew willing to travel to America to establish a branch there. The Drexels suffered from no similar religious or geographic constraints. Francis M. Drexel was at best a passive Catholic; whatever religious impetus existed in the family came from his wife Catherine. If Francis was upset that his first grandchild was baptized a Protestant (and there is no evidence that he was), such concern appears to have been outstripped by his delight at his freedom to resume his travels, now that he had Anthony to mind the store at home. By the time of his first granddaughter's birth in September 1851, Francis was a continent away, chasing a new opportunity for business and adventure alike.

In the early 1850s merchants and capital were pouring into the gold country in California, while gold was pouring out. Perhaps because he perceived great distances as an attraction rather than an impediment, Francis grasped the importance of the new gold fields more readily than other bankers. He resolved to set up a branch house in San Francisco.

Francis was nearly sixty years old, and the treacherous journey across the mosquito-infested isthmus of Panama took at least two months. He arrived in San Francisco early in 1851 and by May had set up the banking house of Drexel, Sather & Church on Montgomery Street. That firm became the depository for California's largest mining company, besides holding the smaller accumulations of individual miners. This business was immensely profitable, because most miners were so unaccustomed to wealth and so grateful for a safe place to store their gold that they neglected to demand interest on their deposits. Like the Drexel house in Philadelphia, the San Francisco house also provided local merchants with the credits they needed to buy goods from the East and from Europe.

Francis Drexel was back in Philadelphia by the fall of 1852, but he maintained his San Francisco partnership until 1857. Over those years nearly all the gold shipped from California to the East and to Europe by way of Panama passed through the Drexel bank, and the family's profits from handling it ran into hundreds of thousands of dollars each year. The only serious loss suffered by the California house occurred when a steamer bearing $300,000 in gold from California was lost at sea.

When Francis Drexel departed for California, he left Anthony to grapple with the most pressing financial challenge of the age: the railroads' growing hunger for capital. Between 1850 and 1860 America's railroads added some 22,000 miles of new track, at a cost of more than $838 million. Never before had any single business required such vast sums of money, far more than mere local capitalists could provide. Yet while many other banks shied from the task, well before his thirtieth birthday Anthony was committing his house to the future of the Iron Horse.

The size of these ventures and the risks involved are suggested by one of Anthony's early clients, the Sunbury and Erie Railroad (later the Philadelphia and Erie). It had been chartered in 1837, shelved during the depression, then revived in the late '40s. But by the early 1850s the road had made little progress, simply because it couldn't secure funding.

As was then customary with railroads under construction, the Sunbury and Erie owned practically nothing but its right-of-way, and it had to finance construction by selling bonds or, more commonly, by using bonds to pay for labor and materials. The Moorhead brothers, William and J. B., were the railroad's construction engineers and also its de facto financial managers. In lieu of cash, the railroad compensated them in stocks and bonds, which they sold for cash or used to buy materials. When they were unable to dispose of the bonds, they attempted to procure bank loans, using the securities as collateral. In 1854 they approached many Pennsylvania banks for such loans, but only three—the Girard Bank, Drexel & Co., and E. W. Clark & Co. (where their previous boss, Jay Cooke, worked)—would help them. The City of Philadelphia also granted them a $2 million, 6 percent loan redeemable in 1892, which the Drexels and Jay Cooke helped to sell to the public in the late 1850s. This funding ultimately financed the completion of Philadelphia's first railroad to Lake Erie.

No merely local bank could fill these awesome capital requirements. The investment banks that evolved in the 1840s and '50s were essentially distribution firms, hired by railroads and governments to peddle securities to wealthy capitalists. Most of these private banks were based in New York, Philadelphia, and Boston because that was where the nation's relatively few wealthy men could be found.

To extend their reach, large private banks of the 1850s tended to build branch organizations—semi-independent enterprises with firm names of their own, in which some of the partners of the mother firm were part owners or managers. Drexel & Smith—launched in Chicago in the early 1840s, shortly after Chicago itself was incorporated—was the Drexels' first such branch. Their San Francisco firm of Drexel, Sather & Church was a classic case of bankers going where the money (in this case, gold deposits) was. The Drexels gained their first foothold in New York in 1855 by acquiring an interest in an established Wall Street house, J. T. Van Vleck, Read & Co., which promptly became VanVleck, Read, Drexel & Co. Through this house the Drexels expanded their role in government finance. In 1858, for example, Van Vleck Read & Drexel took $400,000 worth of 4.5 percent U.S. Treasury notes and bid on another $1 million worth of Treasury notes, of which the firm was allotted $137,000. The same year, Drexel & Co. of Philadelphia took $500,000 in U.S. bonds—possibly Drexel & Co.'s first government financings since the Mexican War eleven years earlier.

But these domestic branches were no substitute for the firm's most pressing need: connections in Europe, then the world's wealthiest continent. For the first hundred years after the American Revolution, the U.S. was a debtor nation that relied heavily on foreign investment. In the 1850s Englishmen were the largest buyers of American securities, and most of the world's trade was financed through bills of exchange denominated not in dollars but in pounds sterling. As of 1853 Europeans held about $222 million in American securities—19 percent of all outstanding U.S. stocks and bonds. Three years later, the Treasury Secretary estimated that foreign investment in U.S. railroads alone amounted to nearly $83 million. If the Drexel bank hoped to grow, closer ties with London's money and credit markets were essential.

Like most banks, the firm developed its first foreign connections through correspondents—that is, banks that held each other's deposits in order to earn interest, provide local representation in each other's cities and nurture mutual sources of information. Many British investments in the United States were represented by Baring Brothers, the legendary London bank that helped Thomas Jefferson finance the Louisiana Purchase in 1803. By 1850 Barings was one of just three preeminent London banks specializing in Anglo-American trade. A correspondent relationship with Barings, founded in 1762, would have been a prize plum for a fourteen-year-old American house like Drexel & Co. But beginning in 1848 Barings rejected overtures from several American banks, including Drexel & Co. in 1851.

Baring Brothers' logic in rejecting the Drexels demonstrates the disproportionate weight attached to reputation and hearsay in an age when solid financial information was hard to come by. The Barings themselves had never heard of Drexel & Co. at that point; they left the matter up to their U.S. agent, Boston banker Samuel G. Ward. He declined to open an account with Drexel & Co. because, he explained to his London employers, Drexel did not "appear to be a House of the sort of character and standing" Barings desired in its correspondents. But Ward was not really familiar with Drexel & Co. either; *his* opinion was based almost exclusively upon a letter he received that year from Abraham Barker, a genial if unreliable patriarch of the Philadelphia Stock Exchange whose greatest asset was his seemingly endless supply of humorous anecdotes.

Barker described Drexel & Co. as bankers and brokers—"the largest Banknote Brokers in this city, having almost monopolized that business by undermining other dealers by low rates of discount." The Drexel bank's "whole system for years," Barker added, "has been to underbid until at this time the difference between buying and selling is reduced to the very smallest fraction. The effect of this has been to give them a most extensive correspondence throughout the United States and a larger Counter business which notwithstanding the low rates yields in the aggregate very considerable profit." Barker estimated that the worth of the Drexels might reach $200,000 and characterized Francis Drexel as grasping and litigious, though he added that the Drexel sons were considered more amiable.

To a family just on the cusp of respectability, that rejection must have stung. Barker had articulated what the Drexels probably sensed implicitly: that for all Francis M. Drexel's energy and ingenuity, his vagabond persona was impeding the firm's further growth. The Drexels were still outsiders in international banking circles and Philadelphia social circles alike. And precisely because reputation was so critical to acceptance in both circles, the Drexels had to pay closer attention to their image.

As Philadelphia's population expanded, the upper classes moved westward, to the newly fashionable "West End" around Rittenhouse Square. The Drexels resolved to move with them. Anthony and Ellen Drexel moved to the south side of the Square with their two infant daughters in 1853, and two years later Francis and Catherine and their four remaining unmarried children settled there as well, on the south side of the Square at 19th Street. But what truly announced the Drexels' success to the world was the opening of their new office in 1854.

For its first sixteen years in Philadelphia, Drexel & Co. had operated out of the first floor of the fourteen-foot-wide house at 34 South Third Street. Here customers walking in—perhaps from lunch at Mirabella, a decent restaurant in the cellar—found Francis M. Drexel and his sons all working unpretentiously behind the counter. In this cozy environment the sons were routinely greeted by visitors as Frank, Tony, and Joe without their taking any offense.

The Drexels' majestic new building, just six doors north of their old one, conveyed a very different message. At twenty feet wide, eighty feet deep, and four stories high, it was the largest structure on the block. Its Pennsylvania marble facade front was divided by four fluted columns. The legend "Drexel & Co. Bankers" was emblazoned above its entrance. Its designer was Gustavus Runge, the German architect who just three years later designed Philadelphia's Academy of Music in partnership with Napoleon LeBrun.

The Drexels' new banking house, gushed the *Public Ledger,* the city's leading newspaper, "is one of the most imposing business edifices in the flourishing part of the city in which it is to be located," one that "for beauty excels every other private house in the block." But what most impressed the *Ledger* was the building's state-of-the-art working environment.

> The first floor is appropriated to the operations of the firm, and is arranged in the most ingenious manner, the plan having been executed by the head of the establishment, the elder Mr. Drexel. . . . Particular care has been taken to have it properly ventilated, and the result has been most satisfactory to those employed. The counter in the banking room, which is fifty feet long, is elevated about eight inches, on a ventilator extending the whole length, which communicates with flues in the walls. This, with the other ventilators, renders the atmosphere of the room pure and healthy. In the rear of the banking room is the private office, and back of that a spacious apartment for the bookkeepers. . . . Besides the conveniences referred to, the office is well-lighted with windows front and back, and a large skylight immediately above the entrance to the private office. The floor is laid with marble tile. The second, third and fourth stories are each fifty feet deep, furnished with all the modern improvements, and are well-lighted and ventilated.

The new building and its public reception may have enhanced the Drexels' own self-confidence. Undeterred by the Baring Brothers rejection in 1851, Tony Drexel decided to approach another London banking house: George Peabody & Co. This time Tony's emissary would be his own father, returning to Europe for the first time in thirty-seven years.

. . .

Peabody was a Massachusetts native who had made his fortune and reputation as a dry goods merchant and importer in Washington, D.C. and Baltimore before opening a merchant bank in London in 1837. The transition from merchandising to banking was not as illogical as it might seem today. Most of the nineteenth century's great "merchant bankers"—like the Rothschilds, Barings, and Hambros in Europe and the Seligmans, Kuhns, Loebs, and Goldmans in America—began as merchants or traders who discovered, in the process of extending credit to their customers, that the credit business could be more profitable than the merchandise business.

By the summer of 1854, when Francis Drexel paid him a visit, Peabody was fifty-nine years old and one of London's most respected bankers. Whether Peabody was aware that Baring Brothers had rejected the Drexels three years earlier is not known, although such information rarely remained a secret among the small group of London bankers who conducted business with America. But Peabody and Francis Drexel shared at least a few common characteristics. They were contemporaries (Francis was three years older); both had come from obscure backgrounds (Peabody was born into a poor branch of a notable family); both had entered banking from other fields; and both had crossed the Atlantic (albeit in opposite directions) in order to establish themselves. Whatever the reason, when Francis visited London in the summer of 1854, he found Peabody receptive to a possible connection between the two houses.

Peabody was then a bachelor with a net worth of $3 million, but he lacked an heir to assure his bank's continuity. As timing would have it, only a few months before Drexel's visit Peabody had lined up a junior partner and putative successor: the well-established, widely respected Boston merchant Junius Spencer Morgan, then forty-one years old. Morgan had not yet arrived in London; instead he was traveling throughout the East Coast to investigate business opportunities for Peabody. Thus in late August Peabody wrote to Morgan suggesting a possible new contact.

"We shall require an active, clever agent to superintend our interests in the United States after we get well organized," Peabody wrote. Later in the same letter he noted, "Francis M. Drexel who goes in the Steamer that conveys this called on me today and intimated that he might wish to do business with us & I told him I would request you to call upon him. His firm is Drexel & Co., Bankers, Phila."

Shortly afterward, Morgan called on the Drexels in Philadelphia. Only a year

{ 51 }

earlier Morgan might not have been impressed, but now he found Tony living in the city's most fashionable neighborhood and Drexel & Co. doing business in the financial district's most impressive building. As a result of that meeting, Drexel & Co. was named Peabody's Philadelphia correspondent.

With that connection, Drexel & Co.'s focus shifted: Now financing trade and dealing in securities gradually became the bank's primary business. And less than a generation later this first connection with Peabody & Co. would blossom into the most formidable financial banking alliance in the world's history.

The birth in 1851 of Tony and Ellen Drexel's first daughter, Emilie, was quickly followed by the arrival of Frances Katherine in 1852 and Marie in 1854. By this time the young couple's need for space transcended their need for social approval. Now Tony Drexel uncharacteristically declared his independence from both his father and social convention.

After Philadelphia had merged with its surrounding suburbs in 1854, the city's horse car lines had been extended westward across the Schuylkill River, enabling Philadelphians to commute to work from what had previously been the inaccessible rural wilderness of West Philadelphia. Tony and Ellen moved to this virgin land in 1856, acquiring a two-and-a-half-story white stone house on most of a city block along Walnut Street between 38th and 39th Streets for the enormous sum of $20,000. (By contrast, the celebrated new Drexel & Co. building on Third Street was valued at just $5,000 when it went up in its prime location in 1854.)

The Drexels' new home was just around the corner from the equally new Episcopal Church of the Saviour at 38th and Chestnut (then Mary and Oak Streets). Indeed, Tony may have been instrumental in putting it there. The church's first vestry book contains pledges by Tony and other parishioners to pay $500 each to the architect Samuel Sloan for his design of the church, completed in 1856. Tony also contributed the church's huge onyx baptismal font, which is still in use.

Within a year or two the Drexels' stone house was succeeded by an Italianate villa with an asymmetrically placed square tower and projecting eaves supported by scrolled brackets. Its design seems to bear the imprint of Samuel Sloan, the same well-connected architect who had designed the church. Over the next few years this beautiful residence was gradually filled with works of art in bronze, on canvas and out of stone, with wood carvings, ceramic treasures, large shields, rare editions of famous books, upholstery, statuary, paintings— "everything that wealth could purchase or taste could choose," according to one contemporary observer. Like the house itself, the furnishings reflected the judgment of an owner whose interest in art and beauty was genuine but hardly daring or unconventional.

The house soon filled up with more children and servants: Although baby Marie had died at the age of one year in 1855, her death was followed by the birth of Mae in 1857 and Sarah in 1860. And when Tony's brother Frank was widowed in December 1858, Tony and Ellen took charge of Frank's two small daughters, Elizabeth and Katharine, until Frank was remarried in 1860 to Emma Bouvier, the daughter of his father's friend Michel Bouvier.

Unlike Frank's first wife, the liberal Dunkard Hannah Langstroth, Emma Bouvier Drexel was a devout Catholic who quickly steered her husband back into the faith and into philanthropy as well. Three afternoons a week she invited Philadelphia's needy to Frank Drexel's Walnut Street townhouse to receive clothing, medicine, and rent money—some $20,000 worth each year, an astonishing sum for the time. This should have pleased Frank and Tony's mother, Catherine Hookey Drexel, who until Emma's arrival had been the last defender of the faith within the Drexel family. But Emma was so puritanical and reclusive—refusing even to attend family gatherings—that the two women never got along.

The 1860 Census found Tony and Ellen Drexel's household assisted by five live-in servants, four born in Ireland and one in Germany. The move to West Philadelphia reflected Tony's lack of interest in fashionable Philadelphia, his devotion to his family, and his independence from his father. But it also reflected something deeper: his quest for stability. Banking is by its nature a business of intangibles; Tony's relationship with his father was similarly fleeting and uncertain. From the 1850s onward Tony Drexel was one banker who tried, perhaps too hard, to compensate for life's intangibles by surrounding himself with the tangible blessings of a family housed in solid structures he created on land that he owned.

It was about this time that Tony Drexel struck up a relationship whose significance rivaled and perhaps exceeded that of his marriage. George William Childs was born in Baltimore in 1829, apparently the illegitimate son of a prominent father who never acknowledged him. Like Francis M. Drexel, he consciously sought to emulate Benjamin Franklin. He arrived in Philadelphia in 1844, when he was fifteen, with just three dollars in his pocket, and found a position as clerk and errand boy for a bookseller at the corner of Sixth and Mulberry Streets (now Arch). There, for three dollars a week, he sold books, made the fires, swept out the shop and washed the pavement. He began to frequent the evening book auctions, equipped with a wheelbarrow to cart off his purchases. Finally his employer began sending him to book trade sales in New York and Boston, where Childs learned to strike a bargain by calling for the "balance" of the lot offered by the auctioneer.

Four years after his arrival in Philadelphia, Childs had amassed enough capital to set up a business for himself. In 1848 he opened a candy shop on Market Street. A few months later he switched to selling patent medicines from a one-room shop in the *Public Ledger* building. The *Ledger*, founded in 1836, was already one of America's most respected newspapers, and the ambitious young entrepreneur (as Childs himself later recounted the story) vowed that he would own it one day.

But not quite yet. Childs's medicines were designed to prevent cholera, which never invaded the city, so he abandoned medicine and at age twenty-one became a clerk with the retail merchant Robert E. Peterson, at a salary of $600 a year. Within two years he was Peterson's partner, and the firm—soon renamed Childs & Peterson—had abandoned retailing to publish textbooks for ministers and lawyers as well as cookbooks and reference works.

Childs wasn't interested in fortune alone; he yearned for fame as well. He was willing to risk both his own and his partner's profits to publish more exciting, colorful books that would appeal to a wider public, offering what he called "amusement as well as instruction." He displayed a flair for dramatic advertising.

Childs's first introduction to Tony Drexel, perhaps about 1853, may have occurred through Peterson, who in the 1830s had practiced law on Sixth Street, just eight doors down from Francis Drexel's home. Or Childs may have approached Drexel to finance one of his ambitious book publishing projects, like S. Austin Allibone's 1,000-page *Critical Dictionary of English Literature* or the explorer Elisha Kent Kane's two-volume *Arctic Explorations*, complete with more than 300 engravings.

In many respects Childs was everything Tony Drexel was not: self-made, independent, rootless, and extroverted. Where Drexel sought privacy, George Childs relished publicity. Yet precisely because their personalities complemented each other, Drexel and Childs quickly developed a close friendship. It blossomed into the self-sacrificing sort of David-and-Jonathan, Damon-and-Pythias male relationship that might cause raised eyebrows today but was esteemed in Victorian society. In the words of one contemporary observer, the friendship of Drexel and Childs was "such an example of the better things of life as must have quickened a desire for a like relation in every man who saw its long unbroken consistent beauty."

In a quaint surviving daguerreotype from the mid-1850s, in the Drexel family files, Drexel and Childs sit side by side on the photographer's bench, staring into the camera with solemn faces, long hair and constrictive waistcoats, almost like a newly married couple on their wedding day. It is a poignant statement of two young men, both still in their twenties, who have committed their lives to each other. Over the next forty years Tony Drexel would provide George Childs what he needed most: financial support, social acceptance and a surrogate family. And Childs in turn would provide Drexel what *he* needed most: a front man who would happily absorb the limelight, enabling Tony Drexel to function behind the scenes and removed from public view.

The California Gold Rush and the growth of the railroads brought unprecedented prosperity to the nation and especially to its business owners. By 1857 Philadelphia's millionaire count had increased to at least twenty-five by one estimate, from just ten in 1845. Francis M. Drexel was one of only two brokers on that list. But the explosive quality of this new wealth inevitably changed both the way in which fortunes were made and the people who made them. A voyage to California was no longer necessary to strike it rich overnight; manipulating railroad stock would do just as well. These stocks were favorites of European investors, who lived too far away to effectively monitor their investments. Who in London or Paris would notice if a few extra shares were missing in New York or Philadelphia? For some railroad chiefs, the temptation to water stock was simply too great to resist. In 1854 Robert Schuyler, president of the New York and New Haven Railroad, issued almost $2 million worth of fraudulent stock in his own company. Shortly afterward, Alexander Kyle, president of the New York and Harlem Railroad, issued bogus certificates for 3,000 shares in *his* own company.

At the same time, the enormous quantities of gold mined in California eventually produced a glut of small chartered Western banks, many of which issued far more notes than their deposits could cover. Construction projects, many of them financed with borrowed money, mushroomed across the country, creating a credit bubble that was bound to burst sooner or later. In August 1857 the Ohio Insurance and Trust Company failed in Cincinnati, leaving about $5 million in unpaid liabilities. The confusion quickly spread to New York insurance companies, which made cash demands on their banks, which reacted by calling in loans to cover their own positions. The Panic of 1857 was under way, just months after Francis Drexel, with what was either remarkable luck or remarkable foresight, returned to San Francisco to withdraw from his partnership there.

While riding the horse-drawn public omnibus into town on the last morning of September 1857, the aristocratic Philadelphian Sidney George Fisher noticed crowds gathered around several Chestnut Street banks. When he entered the Bank of Commerce to make a deposit, Fisher found himself in the midst of a run on the bank. The bank, he learned, was still paying its own notes but refusing payment for checks from other banks. By the next day every Philadelphia bank had ceased making payments altogether.

"In 1817 there was a crash," Fisher reflected in his diary that night, "another in 1837, and now another in 1857." Popular wisdom blamed these disasters on banks, but Fisher understood that banks were "merely instruments" that reflected the society they served—a society whose embrace of fast trains had mutated into a love of fast money.

A prudent people would make prudent banks, a wild and reckless people make rash and headlong banks, and we are a wild and reckless people. We like to make money fast, because the circumstances of the country tempt us to make money fast by offering unprecedented facilities for doing so. This creates a demand for capital beyond the supply and therefore fictitious capital is created. So long as confidence is maintained all is well, but a failure must at length occur, and then the fiction becomes apparent. A bank is a machine to facilitate trade, just as a railroad is. Our people require a machine to make money fast altho now and then it produces bankruptcy and confusion, and they require a machine by which they can travel fast and cheaply, altho now and then a collision occurs, by which fifty or a hundred people are killed or maimed at a blow. In each case the end is attained. Banks do enable men without capital to speculate and trade and grow rich and the country is developed thro the great West, but every twenty years the merchants and capitalists fail in the great cities; and railroads enable the masses to travel twenty miles an hour and carry emigrants beyond the Missouri at a low rate, but some 600 to 1,000 are killed by them every year.

For all Fisher's perceptiveness, the notion that bankers might stabilize such a "wild and reckless" society did not occur to him or to his contemporaries. Nor did it occur to the otherwise astute Francis M. Drexel, who throughout his life was driven by his insecure belief that he was helpless to change a threatening world and so must look out above all for himself and his family. But Tony Drexel was beginning to grasp the revolutionary notion that a banker might indeed change his world for the better. His timing was propitious. A threat to the nation far greater than the Panic of 1857 lay just around the corner.

PART III

STRUGGLE

"The Yankees Did Not Whip Us in the Field"

A HEAVY RAINSTORM battered the Atlantic coast throughout the second week of April 1861, preventing most sailing vessels from leaving port. Along Philadelphia's wet and dirty streets, pedestrians dodged umbrellas and the splashing of horses' hooves. In the city's muddied parks, grass had barely begun to sprout.

The gloomy weather was compounded each day by disturbing news from Washington and the South. The newly created Confederate government in Montgomery, Alabama had demanded that Major Robert Anderson's federal garrison abandon Fort Sumter in Charleston harbor. Each day that week, Philadelphia's customarily phlegmatic residents anxiously scanned the newspapers and bulletin boards for the latest dispatches. "I had no idea I would care so much," the young wife of a Philadelphia lawyer confided to her diary. "I felt a shock & thrill of terror, surprise & dread of all that may be coming, & then indignant defiance & a feeling that *we must* come well out of it."

The climax came on the last day of the week—Saturday, April 13—with the news that South Carolina had fired on Fort Sumter the day before. This first announcement that the Civil War had finally begun brought mobs swarming to the newspaper offices downtown. Oblivious to the rain, Philadelphians gathered far into Saturday night and through Sunday in crowds so large that people standing nearest the bulletin boards read the announcements aloud, to be passed by mouth to those standing on the periphery. Many Philadelphians who had never read a newspaper before now snatched and devoured the Sunday papers. One Southern sympathizer was chased from Third and Chestnut Streets to Doctor Jayne's drug store three blocks away, where he was eventually rescued by police.

In the excitement, everything else was forgotten over the next few days. Little or no business was conducted at the Stock Board or the outdoor commercial markets. But beyond diverting 600,000 Philadelphians from their dismal weather, the first Confederate gun fired on Fort Sumter also accomplished what no one in Washington had been able to achieve: It united Philadelphians behind the federal government.

Before that week in April Philadelphians had been divided and apathetic on the subject of Southern slavery. The South was one of the city's best customers. Goods produced in Philadelphia were shipped down the coast or sent by rail in an endless procession of freight cars through Wilmington and Baltimore. Philadelphia in turn used Southern products such as lumber, turpentine and cotton. Hundreds of Southern students attended Philadelphia's medical colleges. Although Philadelphia Quakers had organized the nation's first antislavery society even before the Revolution, by 1861 the city's defenders of racial equality were in a distinct minority. Most Philadelphians (like most Northerners) felt more apprehensive about antislavery agitation than they felt about slavery itself. When John Brown's body passed through the city on December 4, 1859, a mob of Philadelphians reacted by holding a proslavery demonstration at the Broad and Prime Streets railroad station. But once the war was under way this ambivalence vanished. Philadelphia hastily organized its troops and sent them away with a band and a blessing.

The federal government that now belatedly commanded its citizens' passion enjoyed no similar hold on their money. Because of the depression that had begun in 1857, the government in Washington had operated in the red for four years, borrowing to make up the deficit. The national debt, only $28.7 million in 1857, more than doubled to $64.8 million by 1861. In December 1860, when South Carolina became the first of eleven Southern states to secede from the Union, there was not even enough money in the Treasury to pay Congressional salaries. Since that crisis, foreign investors, anticipating war, had been selling their American securities and taking cash out of the country, causing a flight of gold. The stock market plunged to low points not seen even during the panic of 1857.

The federal government's expenses in December 1860 had averaged only $172,000 a day, but the war quickly pushed them to $1 million a day by early summer 1861 and to $1.5 million by December. Taxes could cover only about 25 percent of these expenditures. The rest would have to be borrowed.

At first the U.S. Treasury tried to raise funds by marketing loans through competitive bids—the method used in the 1840s to finance the Mexican War. In effect, bankers and wealthy individuals would assume the government's financial risk by buying Treasury bonds at a discount and marketing them to wealthy customers, just as Francis Drexel had assumed merchants' risks by buying bank notes at a discount back in the 1830s. But this government was unwilling to grant the discounts demanded by the nervous financial markets. In February 1861, when the government offered a 6 percent, twenty-year loan of $8 million, it received bids totaling more than $14 million from 156 individuals and banks, mostly in New York, Boston, and Philadelphia. The bids ranged from 75 to 96 percent of the par (that is, full face) value, and because it was oversubscribed the government was able to place the entire loan at no less than 90 percent of par. But the following month, when the government offered another $8 million loan, it rejected all bids below 94—and consequently sold barely $3 million worth of bonds.

The offering left a sour taste in the mouths of many bankers, who felt that Treasury Secretary Salmon Chase would have been better off selling the bonds for whatever the market offered. The government didn't seem to appreciate that the bond market was the nineteenth-century equivalent of public opinion polls. The bankers who offered low bids for government bonds were neither arbitrary nor greedy; they were simply concerned about their ability to market the bonds to investors. Most bankers had relatively little working capital and could easily be ruined by loans of such magnitude if they were forced to swallow the bonds themselves.

One such disturbed banker was Tony Drexel, not yet thirty-five at this point but head of what was already the largest and most influential private bank in Philadelphia, if not the United States. In February Drexel & Co.'s New York affiliate, Read, Drexel & Co., had taken $1,345,000 of the government's $8 million loan with a bid of 90.1 percent of par. In the March offering Drexel's Philadelphia and New York houses had raised their bid to 93.17 for $3.3 million in bonds—but their bid was refused because of the Treasury's arbitrary cutoff at 94.

Drexel & Co. at this point possessed between $1 and $2 million in capital, a sizable amount for a private bank but a slender foundation from which to rescue a government that was spending that much every day. Tony had spent fourteen years building up Drexel & Co. by taking judicious risks, eliminating uncertainties wherever possible, and avoiding politics and politicians. To his analytical mind, he could not find investors for Treasury bonds at 95 or higher—the price he would need to charge if his cost was 94. Having brought Drexel & Co. so far, Tony was in no position to risk everything he had assembled on the awesome gamble of financing the Civil War. That task would require someone hungrier and pushier, someone who was more of a political animal and had little to lose. And one day, shortly after Fort Sumter surrendered, such a financier presented himself at Tony Drexel's office.

Jay Cooke was in many respects Tony Drexel's opposite in temperament as well as background. He was an extrovert, a hail-fellow-well-met, a sunny optimist endowed with a glib confidence in his salesmanship as well as his ability to make any man his friend. Just as investment bankers could be divided into two groups —honest and corrupt—so the honest bankers could be further broken into two more types. The first was exemplified by men like Tony Drexel, who were, in the words of one unsympathetic observer, "international and realistic . . . cold and calculating." For them, "emotion plays but little part; even patriotism is not the most reliable factor." The second type, exemplified by Cooke, "is lacking in realism and tends to neglect caution. It can be enthused even with patriotic emotion. . . . It is suspected of not being orthodox and reliable. The time will come when its members will get into difficulty."

Cooke was born in Sandusky, Ohio in 1821, a lineal descendant of Francis Cooke, who arrived in America on the Mayflower in 1620 and built the third house in Plymouth, Massachusetts. As one of Jay Cooke's admiring biographers later portrayed the contrast, Tony Drexel "came from a cosmopolitan home with its immediate roots in the culture of Europe," whereas Cooke came from the Midwest, "from a family that had for generations been busy building America, paying the price in the narrowness of its culture." From this bizarre perspective, it was the second generation Tony Drexel and not the *Mayflower* descendant Jay Cooke who enjoyed the superior pedigree.

In the spring of 1838, Cooke arrived in Philadelphia as a sixteen-year-old clerk for the Washington Packer and Transportation Company, whose president was his brother-in-law. Here young Cooke kept the books and solicited business. He also handled the firm's advertising, a craft that was then still in its infancy. Cooke's ads suggest that even in that primitive stage he grasped the field's possibilities: While advertisements for other packets companies merely announced schedules and rates, Cooke's efforts took the form of sales pitches that emphasized the Washington line's comfort and speed. (Passengers to Pittsburgh, his ads noted, arrived there at least a half day earlier than by any other line.) But Cooke's ingenious ads failed to offset the effects of the panic of 1837; late that summer of 1838 the firm closed.

After returning to Ohio, Cooke came back to Philadelphia in 1839 to work for E. W. Clark & Co., a Third Street firm engaged in the currency exchange and stock commission business. In the 1850s Cooke helped the Clarks sell securities for some of the first railroads. He left Clark during the panic of 1857 and spent the next four years as a freelance financier, reorganizing canal and railroad companies damaged by the panic. By January 1861 he had accumulated about $150,000 in capital, enough to open his own banking house in the first floor of a brownstone building at 114 South Third Street, a block south of the Drexels. But the Civil War put an end to his work in transportation finance. Cooke needed a new specialty; in the federal government's desperate financial situation, he saw his opportunity.

Cooke and Tony Drexel were already well known to each other. Both men had been active in Third Street banking circles since 1839. Because banking houses didn't provide meals to their clerks and principals, in the mid-1850s Cooke, Tony Drexel, the Clarks, and a few Third Street brokers had organized a small dining club where they took their lunches. To pay their expenses, the group began dabbling in the stock market. When their first investments met with success, they grew bolder. Among other things, they entered a joint venture to purchase warrants for prairie lands in Iowa, Minnesota, and Missouri, which involved the challenging task of selecting the best sites on endless prairies and then securing title to them. They also acquired a large interest in the Vermont Central Railroad, a stake that in 1860 led Cooke and Drexel to fight unsuccessfully to remove the railroad's corrupt management.

Cooke had supported himself during his freelance years by borrowing from Drexel & Co. and one other bank, giving bonds as security. By 1861 Drexel and Cooke were "Tony" and "Jay" to each other, but Drexel was widely perceived as an elder statesman and Cooke as a youthful upstart, even though Cooke at thirty-nine was actually five years older than Drexel.

Cooke's brother, Henry D. Cooke, was a political friend of Treasury Secretary Chase, which may explain why Cooke saw possibilities for his firm in government finance. Like Drexel & Co., Cooke's bank subscribed to an offering of Treasury notes in April 1861—$200,000 worth in Cooke's case. Shortly afterward Cooke joined forces with Drexel to secure bids for more Treasury notes and for a $9 million, twenty-year loan. But the response from the two bankers' customers was so weak that Drexel and Cooke were able to bid for only $159,000 in bonds, at 85 to 88 percent of the par value. Indeed, the Treasury received subscriptions for only $7,441,000 of its $9 million loan, at from 60 to 93, bids that suggest how rapidly the government's credit was falling. Of the $1,684,000 in a separate issue of Treasury notes sold at par at the same time, Drexel & Co. and Jay Cooke & Co. took $141,000 for four banks and one individual in Philadelphia.

"I am sadly disappointed this day in not being able to make a larger bid for loan and Treasury notes from Philadelphia," Cooke wrote his brother Henry on

May 24. "Toney [sic] Drexel and Company and myself have spent most of the time this week in pulling the wires of our banks and have only succeeded in getting 300,000 bid for."

These experiences convinced Cooke that the old way of selling government loans—to hard-nosed bankers and capitalists—could not serve the Treasury's coming needs. Long before Freud, Cooke keenly appreciated the importance of the irrational in human behavior; now he visualized the great possibilities of an emotional appeal to Americans' patriotism as an incentive toward purchasing the loans. Cooke's revolutionary idea was a "popular loan" that the Treasury would market directly to its ordinary citizens, using Cooke as the conduit.

His first opportunity to try this idea arose early in the summer of 1861. Pennsylvania had decided to raise a $2 million loan for the state's military defense, but the state was still distrusted by investors because it had repudiated its bonds during the depression in 1841. The loan was to have been offered for the best price the market could bear—which, given Pennsylvania's poor credit standing, might be as low as 75. Utilizing his political connections, and capitalizing on Drexel's respected reputation, Cooke convinced state officials to try to sell the loan at par—that is, at 100—on patriotic principles. On May 28 Jay Cooke & Co. and Drexel & Co. were appointed general agents for the sale of this loan, with Cooke principally in charge. This transaction offered little profit for Cooke and Drexel, whose banks would make only pennies on the sale of each bond. But in exchange for this altruism, Cooke—who had no working capital to speak of—persuaded the state treasurer Henry D. Moore to name his bank as an official state depository. This action instantly solved Cooke's capital needs, although it provided no benefit for Drexel.

Tony Drexel clearly had mixed feelings about his alliance with Cooke. On the one hand, he recognized that Cooke was on to something in his insistence that the government's traditional financing methods no longer worked. And Drexel perceived, as Cooke did, the opportunity that an innovative approach would offer for solidifying his bank's leadership in the exploding field of government finance.

On the other hand, Tony detested politics. And Tony sensed the huge risks that Cooke's scheme posed, not only for the two banks but for the state and federal governments as well. In many respects Jay Cooke was the second coming of Tony Drexel's impetuous father: a decent man but impulsive, adventurous and impatient to jump into things without much investigation. Cooke was a man who thrived on crises; Drexel labored to *avoid* crises. Indeed, Drexel went so far as to caution State Treasurer Moore not to deposit money with Cooke's house because, Moore wrote to Cooke years later, "you had no cash capital and that I would run great risk if I did it."

Few bankers thought the Pennsylvania loan could be sold to anyone at its par value. But then, few bankers could imagine Cooke's talent as a salesman. To market the bonds he used such novel methods as ads inserted in newspapers and circulars distributed throughout the state, all stressing not only the financial return but the patriotic issues. Drexel & Co. and Jay Cooke & Co., said one handbill,

> respectfully appeal to the patriotism and State pride of Pennsylvanians in this hour of trial, that they come forward and manifest their love of the old Commonwealth by a prompt and cordial response to her call. But independent of any motives of patriotism, there are considerations of self-interest which may be considered in reference to this Loan. It is a six per cent Loan free from any taxation.

Cooke sent agents throughout the state to see bankers and other potential investors. When bankers protested that the loan wasn't worth taking at par, Cooke matched their financial skepticism with his patriotic fervor. Throughout this campaign Cooke was the front man and Drexel, as he preferred, was the silent partner. Drexel's contribution was summed up years later in a letter to Cooke from State Treasurer Moore. While Tony Drexel "did not take an active part in the details of the work," Moore wrote, "yet we had the valuable aid of his counsel and advice, and his name was of great assistance to us because of the high character and standing of his house." The loan was oversubscribed.

Cooke's Pennsylvania success emboldened him to make a similar pitch to the federal Treasury. Cooke wrote to Treasury Secretary Chase that Drexel & Co. was willing to join Cooke's bank in opening "a first class banking Establishment in Washington, *at once* trusting to our energy, capital & credit for success, as well as those natural advantages that would legitimately & honestly flow towards us from your personal friendship & the fact that our firm was ardently & fully with the Administration." They proposed to make Treasury operations their main business. Cooke's July 12 letter to Chase suggests the extent to which he depended on Drexel's credentials for his own credibility.

> We would refer to Drexel & Co. as the heaviest house in Philadelphia, with correspondents all over the land & doing also a heavy business in Germany. Mr. Reed [sic] their New York partner . . . had probably transacted more busi-

ness in Gov. Loans & Treasury notes than any other New York firm & is the particular friend of Mr. Cisco [head of the U.S. sub-Treasury at New York] and stands very high as a business man.

To raise the hundreds of millions that the government needed, Cooke suggested that Secretary Chase arrange to pay a very modest commission of 0.25 percent on sales and engage the Cooke-Drexel combination to manage the sale of the loans. They would save the government large sums "besides *insuring* prompt success."

Cooke didn't send the letter directly to Chase. Instead he sent it to his politically connected brother Henry with instructions to read it to Chase and elicit Chase's reply. He explained to Henry that he wanted assurance that Chase would give them management of the loans, because Tony Drexel was unwilling to join them in a Washington banking house "without some definite understanding."

Cooke's proposal required monumental nerve: A Philadelphia broker with negligible capital and a minuscule organization sought the authority to sell hundreds of millions of dollars' worth of government bonds. True, in partnership with the Drexels he could command broad influence plus capital of more than $2 million—as Cooke pointed out in his letter to Chase. But nobody in the U.S., regardless of his capital, knew how to sell hundreds of millions of bonds; such a thing had never been done before.

On July 21—nine days after Cooke's letter to Chase—the Union army suffered a stunning defeat at the first battle of Bull Run. With that disaster came the realization that the war would be a long one. Cooke was the right man at the right time.

While the Drexels and Jay Cooke struggled to provide the government with the funds it desperately needed, hordes of politically connected speculators—most of them unknown before Fort Sumter—basked in a golden era of corruption. Instant fortunes could be made in weapons, uniforms, provisions, and anything else in short supply that the government needed quickly. In the war's first months the federal government bought 5 million pairs of substandard shoes from suppliers who pocketed more than $3 million in profit. Through his open line to New York's Democratic machine in Tammany Hall, Jim Fisk sold the army shoddy blankets by the tens of thousands. When shipping became essential to blockade Southern ports and carry merchandise across the Atlantic, Cornelius Vanderbilt offered his fleet of 60 vessels for as much as $2,500 a day. By involving himself in Republican politics, a Philadelphia butcher named P. A. B. Widener netted $50,000 on a contract to supply mutton to Union troops (proceeds that Widener later used to develop streetcar lines in Philadelphia, Chicago, New York, Pittsburgh, and Baltimore). Tony Drexel may have been uncomfortable with Jay Cooke's slick salesmanship of Treasury bonds, but Cooke's relative honesty and selflessness placed him head and shoulders above these profiteers. Like Treasury Secretary Chase, Tony Drexel felt he had no choice at this point but to throw his support behind Cooke and hope his gambit succeeded.

Armed with his authority as the federal government's sole financial agent in negotiating $500 million worth of loans, Cooke sprang into action in the fall of 1862. He unleashed a barnstorming sales machine that employed brass bands, newspaper advertising, and a nationwide army of some 2,500 salesmen—mostly small-town bankers, insurance agents, and real estate brokers, all coordinated by Cooke via telegraph. Eventually this team disposed of some $360 million, or nearly 75 percent of the Union's bond issues, sometimes raising as much as $2 million in a single day. Bankers visiting Cooke's Third Street office gaped at the legions of clerks processing the millions of dollars pouring in over the counter from loyal Americans in exchange for U.S. Government 6 percent bonds at 100 percent of their par value. And Cooke's efforts were just beginning.

When the doors of Cooke's Washington banking house opened for business in February 1862, Tony Drexel's father was nearly seventy years old. At this advanced age Francis Martin Drexel found himself increasingly venerated in Philadelphia as a civic elder statesman and a liberal philanthropist, but he remained as footloose as ever. In 1858 or 1859 he had returned to Austria to visit his family; his father had died in 1836, but Francis found his brother Anton, four years his junior, still living in Dornbirn.

From the 1840s onward Francis had invested heavily in Philadelphia real estate, Pennsylvania copper mines, and other ventures throughout the state, which he visited frequently. After one such errand to Pottstown on the afternoon of June 5, 1863, Francis returned with a portfolio of documents under his arm. As his train pulled into the Reading Railroad's Philadelphia depot at 17th and Willow Streets, he asked a boy to hold this package while he alighted from the train. Francis stepped down to the platform, but as he reached back for his portfolio the train began to move. In that instant Francis lost his balance and fell beneath the wheels. The train passed over his legs, mangling one and severing the other completely.

A carriage took Francis to his home at 19th Street and Rittenhouse Square, where his physician—Tony's brother-in-law, Dr. John Livingston Ludlow—stanched the bleeding and administered cordials and stimulants to ease the pain. Two surgeons were summoned, but both quickly agreed that the case was hopeless and departed. Francis, who remained conscious, was informed that his injury was fatal; he received the sacraments of the Catholic Church; and at 10:15 that night Francis Martin Drexel's global Odyssey quietly reached its end, seventy-one years and 4,000 miles from the Austrian village where it had begun.

When Francis died, Tony had for all practical purposes functioned as head of the family bank for a dozen years, and the bank's standing had never been higher. Francis Drexel "died worth over a million $ & the sons are worth $300m [$300,000] independent of that," the credit agency R. G. Dun & Co. estimated in the first of its periodic credit reports on Drexel & Co.

> They do a very fine large bus. Are careful & judicious bus. men, wield their large capital & monetary influence with great ability & make money rapidly & safely. Stick closely to their legitimate bus. & great confidence is reposed in them, own val. real estate, have an undoubted credit & perfectly good & strong beyond a doubt.

But the loss of the family patriarch came at a threatening moment. The Confederate General Robert E. Lee was assembling an army of 75,000 men to invade the North. He planned to strike into central Pennsylvania, cut off Philadelphia's rail connections to Western Pennsylvania's coal fields and, in the process, intensify the pessimism and defeatism already spreading through the demoralized North.

The country's financial conditions were just as uncertain as the Union's military condition. Four months before Francis Drexel's death, Congress had passed the National Banking Act, which introduced a new system of national banks and a new currency. The law (which remained the country's cornerstone banking statute until 1913, when Congress created the Federal Reserve system) added still more confusion to the country's paper money, at least temporarily. Meanwhile, the Union government's heavy borrowings to pay for the war were sucking up virtually all the available capital for other public and private ventures. And the war's disruption of trade had devastated Drexel & Co.'s business in commercial credits.

Tony's first response was to close Drexel & Co.'s Chicago branch, which his younger brother Joe had reopened in 1861. Now Tony summoned Joe home to replace their father as the firm's road agent. Four weeks after Francis Drexel's death, as the Union armies engaged Lee in the first day's battle at Gettysburg, the three Drexel brothers drew up a new partnership agreement. Frank and Tony would each contribute 40 percent of the capital and take 40 percent of the profits; Joe would get the remaining 20 percent.

Although Drexel & Co. took in its first outside partners less than two years later, this new partnership agreement of 1863 essentially spelled out (albeit between the lines) the relationship among the three brothers for the rest of their business careers. Tony remained in charge but shared all profits equally with his older brother Frank, who continued as the firm's titular head. Joe, gentler and less driven than Tony, essentially became a representative for his older brothers, setting up new branches and carrying out other needs in exchange for his lesser share of the profits.

The closing of their Chicago office sensitized the Drexels to the need to strengthen their sole remaining branch in New York. On that same July 1, 1863 the Drexels dissolved their New York partnership of Read, Drexel & Co. and opened a new branch there, known as Drexel, Winthrop & Co., in which the Drexel brothers held a two-thirds interest and Robert Winthrop, the firm's resident partner in New York, one-third. Winthrop was a proud, wealthy man with many business interests and seemingly solid connections: His father-in-law, Moses Taylor, then sixty-five, was president of the National City Bank. Whether Winthrop possessed the most critical quality—a sufficient hunger to expand the business—would remain a constant concern for Tony.

Lee's defeat at Gettysburg on July 3, 1863 coincided with the victory of Union forces at Vicksburg, Mississippi. Within a single critical week, Confederate armies had been driven from the North while surrendering control of the Mississippi River. Shortly afterward, the hero of Vicksburg, General Ulysses S. Grant, came to the Philadelphia area to visit his wife and children, who were living in Burlington, New Jersey, where Grant's sons were attending school. During this visit Grant met George W. Childs, by then one of America's leading book publishers and a man who cultivated the company of celebrities. Childs in turn introduced Grant to Tony Drexel.

It was the beginning of a long and close friendship in which the future U.S. president often stayed with Childs or Drexel, either at their Philadelphia homes or at their adjoining summer cottages in Long Branch, New Jersey. Childs' hospitality and connections were no doubt attractive to an unworldly soldier like Grant.

But the relationship between Grant and Tony Drexel was more subtle. Grant had modeled himself after "Old Rough and Ready," General Zachary Taylor, his commander in the Mexican War. "No soldier could face either danger or responsibility more calmly than he," Grant wrote years later in his military memoirs.

> These are qualities more rarely found than genius or physical courage. . . . General Taylor never made any great show or parade, either of uniform or retinue. But he was known to every soldier in his army, and was respected by all. . . . Taylor was not a conversationalist. But on paper he could put his meaning so plainly that there could be no mistaking it.

Consciously or subconsciously, Grant was describing himself as much as Taylor. But he also could have been describing Tony Drexel's qualities as a business leader. In Tony, Grant had found a kindred spirit. For a military hero, unschooled in the civilian world and increasingly surrounded by fawning sycophants, that was no small discovery.

Before Jay Cooke's sales machinery could be stopped in January 1864, an additional $11 million worth of the government's $500 million bond issue was sold, bringing the total raised to $511 million. Before the Civil War ended Jay Cooke had sold the lion's share—some $700 million—of two more government loans. The last whirlwind operation was accomplished in just 140 days over the winter of 1864–65, sustaining the Union until Lee's surrender at Appomattox that April.

By this time, no longer in need of Drexel's good offices, Cooke was operating on his own and had negotiated a commission three times his original 0.25 percent. Financing the government was now both more lucrative and less risky than it had been in 1861. As the subscriptions poured into Cooke's Third Street office from points around the country, rival financiers sprang up to bid for the business. Cooke's operation was so overwhelmingly successful that to many observers it seemed like theft from the government to pay Jay Cooke 0.75 percent merely for receiving and processing the public's money as it flowed in. Several bankers wrote to the new Treasury secretary, Hugh McCulloch, assuring him that he could secure money at much cheaper rates. One of these, Cooke was advised by his Washington partner Harris Fahnestock, was "from your friend (?) —this in confidence—Tony urging that by withdrawing the loan from the market he could obtain money at a lower rate." According to Cooke, Tony Drexel even offered Cooke "his gratuitous advice not to become agent for the loan."

These must have been frustrating times for Tony. Having supported Cooke against his better judgment, he now found himself cut off by Cooke once Cooke's scheme had succeeded. Cast adrift as well from his father's moorings—however uncertain they may have been—and buffeted by the uncertainties of a wartime economy, in October 1864 Tony committed a misjudgment that might have devastated his firm's long-term future, not to mention that of the U.S. economy. Only days after Junius S. Morgan had taken over George Peabody's firm in London, Tony withdrew Drexel's account from Morgan's firm and transferred it to Brown, Shipley & Co., the London affiliate of Brown Brothers in New York. The reason, as Tony explained in a letter to Morgan, was simply a matter of price: The Brown firms' commission rate of 0.25 percent was half what Peabody & Co. always had charged.

This shortsighted decision ran the risk of stamping Drexel & Co. as a firm of bargain-hunters who cared only for price. Tony compounded this problem soon afterward by finding another London house that charged an even smaller commission than Brown, Shipley and sending all Drexel & Co.'s most credit-worthy bills to that firm, leaving Brown, Shipley only the more troublesome ones. This move seemed so out of character for Tony—more reminiscent of his father's early days as a tightfisted currency broker—that an observer can only conclude that during this period he was under severe pressure to cut his costs.

Jay Cooke did not make a fortune selling the government's war loans. After four years of operation, Cooke's Philadelphia house had profits of $1.1 million and his Washington branch $750,000. All told, Cooke personally made slightly more than $1 million for selling more than $1 billion of Treasury war bonds. That amounted to about 0.1 percent for the most remarkable feat in the world's financial history to that point—a feat that, not incidentally, saved the Union. "The Yankees did not whip us in the field," noted one distinguished Confederate leader. "We were whipped in the Treasury Department."

Cooke's relatively meager commissions hardly compensated him for the risks he took, but his real reward came from the exposure he gained. Suddenly the flamboyant Jay Cooke and Co. was America's best-known investment bank, using its proprietor's fame and his government revenue stream to compete effectively with older houses for private and corporate banking business. A Philadelphia financial column in *Forney's War Press* of July 2, 1864, noted that Jay Cooke & Co. was quoting a gold market of 223 bid, 225 offered, and Drexel & Co. 238 bid, 240 offered, causing the *Forney's* columnist to comment: "To those desirous of making a profitable speculation, we would suggest the propriety of purchasing gold from Mr. Jay Cooke, and selling it at once to Mr.

Drexel." In the face of such competition, and for reasons neither man ever fully acknowledged, the relationship between Drexel and Cooke gradually crumbled.

The Drexels had not suffered during the war. According to a published list of Philadelphia and Bucks County incomes for the year ending April 30, 1865 (a list made possible by the wartime federal income tax, which not only taxed but publicly disclosed all personal incomes above $10,000), Tony Drexel and his brother Frank both ranked among the ten highest incomes in Philadelphia, with $131,631 and $128,349 respectively, and their younger brother Joe earned $42,435. (Cooke's name did not appear on the list, perhaps because he may have filed in Washington.) But the three brothers' combined income of some $302,000 for that year suggests that Drexel & Co.'s profits were probably exceeded by Cooke's that year, if not throughout the war.

Tony Drexel probably felt about Cooke much the way a twenty-first-century chief executive of General Motors or IBM might feel upon learning that his company's market value has been exceeded by an Internet startup company that has yet to earn a cent of profit. Although Drexel & Co. was older, better capitalized, and more soundly organized, it was no match for Cooke when it came to seizing the public's imagination. But then a businessman brought Tony a proposition that inadvertently helped him to level the playing field. This time the eager entrepreneur was not Jay Cooke but another acquaintance who was every bit as ambitious, flamboyant and noble-hearted as Cooke: Tony's best friend, George Childs.

CHAPTER SIX

The Rise of George Childs

AT THE OUTBREAK OF THE CIVIL WAR George Childs was thirty-two and seemingly on track in his effort to emulate the rise of his hero, Benjamin Franklin. He had succeeded as a book publisher, married his boss's daughter, and then severed his partnership with his father-in-law to search for greater opportunities. In April 1863 Childs bought the *American Publishers' Circular and Literary Gazette*, a trade paper founded in 1851. Childs broadened its scope, developing what had been primarily an advertising sheet into a professional and literary journal. (He owned it until 1872; it still exists as *Publishers Weekly*, the bible of the book publishing trade.) But Childs yearned for a wider audience. His obsession with the *Philadelphia Public Ledger*, first expressed when he rented a one-room office in that newspaper's building in 1848, remained with him. "I will yet be the owner of the *Public Ledger*," Childs remarked to one friend in 1855.

When Childs made that vow the *Ledger* was an American legend. At the time of its founding in March 1836 virtually all newspapers sold for the high price of five or six cents a copy and appealed to small and elite audiences: The combined circulation of all Philadelphia newspapers then was said to be less than 8,000. But the *Ledger*'s founders—two printers from New York, William Swain and Arunah S. Abell—had a radically different idea. Their *Ledger* sold for only one cent and thus would need to reach a broad audience to survive. The new paper was a cleaned up imitation of the first of America's penny papers, James Gordon Bennett's *New York Herald*—full of sensational news, but without the *Herald*'s extreme bad taste. The *Ledger* had a crusading editorialist in Russell Jarvis and one of America's first financial columnists in Joseph Sailer, who began writing his daily "money article" in 1840 and continued it for more than forty years.

The *Ledger*'s novel formula succeeded from the start. By 1840 it claimed a circulation of 15,000; by 1845 it enjoyed by far the largest circulation in the state; by 1850 its circulation had risen to 40,000.

Like the *New York Herald*, the *Public Ledger* was a technical pioneer as well as a journalistic innovator. In 1837 Swain, the dominant partner, installed the finest equipment then obtainable: a steam-powered Napier single-cylinder press. A year later Swain had to order another press, this time a double-cylinder machine (that is, its output could be doubled by using two cylinders at a time). But even these presses were not fast enough to meet the demand for the *Ledger* and its penny paper imitators in other cities. In 1846 the *Ledger* became the first newspaper to install Richard Hoe's revolutionary revolving-type press, which replaced the old flat-bed press with horizontal cylinders capable of printing all four of a paper's pages in a single high-speed press run.

One other important characteristic distinguished the *Ledger* from its Philadelphia rivals: it was not political. Most newspapers of the day functioned primarily as party organs, publishing party propaganda in exchange for political ads and government jobs. The *Ledger*, by contrast, took no government advertising other than lists of unclaimed letters left at the post office—work that was awarded by statute to the local paper with the largest circulation.

During the Civil War most Republican papers, liberally subsidized by job appointments and advertising, defended war profiteers. The Democratic papers that might have challenged these excesses virtually collapsed with their loss of patronage after President James Buchanan left office in 1861. In Philadelphia only two papers departed from this pattern. The *Inquirer*, although enjoying Republican patronage, mixed its support for the war with criticism of party hacks and crooked government contractors. The *Ledger* alone remained non-partisan. It generally supported Lincoln's administration, and it assiduously aided Jay Cooke in promoting the sale of government securities, frequently printing editorials prepared by Cooke's agents to cajole the public into buying the national loan. But the *Ledger* had nothing material to gain from this support, and by 1864 it was paying a heavy price for its independence.

Although the war had doubled the cost of materials and labor, the *Ledger*'s owners had stubbornly stuck to their original penny price—which in an inflationary year like 1864 was tantamount to giving it away. Unknown to the general public, this newspaper of immense circulation, crowded with ads, was losing $480 per issue—nearly $150,000 a year. Its once famous printing presses had deteriorated to the point where the *Ledger*'s appearance was the sloppiest of Philadelphia's newspapers. Swain had been at the paper's helm for more than a quarter-century and at age fifty-five was losing interest; his partner Abell was preoccupied with a paper he had started in Baltimore; and a third inactive partner was dead.

Childs saw his chance but lacked the $150,000 purchase price. At this point

Tony Drexel stepped in with the solution. In partnership with his brothers, Tony would buy the *Ledger* for his friend Childs. Childs's name would appear on the masthead as the paper's proprietor; for his management efforts he would receive a one-third interest in the paper. The Drexel brothers would own the remaining two-thirds but would function as passive (and silent) investors. It is unclear whether Childs put up any money at all, but in any case Tony minimized Childs's risk by guaranteeing that he or his estate would buy back Childs's interest at the prevailing market value upon Childs's death.

Childs was a novice when he took charge of Philadelphia's largest and most respected newspaper on December 5, 1864. Alone among Philadelphia newspaper publishers, he had served no apprenticeship in either journalism or politics. Yet, as Tony perceived, his friend was eminently well suited to the challenge of saving the *Ledger*. Childs immediately relinquished his career as a book publisher to throw his energies into his new property.

In his first issue Childs pledged that the *Ledger* would "always raise its voice clearly and unmistakably in support of the Government." A week later, he doubled the price of a copy (to two cents) and increased the advertising rates. Next he set out to make the *Ledger* so indispensable that Philadelphians would happily pay his higher rates. He cleaned up the paper's visual appearance, beefed up its reporting staff, and eliminated anything that might offend a family audience.

At first the higher rates caused subscribers and ads to fall off. But within a month the tide turned and revenues increased. Now Childs was able to reduce the *Ledger*'s cover price slightly, from two cents a day to ten cents for a week of six issues.

Under his command, the *Ledger* became one of the country's foremost daily family newspapers, a nineteenth-century forerunner of respected independent twentieth-century papers like the *New York Times* and the *Philadelphia Bulletin*, papers famous for emphasizing substance over style. With its prudish standards and its refusal to use large "display" headlines, the *Ledger* struck many Philadelphians as stiff and Quakerish; its rivals disparaged it as "the servant girls' organ." But readers knew that no local competitor could get a scoop on the Ledger.

When Childs bought the *Ledger* there were three other newspapers in Philadelphia selling for a higher price; within 20 years all went into bankruptcy or changed hands, while the *Ledger* became the second most profitable daily newspaper in the United States. The paper that had been losing nearly $500 a day when Childs bought it subsequently showed a profit of $2,000 a day for many years.

"The *Philadelphia Ledger* has the largest circulation of a daily paper in the

U.S., if we except the *Herald*," an envious New York paper wrote in March of 1865, just four months after Childs bought it. "There are about 70,000 houses in Philadelphia, and the *Ledger* prints about 70,000 copies, which is just one copy for each house."

The *Ledger*'s turnaround was not merely Childs's doing but Tony Drexel's as well. "The rules which governed the newspaper and the banking house were in many respects identical," one observer later remarked. Some sense of Tony's involvement in the *Ledger* can be gleaned from a letter he wrote to Childs in March 1869, when Childs was in Europe.

> The *Ledger* is in "fine" order & condition with an increased circulation of about 4,000. . . . I think Mr. McKean [William V. McKean, the paper's general manager] has been most faithful in his trust in every way and as you so often say we must *judge by results*, which have been most satisfactory in every way . . . . I have never sacrificed a day when in town for stopping at the office. I have endeavored to watch things from the statements & closely.
>
> I hope upon your return you will carry out your plan to have a private office upstairs to keep out of the way of the boxes and that you will never go to the office at night again. I think I have a just and true conception now of what is required and I am quite satisfied that night attendance on your part is *not* requisite, and that it will only injure your health without doing any good to the paper.

In an age when medicine was still more art than science and antibiotics were unknown, preventive health care was a constant preoccupation for Tony. At the time of this letter his concern was heightened by the illness of his oldest son Frank, then eight years old:

> My poor little Frank continues very sick. He has a low fever & is reduced to a severe bundle of bouet. Dr. Ludlow says he is doing well & I hope he will get over it, but I am *very* anxious.

Tony's anxiety was justified: Frank died a month later, April 25, 1869, the first of four grown children Tony and Ellen would bury. The more cheerful news, Tony informed his friend, was the newest member of the family, Tony's and Ellen's ninth and last child: "G.W.C.D. is a splendid little fellow, admired by everybody. He has two teeth and is getting more." The initials stood for George W. Childs Drexel, then eight months old. Since Childs himself had no children, Tony had created, first in name and subsequently in upbringing, a surrogate son for his closest friend.

With the *Ledger* purchase, Tony had in a single stroke rescued a vital civic institution while providing his best friend with both the calling of his dreams and personal financial security. But consciously or subconsciously, Tony's interest in the *Ledger* may have stemmed from less altruistic motives as well. An intangible business like banking succeeds or fails largely on perception. Jay Cooke had shrewdly demonstrated the importance of the press in shaping public attitudes on financial issues. It could not have displeased Tony to know that the city's most responsible and respected newspaper was now in the hands of his closest and dearest friend.

Uniquely among newspaper owners of the day, Tony scrupulously avoided interfering with the *Ledger*'s editorial policies for the next thirty years of his partnership with Childs. But of course he didn't need to. Around this time, Tony Drexel and George Childs began their daily practice of meeting each morning and evening to walk from home to work and back, and again at noon to take lunch. In this way one man's ideas blended with the other's; Childs became, in effect, Tony Drexel's public alter ego. Indeed, he may have become overprotective of Tony in the *Ledger*'s pages in ways Tony never desired or intended.

Childs's purchase of the *Ledger* at the end of 1864 coincided with the launch of Jay Cooke's third and final government loan campaign. Cooke's first two campaigns had depended heavily on cooperation from the press. The nation's newspapers had been only too happy to help, printing the constant stream of news reports and editorials prepared by Cooke's agents. But now the *Ledger*, alone among Philadelphia's newspapers, refrained from printing notices touting the progress of the government bond sales or anything favorable to Cooke's marketing efforts.

This passive dissension by a respected newspaper infuriated Cooke in much the same way as, say, Thomas More's silent refusal to approve the king's marriage had so incensed Henry VIII in the sixteenth century. Convinced that his own motives were pure and that therefore Childs's motives must be malign, Cooke impulsively burst into Childs's office to complain, shouted some angry words, and stormed out. Before returning home that night—explaining to friends that it was his personal rule never to let the sun go down on his anger—Cooke returned to the *Ledger* office to apologize. But this time Childs refused to speak to Cooke. What had begun as an imperceptible breach was now out in the open.

Civic-minded businessmen who survived the Civil War found themselves flush with money—in many cases thanks to government contracts—and eager to demonstrate their gratitude to the Union's saviors. During a visit to Philadelphia in 1864, General Grant remarked in passing to his friend George H. Stuart, a prominent local dry goods merchant, that he was thinking of renting a house in Philadelphia. Stuart resolved to solicit funds to buy Grant a house outright. He raised $50,000 from nine Philadelphia boosters, including Tony Drexel and Jay Cooke, and purchased a mansion at 2009 Chestnut Street. When Grant came to Philadelphia on April 12, 1865—just three days after Lee's surrender at Appomattox—he found himself the guest of honor at a surprise gathering where the house was presented to him along with an embossed deed in a jeweled case. But the celebration was short-lived. Two nights later President Lincoln was shot to death, and shortly afterward Grant set up residence in Washington. He never lived in the Philadelphia house. He was drifting toward a political career at the very moment that financiers and captains of industry were replacing generals and statesmen as the nation's driving forces.

The Delusions of Jay Cooke

SLAVERY AND THE SOUTHERN PLANTATION SYSTEM were dead, along with half a million soldiers on both sides. But the Northern society of farmers and shopkeepers who had marched off to battle four years earlier was gone as well. The federal government's massive wartime investment in railroads to carry troops and supplies now linked goods and services with customers in distant states. The need to supply and feed soldiers had created a huge boot and shoe industry in New England as well as new packing plants in Chicago. Iron and steel mills, expanded during the war to produce guns and cannon balls, could now make the cables capable of supporting the first giant suspension bridges. Steam engine technology that had powered U.S. naval ships would now foster transatlantic steamship travel. The Bessemer steel making process, invented in the late 1850s, could now be put to productive peaceful uses, leading to the internal combustion engine, the acetylene torch, and the electric motor, which in turn provided the foundation for skyscrapers, railroads, and modern factories.

The unprecedented scale of the government's wartime spending had also demonstrated the effectiveness of large scale organizations, in business as well as government. In the years following Appomattox both the number and volume of security issues grew significantly. The federal government, no longer a credit risk, floated huge offerings to refund its Civil War loans at lower interest rates, which Drexel & Co. helped sell. But the securities markets were also called upon to place the issues of many states, counties and cities, not to mention the railroads, who were still the largest corporate borrowers.

To meet these needs, dozens of new investment banking houses sprang up after the war. Banking became a field dominated by new faces. At the close of the war the famous Jay Cooke & Co. was only four years old. The German Jewish Seligman family of New York, clothing manufacturers when the war started, had become bankers only when the government paid for uniforms in war bonds, forcing the family to peddle the bonds in Europe; just three years later their J & W Seligman & Co. had already opened European branches in Frankfurt and London.

So if only by virtue of its survival, Drexel & Co. enjoyed a unique position in 1865. Of all the leading investment bankers after the Civil War, only the Clarks and Drexels of Philadelphia and the Vermilyes of New York were "older" firms. Of these three houses, E. W. Clark & Co. had undergone a reorganization and Vermilye & Co. had been insignificant when the Civil War began. That left Drexel & Co., after twenty-eight years in business, as the only leading investment banker with a relatively long and respected track record.

This prominence was valuable but far from essential. For certain clients, notably the Pennsylvania Railroad, Drexel & Co. sold so many loans after the war that it became the carrier's unofficial recognized banker. But many of the new corporate issues were so large that no single banking house dared undertake the entire operation without help from other firms. Necessity dictated cooperation among them, and the device the bankers employed to minimize their risks and sell their loans rapidly was the syndicate—the same practice employed today to underwrite and distribute large security offerings.

In effect, syndication meant that even as investment banks competed with each other for clients and capital, they had a vested interest in each other's survival (just as, say, a shopkeeper attracts more business on a street bustling with many other shops than with the entire block to himself). On three occasions in 1867, Drexel & Co. joined with two other Philadelphia houses—E. W. Clark & Co. and Jay Cooke & Co.—first to sell $23 million of Pennsylvania state bonds, and then to finance the Lehigh Coal & Navigation Co. and the North Missouri Railroad.

Despite its longevity, Drexel & Co. now found itself overshadowed by Jay Cooke's upstart house. After the war Cooke lost no time exploiting his reputation as a miracle worker to build a private banking network of seemingly unrivaled reach, with its parent office in Philadelphia and affiliates in New York and Washington. By 1870 Cooke had a London branch as well, with the creation of Jay Cooke, McCulloch & Co. His resident London partner was his old friend Hugh McCulloch, who as U.S. controller of the currency during the war and as secretary of the Treasury after the war had eased Cooke's entrée into Washington's corridors of power. McCulloch established strong European ties for Cooke with the Rothschilds, who in turn instructed their New York representative, August Belmont, to support Cooke's future bond operations in alliance with the emerging New York German-Jewish firm of Kuhn, Loeb & Co.

Thus Tony Drexel now found himself playing tortoise to Cooke's hare. The

First National Bank of Philadelphia, the very first bank chartered after the National Banking Act of 1863, was largely a Cooke-Clark operation; Drexel & Co. was merely one of its 73 minor incorporators. And when Cooke organized the Washington and Georgetown Street Railroad Co., the first street rail line in the nation's capital, Drexel & Co. was again merely a minor shareholder.

But Cooke's peripatetic activity concealed a fundamental flaw in his method. To save the Union during the war it had been necessary and even brilliant to whip the public into a patriotic bond-buying frenzy, as Cooke had done. The Union's survival, after all, was a cause in which every citizen had a stake. But the success or failure of a railroad, bank, or streetcar line, for the most part, affected only the particular company's investors. Yet many investors were seduced by their faith in Cooke's infallibility at the very time that corporate managers were discovering the easy profits they could make from fleecing investors.

Speculators like Daniel Drew roamed the stock exchanges of the North, searching for companies they could seize and plunder. Before Drew died in 1867, he taught his protégés Jim Fisk and Jay Gould that an executive could make more by looting his own corporation than by adding value to it. When Fisk and Gould took over the Erie Railroad in 1869 they treated themselves like royalty—operating out of an opulent building on Broadway in New York that became something of a tourist attraction, maintaining female "assistants" on the payroll at as much as $1,000 a month, and financing this life style by printing and peddling new stock certificates that diluted the holdings of their existing stockholders.

Against swindlers like these, government offered investors little protection. Legislators from both parties routinely accepted cash, stock, free passes, directorships, and other financial favors from railroad promoters. At one point four different railroads were paying Republican National Committee Chairman William E. Chandler. Liberal Republican Lyman Trumbull sat in the Senate while on retainer from the Illinois Central. Nor could investors expect help from the press, which with a few exceptions (like George Childs's Philadelphia *Public Ledger*) remained dependent on political patronage. By encouraging investors in effect to speculate with their hearts instead of their heads, Cooke was treading on dangerous ground. Yet like many another promoter he came to believe his own glowing press notices.

Next to the charismatic Jay Cooke, the reserved Tony Drexel must have looked like a fussbudget. Where Cooke seemed unconcerned about the fate of the investors who purchased his securities, Drexel shouldered that burden constantly (indeed, it eventually killed him, whereas Cooke lived to a ripe old age). Cooke came to believe in the late 1860s that Tony Drexel was jealous of

Cooke's spectacular rise, as no doubt Tony was. But Cooke's belief may have reflected his own subconscious jealousy of Tony's superior underlying resources.

Since Cooke's promotional tactics were his primary stock in trade, he could not easily abandon them even if he wanted to. Cooke had made his national reputation by devoting five years almost exclusively to government finance, but in the process he had neglected his railroad connections. When the government bond business dwindled in the late 1860s, he found the railroads largely locked into relationships with other bankers, like the Drexels. During the war Cooke had performed a patriotic service at great risk in return for negligible commissions, but after the war, when he tried to exploit his government connections for profit, he found himself criticized for trying to monopolize a lucrative business. In the heat of the Civil War, the press and the public had overlooked Cooke's practice of reinforcing his government contacts by performing personal favors for public officials, but now, when he took out a mortgage for House Speaker James G. Blaine or sold land at a steep discount to Ohio Governor Rutherford B. Hayes, he was fair game for criticism just like any other influence seeker.

Cooke continued to contend, as he had during the Civil War, that the government could save large amounts on its funding needs by privately negotiating with a single friendly agent like himself rather than placing itself at the mercy of the investment banking community. In those days of weak government and nonexistent antitrust laws, this argument made some sense. Whenever the Treasury Department advertised its intentions openly beforehand, Cooke argued, dealers and speculators conspired to make the purchase or sale as advantageous to themselves and as disadvantageous to the government as possible. But Cooke's implication—that government agencies function best in secrecy—was shortsighted, naïve, and outdated, especially for a man who prided himself on his public relations skills.

Not surprisingly, one of Cooke's leading critics on this issue was George Childs's *Public Ledger*. Early in 1869, just before Grant took office as President, Senator Roscoe Conkling of New York introduced a bill to prohibit secret sales of gold and bonds by the Treasury. The *Ledger* and most reformers, including Tony Drexel, supported the bill; Cooke opposed it, perceiving it (perhaps correctly) as a personal attack on him. A *Ledger* editorial about the bill appeared to target Cooke when it remarked:

> Indeed it may be said that no other measure is supported with so near the approach to unanimity among solid business men, there being no opposition to it except so far as it may come from those who do not look to the public

interest, but to their own private advantage in maintaining the existing system which gives them a monopoly of the mischievous manipulation of the public funds.

Cooke had of course already burned his bridges with Childs during his shouting match at the *Ledger* in 1865. So when he read this editorial he sat down and wrote instead to Tony Drexel, with whom he still had a business relationship as well as a surface (albeit fading) friendship.

Dear Toney,

Do you think if I should start a newspaper, or rather own one, I would permit its editors and conductors to persistently and constantly misrepresent and injure the position of a neighbor and life-long friend?

The enclosed article is but one of a series of wicked and malicious misrepresentations of facts, and I cannot think it true, as some think, that they are instigated by my old friends, Drexel and Company.

As ever, yours sincerely,
Jay Cooke

Tony Drexel, sitting in his office one block up Third Street, replied immediately by messenger.

Dear Jay:

I have just received yours of today's date. . . . Now I want you to understand that, although we have an interest in the *Ledger*, I entirely deny that I, or any of Drexel and Company, ever interfere or influence the course of that paper in any way, and so you can always assume that anything you see in that paper is not, as you do us the justice to think, instigated by Drexel and Company or by any member of the firm. Have you ever seen anything in the *Ledger* in favor of any bonds we sell or in our favor in any way? I took that ground from the day we became interested in the paper, and will always stick to it, and I have quite enough to do in my own business. As to the article in question. . . . I can't see any attack on you in any way. . . . The article simply attacks the system of secret sales, which 99 per cent of the business men of the country condemn and in which I fully concur. . . . I will make it my business to see Mr. McKean on the subject, and in the meantime let me assure you that there is not the slightest disposition on the part of the *Ledger* to misrepresent facts or to allude to you in any way, etc., etc.

Very sincerely your friend,
A. J. Drexel

The next day the *Ledger*'s manager, William V. McKean, did indeed write Cooke to corroborate Tony's statement and to declare that Tony did

> not in any way control or interfere with the editorial direction of the paper, but studiously abstains from such interference, and as to the particular article you refer to, neither Mr. Drexel, nor any other person except the editors and printers of the paper knew anything about it until it appeared in print.

These denials failed to appease Cooke, since Tony had declared that he agreed with the *Ledger*'s policy. And Cooke was further enraged the next day when the *Ledger* characterized the opponents of the "secret sales" bill as the "stock jobbing ring of gamblers in gold and bonds who have little regard for government credit and indeed for anything except their own personal profit."

Cooke and his brother Henry fought the bill in Congress. Having heard in the course of his lobbying that Tony Drexel was also seeing Congressmen, Cooke made a revealing comment:

> I have not much fear of these fellows—They make a noise, but don't know where to take hold—nor which ropes to pull—like landsmen in a gale of wind at sea. If it were not for their salt-water allies—Hooper, Conkling, &c., I could snap my fingers at the whole crew.

Those words suggest the extent to which Cooke—an emotional man to begin with—had deluded himself about his own rectitude and power. In this case Cooke won the battle but lost the war. Despite support from the *Ledger* as well as Tony Drexel, Conkling's bill to prohibit secret Treasury sales failed to pass. But in deference to public opinion Treasury Secretary George S. Boutwell began his administration by openly announcing his purchases and sales. Jay Cooke still had a hand in public operations when Boutwell authorized them, but he no longer enjoyed a monopoly shielded from public view. This incident is noteworthy not so much for the Drexels' opposition to Jay Cooke but because it reflects Cooke's feeling that they were beginning to stand in his way.

As the federal government's funding needs scaled down in the postwar years, Cooke turned his attention to his old prewar specialty, marketing transportation securities. But he knew little about building or managing the vast railroad lines now being planned, nor had his experience peddling war bonds to patriotic crowds prepared him to raise tens of millions of dollars in a saturated market against hardened railroad operators like Cornelius Vanderbilt, Jay Gould, and Collis P. Huntington. Cooke's penchant for grandiose schemes, combined with his resources and connections, struck Tony Drexel as a formula for disaster. But for the moment the Drexels were helpless to compete.

Although on paper Drexel & Co. had the trappings of an impressive transatlantic banking network, Tony Drexel knew better. His New York branch—Drexel, Winthrop & Co., organized in 1863—lacked a forceful manager capable of competing with Manhattan's new and aggressive banking houses for the investment dollars of that city's burgeoning capitalist class. In London he had transferred his account from J. S. Morgan & Co. to the less expensive Brown, Shipley, but had then jeopardized that relationship by sending his best business to an even cheaper firm. In Germany he still enjoyed scattered banking connections—set up by his father and later tended by Tony's brother Joe—that provided commercial credits and currency exchange services for traveling business clients, but no securities operations. And in Paris, then one of the Continent's most important capital markets, he had no representation at all.

Methodically but quickly, Tony moved to correct all these deficiencies. First he expanded his German operations to include securities transactions. Then, late in 1867, at a time when there were probably fewer than a half dozen American banks in Paris, he dispatched his younger brother Joseph there to open the Drexels' own house to compete with Munroe & Co., Seligman Frères, and Lazard Frères, then the three most prominent American financial firms in the French capital.

Like the other American private banks in Paris, the new Drexel, Harjes & Co. was technically a separate partnership operating under its own name. But in practice the mother firm in Philadelphia actually owned the house and set its policies. The Drexels' Philadelphia and New York partnerships were general partners in the Paris firm, and Joe Drexel was assigned to represent their interests. But Tony seems to have sensed that Joe lacked the necessary forcefulness to pull in Parisian capitalists. Instead, Tony assigned two other resident general partners to the Paris house: Eugene Winthrop, brother of the Drexels' New York partner Robert Winthrop, and Tony's Philadelphia friend John H. Harjes, who effectively became the new Paris firm's "senior."

Harjes was not a member of the Drexels' family or bank, but he seemed like one. The Harjes family's story was similar to the Drexels', albeit a generation removed: Harjes was born in Bremen of Danish parents, who emigrated to America in 1849, stopping first in Baltimore before settling in Philadelphia. In 1853, at the age of twenty-three, Harjes began his financial career with Harjes Bros., his family's bank. Like the House of Drexel, this firm started by trading American bank notes, then graduated to foreign exchange and general banking. John Harjes was four years younger than Tony, and they had known each other and transacted business together for almost twenty years.

The Paris house's original partnership agreement of January 31, 1868 reflects the Drexels' willingness to reward their key people with what the twentieth century would call "sweat equity." Of the firm's initial capitalization of 500,000 francs, Drexel & Co. contributed five-sixths and John Harjes one-sixth, but Harjes was entitled to one-third of the profits and Eugene Winthrop (who contributed no capital at all) to one-tenth. Moreover, Tony personally pledged to advance Harjes the funds necessary for his share of the capital. In effect Tony bankrolled Harjes's new career, just as Tony had done for George Childs at the *Ledger*. And like his investment in the *Ledger* for Childs, Tony's choice of Harjes for Paris was another good example of his sound instincts in people.

Under Harjes's steady hand and watchful eye—it was said that he never missed a day at the office when in Paris—the firm gradually became the bank of choice for American tourists and U.S. citizens residing in Paris. And gradually it developed a market in France for American securities—first the bonds of the U.S. government issued to refinance the Civil War loans, then the debt offerings of American railroad companies.

At the outbreak of the Franco-Prussian War in July 1870, many travelers and tourists bearing Drexel letters of credit in Europe found themselves cut off from communication and unable to travel elsewhere, because the French and Prussian governments alike had seized the railways and telegraphs for exclusive government use. In this emergency, the Drexels' Paris house dispatched gold shipments to Geneva and other European cities to protect their letters of credit, and issued authorization that holders of Drexel letters of credit, wherever they were, could draw funds through local banks, in whatever currency would be most available to them. This action cost the Drexels a great deal of money, but it provided instant relief to the holders of their letters and enhanced the bank's reputation for standing behind its guarantees at any cost.

Harjes himself distributed 2,000 pounds ($10,000) of relief funds raised in New York to suffering Parisians during and immediately after the War. The French government subsequently decorated him with the order of the Chevalier of the Legion of Honor. The Franco-Prussian War established the Drexels as an important presence in Paris, even if that presence wasn't as forceful as Tony would have liked.

In London, where Tony's relations with his correspondent bank Brown, Shipley were deteriorating, he patched up his differences with Junius Morgan and moved his account back to J. S. Morgan's bank in 1868. The fact that Morgan welcomed him back after Tony had deserted him four years earlier suggests that at this point Morgan may have needed Drexel as much as Drexel needed him. His J. S. Morgan & Co. had succeeded George Peabody & Co. only four years earlier, and, while it continued to use Peabody's capital, the new firm's capital was considerably smaller than that of some of its principal competitors. With the opening of Drexel, Harjes & Co., Tony could now offer something Junius Morgan's firm lacked: a strong tie to Paris.

Morgan was turning his London house into a major distributor of American securities, but much of his business with U.S. clients was conducted in New York through Morgan's son Pierpont, then thirty-one, who Junius felt lacked both the necessary experience and character. Tony Drexel probably appealed to Junius on both grounds. Although Tony was thirteen years younger than Junius Morgan, he was actually the more experienced financier. Junius hadn't become a banker until 1854, had effectively run Peabody's house only since 1858, and had led his own house only since 1864. By contrast, Tony Drexel had been steeped in one form of banking or another since 1839 and had effectively run his family's house since 1851, if not earlier. And of course Junius Morgan's relationship with Tony stretched back to Junius's visit to Philadelphia in 1854—ancient history by the standards of these fast-changing times.

By coincidence, it happened that at this moment the weak link in Tony's network was the same as Junius Morgan's: New York. The New York house of Drexel, Winthrop & Co. lacked an energetic senior partner, someone with wide experience and strong European connections, capable of commanding the respect and attention of corporate clients and government officials. Neither Robert Winthrop nor Tony's younger brother Joseph fit that description. Winthrop was too cautious, and Joseph Drexel, despite his loyal service in Chicago, Germany, Paris, and Philadelphia, lacked the interest and drive Tony considered necessary to run the New York operation.

For that matter, all the Drexels' resident partners in both New York and Paris were either too cautious or too preoccupied with administrative matters to raise the firms' profile. As effective as John Harjes might be in managing the Paris firm, he was not the kind of strong leader who could bring the house new business.

There was no time to lose. Jay Cooke had gained control of the newly created Northern Pacific Railroad and had set out to raise a staggering $100 million to finance its construction from Duluth through the Rockies to the West Coast.

That bond issue threatened to divert badly needed capital from worthwhile projects to an overblown railroad scheme that might not reach fruition for years, if ever. If the Northern Pacific failed, the credibility of American investments in the eyes of European capitalists could be damaged for years. To counteract this threat, Tony needed more than a mere presence in New York; he needed a house that would be recognized among the best on Wall Street. He resolved to find a man capable of accomplishing this goal.

Such a man did indeed exist. But at this moment that man was laboring in confused obscurity in the bowels of lower Manhattan, waiting for someone to unleash his potential: Junius Morgan's son J. Pierpont.

PART IV

POWER

"A First-Class Businessman"

THE MORGANS CAME FROM an old New England family that traced its roots to Miles Morgan, the son of a Welsh merchant, who settled in the Connecticut River Valley in 1636. Junius Morgan's father Joseph, the first of the Morgans to give up farming, moved to Hartford in 1817 and opened a coffee house that became a gathering place for local merchants. From this shop Joseph helped organize the Aetna Fire Insurance Company in 1819 and invested in a Hartford bank. Until his death in 1847, when he was 67, Joseph remained an Aetna director, recruiting policyholders and investigating and settling claims.

Joseph's son Junius was apprenticed at age sixteen to a merchant and banker in Boston—the customary preparation for a business career in an age when colleges existed mostly to train ministers. By 1836, when he was twenty-three, Junius was a partner in the Hartford wholesale dry goods house of Howe Mather & Co. In the Jacksonian era large merchants like Howe Mather were regarded as the nation's commercial elite, and Junius remained there for the next fifteen years.

In 1851 he moved to Boston, joining forces with James M. Beebe, who owned one of the country's largest wholesale dry goods and importing houses, and future U.S. Vice President Levi P. Morton in a new firm called J. M. Beebe, Morgan & Co. But barely two years later, while visiting London on business, Junius met George Peabody, a former Baltimore dry goods importer who had moved to London to establish his own merchant bank. Peabody was by then a well-respected international banker, but he was also fifty-eight and in poor health. Some months later he offered Junius a partnership, and in 1854 Junius accepted and moved to London.

This move disrupted, among other things, his unusually close relationship with his son J. Pierpont, then seventeen. Pierpont's poor health, as well as his outbreaks of facial rashes, had kept him out of school until he was eight years old, and during those years he had spent almost all his time with his parents and grandparents (in marked contrast to Tony Drexel, whose own father was away for much of his childhood). After Junius moved to London, Pierpont attended school on the Continent until 1856, studying French and German and spending five weeks in London learning the ropes at his father's firm. In 1857 Junius arranged a clerkship for Pierpont at Duncan, Sherman in New York, where Peabody & Co. conducted most of its U.S. business.

As a result of this upbringing, from his earliest days in New York Pierpont commanded far more deference on Wall Street than a twenty-year-old novice could normally expect. He was rich and well connected, but he was also intelligent, well educated, cultured, and well informed, a seasoned traveler known to many leading merchants and bankers on both sides of the Atlantic. And Pierpont enjoyed the independence of a man who functioned in two roles: as clerk for Duncan, Sherman and as representative and confidential agent of Peabody & Co., his father's London house.

In some respects this separation from his father added a new dimension to their relationship: Now father and son communicated through long and informative letters. Yet the letters also reflected Junius's reluctance to accept his son as a self-sufficient adult. "You are altogether too rapid in disposing of your meals," Junius scolded twenty-one-year-old Pierpont by transatlantic mail in March 1859, "and then there is the great irregularity in the matter I so often spoke to you of when in New York. You may depend upon it you can have no health if you go on in this way. I would *urge* you to correct it at once—If you do not, dyspepsia with all attendant evils is sure to be upon you."

In 1861, just as the Civil War was beginning, Pierpont left Duncan, Sherman and started his own business with $300,000 in capital provided by his father. J. Pierpont Morgan & Co. operated out of a one-room office at 53 Exchange Place, which Pierpont shared with a colleague and a clerk. Here he unwittingly became involved in one of the early Civil War profiteering scandals, the "Hall carbine affair."

In August 1861 Pierpont lent $20,000 to Simon Stevens, a politically connected lawyer. Stevens used the loan to buy 5,000 carbine rifles for resale to General John C. Frémont, then commander of the U.S. Army's Department of the West, who desperately needed small arms. These "Hall carbines" had originally been ordered and bought by the government, which found them serviceable but obsolete. Consequently, in June 1861 the War Department had sold them for $3.50 each to the arms dealer Arthur Eastman. At first Eastman found no takers for them, but after the First Battle of Bull Run six weeks later, when the Union's defeat put a premium on all weapons, Stevens offered to take all 5,000 carbines at $11.50 each. Stevens in turn immediately telegraphed

Frémont, whom he had known for a half dozen years, offering him the guns at $22 each. That is, Stevens proposed to buy the government's guns at $11.50 each and sell them back to the government at $22 each. General Frémont readily agreed to the price. Stevens turned to Morgan for the $20,000 he needed for his first payment, the balance ($37,500) to be paid when the sale was completed.

During the loan's 38-day period, Pierpont held title to the carbines and prepared them for shipment to Frémont's headquarters in St. Louis. Only after the loan had been made did Pierpont learn that the carbines Eastman had pledged to sell still belonged to the government and were stored at an army installation in New York harbor. But it was Pierpont who received the $55,000 payment that September from the Army ordnance office in St. Louis. This payment he forwarded to Stevens's bankers after deducting his own principal and fees. For his time and trouble in this transaction, Pierpont received a commission of $5,400 plus standard interest on the $20,000 loan of 7 percent ($156.04) for the 38-day period.

A subsequent investigation of the affair exonerated Pierpont of blame; his only offense was naively allowing himself to be used by Stevens to conceal the transaction. (Pierpont's commission, large as it may seem today, was justified in light of the shortage of private capital at a time of great risk and uncertainty.) But the affair seems to have persuaded Junius Morgan in London that his son needed closer supervision. At his urging, in September 1862 Pierpont reconstituted his firm, making his cousin James J. Goodwin a partner, and in the ensuing years Junius gradually transferred the London firm's New York accounts to J. P. Morgan & Co. But Goodwin—all of twenty-seven years old at the time—was hardly a suitable mentor. He was only two years older than Pierpont and powerless to restrain his cousin when Pierpont found speculation too tempting to resist.

Late in the summer of 1863 Pierpont quietly began buying gold on joint account with Edward Ketchum, a family friend from his Connecticut days. By early October they had accumulated a gold cache worth over $2 million, financing the venture by borrowing against the gold and betting that they could sell it for enough to clear the debt and make a profit. In mid-October they shipped $1.15 million of their gold hoard to England. This move caught the markets by surprise and created a temporary gold shortage in New York, driving the price of gold upward. Pierpont and Ketchum sold the rest of their gold as the price climbed, netting $132,407—more than $66,000 for each of the two friends. Ketchum was later arrested for another matter: stealing $3 million in securities from his father's bank and forging an additional $1.5 million in gold certificates, some of them in Pierpont's name.

To the horrified Junius Morgan in London, Pierpont seemed incapable of heeding his father's constant strictures about character and reputation. So in 1864 Junius found his son a new would-be mentor in Charles H. Dabney, then fifty-seven, who had taught Pierpont to keep accounts at Duncan, Sherman. The newly rechristened Dabney, Morgan & Co. opened in November at Pierpont's old offices at 53 Exchange Place. Two years later the partnership was revised again when George H. Morgan, Pierpont's twenty-six-year-old brother-in-law (the husband of Pierpont's sister Sarah), was made a partner.

But within his firm as well as on Wall Street, Pierpont remained an anomaly. In an age that perceived work as a necessary evil, he was a man who worked for a living when he didn't have to, a man oddly endowed with both material wealth and an innate drive to make more. He was indeed earning good money, and he was perceived to be doing even better than he was: By 1869 a credit report from R. G. Dun & Co. estimated Pierpont's net worth at between $600,000 and $700,000, when in fact he was worth about $350,000. The Dun report cut to the heart of Pierpont's problem on Wall Street: Although he was considered "of excellent character, extra ability, shrewd, quick of perception," his house was also "unpopular with many" due to Pierpont's erratic nature and "his peculiar brusqueness of manner." Meanwhile, within his own firm another problem plagued Pierpont: the lack of initiative displayed by Dabney, by his cousin Jim Goodwin, and by his brother-in-law, all of whom approached the business largely as a sinecure.

Pierpont's frustrations were no doubt exacerbated by his father's risky 250-million-franc loan to the newborn French Republic in October 1870. Although Paris was then besieged by two Prussian armies, within a week Junius Morgan managed to sell out more than half the loan in London. But public sales of the loan weakened after a few months when Bismarck, the Prussian chancellor, threatened to make repudiation of the loan a condition of peace. This possibility, together with the fall of Paris on January 27, 1871, frightened investors, driving the issue's price down to fifty-five pounds, thirty pounds below the original offering price. Junius refused to abandon the operation, buying back much of the loan himself at a heavy discount. Now he needed Pierpont's firm in New York to help him sell the rest of the French loan to Americans, at the very moment that Pierpont and his partners were squabbling among themselves.

Dabney, Morgan's five-year partnership agreement was due to expire in October 1871, and none of the partners were eager to renew it. Dabney was sixty-four and thinking of retirement. Goodwin announced that he too wanted to leave and rejoin his elderly father, then still in business in Hartford. Pierpont viewed his brother-in-law George Morgan as more an impediment than a support. Pierpont's own poor health gave him an excuse to retire gracefully from business altogether without ruffling any family feelings.

None of these developments were known to Tony Drexel when, late in 1870 —with Paris still besieged by the Prussians—he paid a call on Junius Morgan in London. Tony was simply heading home from a European business trip and was eager to seek Junius Morgan's advice about strengthening Tony's own New York and Paris houses. As Drexel's London correspondent, Junius was well informed about Drexel's business; more important, Junius was exceptionally knowledgeable about American finance generally and New York banking in particular. And over the previous few months—as Junius used Drexel's Paris house to transfer the proceeds of the French loan directly to the French government—he and Tony had developed a trusting relationship.

Their discussion continued by mail after Tony's return to Philadelphia. In a "strictly confidential" letter dated January 7, 1871, Junius suggested his own son as a possible partner for Tony's New York firm. Junius also sketched the prospect of a closer connection between the Drexel banks and J. S. Morgan & Co. in London, especially if Tony himself were to take charge of Drexel's Paris office.

It was the sort of offer that the irrepressible traveler Francis Martin Drexel would doubtless have seized with alacrity. But Tony demonstrated again that he was not his father: "My pressing business interests in this country, and a large family, requiring my presence and care, would prevent my living abroad for any length of time," he wrote to Junius on January 27.

But a connection with Junius's son Pierpont was another matter altogether. The prospect of a dynamic banker like Pierpont running Drexel's New York office was attractive on its face, but it paled beside the implied added benefit of an alliance with Junius Morgan in London. "I take pleasure in saying it would be (if the matter could be arranged satisfactorily to all the parties) very acceptable to me," Tony wrote. His enthusiasm spilled out in the balance of this long letter, as he candidly discussed his organization's business and assets with Junius. The New York and Philadelphia houses, Tony said, had jointly made annual profits between $300,000 and $350,000 through most of the late 1860s.

Tony acknowledged that the Franco-Prussian War had impaired the finances of the Drexels' newer and smaller Paris house. But he insisted that the war had advanced the Paris house's reputation: "I think the fact of our paying our acceptances, and obligations, through the siege, while so many others suspended, will help us hereafter very much, as we have most favorable reports from many sources."

Tony proposed to gently remove Robert Winthrop, for eight years the head of Drexel, Winthrop & Co. in New York, and replace him with Pierpont Morgan in a reorganized partnership. The association with Winthrop "has been agreeable in every sense," Tony insisted. But Winthrop, whose father-in-law Moses Taylor was president of the National City Bank, suffered from obvious limitations:

> He was brought up in the house of Denniston, Wood & Co., and was with them at the time of their failure, which has made him so exceedingly cautious in our foreign business as to prevent any progress in that department. Also his very large expectations (being a son-in-law of Mr. Moses Taylor) prevented his pushing the business, as all business should be (when it can be done safely) in these times of great competition.

Tony theorized that if the New York house were to be reorganized, Winthrop would withdraw gracefully and "your son could take his position in the House."

A month later Tony communicated for the first time with Pierpont Morgan, in a three-sentence note alluding cryptically to Tony's correspondence with Junius and adding, "Should these matters strike you favorably, I will be glad to have an interview with you to talk it over. Could you come over here any time next week, or when convenient to you?"

Tony assumed—wrongly, as it turned out—that Junius had already explained the proposed alliance to Pierpont. But Junius had merely advised Pierpont to visit Tony if he was invited. Pierpont—very much in the dark but anxious to please his father—replied the next day asking if Tony could see him in New York. Tony responded on March 4, explaining that "I have just returned home this week after an absence of several days which causes such a press of business on me that I can't see my way clear to go to New York soon." Instead Tony offered to put Pierpont up overnight at his home at the soonest convenient time. Four nights later Pierpont boarded the Pennsylvania Railroad train in Jersey City and Tony, as promised, met him when the train arrived at the West Philadelphia depot at 8:20.

The sprawling three-story, forty-one-room mansion at 39th and Walnut Streets to which Tony conveyed his guest that night incorporated several features common to mid-Victorian Italianate villas: an asymmetrical tower, wide overhanging eaves supported by scrolled brackets, a columned façade, and rounded windows with hood moldings. A dining room beneath a low cupola extended from the house's east side, balanced on the west side by a conservatory with a high-peaked roof. The floors inside were finely carpeted, and the high-ceilinged rooms downstairs were filled with fixtures and artworks. A sweeping and handsomely carved stairway led upstairs, where the rooms—presumably including Pierpont Morgan's guest room—were more simply decorated than those below.

This house Tony and Ellen had built about 1860 now bustled with servants and children alike. Between 1851 and 1868 Ellen had borne nine children, and seven now survived, from nineteen-year-old Emilie down to George (named for George Childs), who was two and a half. Whether Pierpont was exposed to any of the Drexels on this brief first business seems unlikely, especially since his dinner could not have been served much before 9 P.M. that night.

After dinner, Tony took Pierpont into the library and told him that he was dissatisfied with his New York arrangement. "Morgan," he said, according to one account, "I want you to come into my firm as a partner." The Drexels' New York house, Tony proposed, would be reorganized as Drexel, Morgan & Co. The three Drexel brothers and their two other partners would put up virtually all the new firm's capital (Pierpont would contribute only $15,000 out of the initial $1 million), but Pierpont would be entitled to 50 percent of the new firm's profits and no less than 15 percent of the combined profits of the Philadelphia and New York houses.

This remarkably generous offer caught Pierpont completely by surprise. In effect, Tony's proposal addressed every one of Pierpont's business quandaries, plus some he hadn't even thought of. It liberated him from his dead-end partnership at Dabney, Morgan. It established him in charge of his own house with far more working capital than Pierpont or his father could have scraped together. It maintained Pierpont's working relationship with his father in London. It allied the Morgans with the Drexels' somewhat larger, somewhat older, and somewhat more extensive banking network.

Pierpont Morgan, like Tony Drexel, was not a man given to introspection or analysis. His intelligence was perceptual and concrete; it dealt in numbers, objects, actions. But even Morgan may have sensed at some level the most important benefit of all. The proposal offered, in the person of Tony Drexel, the prospect of a respected buffer whose presence might emancipate Pierpont from his father's heavy hand.

Pierpont repeated the same mantra he had been communicating to his father: His health was poor and he had decided to take a year off from business, if not retire altogether. Tony urged him to consider his proposal, praised Pierpont's capacities, promised him a bright future on Wall Street, even agreed to Pierpont's insistence on a long vacation (perhaps the best evidence that Tony, whatever his immediate pressures, was thinking very much in long-run terms).

On the back of an envelope Tony hastily jotted down the proposal's essential points:

Drexel, Morgan & Co.
15 [%] of the whole to be guaranteed to amount to 50% of the nett [sic] profits of the New York house and deficiency to be paid by remaining interests.
Interest to be allowed to Drexel & Co. on all balances.
Interest to be allowed to partners on their balances.
Paris profits or loss to be divided half & [illegible] ratio.

Pierpont pocketed the envelope and took it with him to New York the next morning to study the points and communicate them to his father. Two days later Tony wrote to Junius Morgan that "your son came to see me the night before last & we talked over matters fully." Tony wrote of his eagerness to bring about "the projected change," which "will I think be of advantage to all the parties concerned."

That was an understatement. In the proposed alliance, Tony would gain not only a dynamic partner in New York but stronger ties with Junius Morgan in London and, through him, with the entire London financial community. Tony hoped that Pierpont's involvement would bring stronger drive to Drexel's Paris house as well.

Junius Morgan, meanwhile, gained direct, effective representation in three of the world's principal capital markets—Paris, New York, and Philadelphia. It was the sort of access then enjoyed by only three of his London competitors—the Rothschild, Baring, and Seligman houses—and some half dozen other comparable private international banks (including, of course, the Drexels). Perhaps most important, in Tony Drexel Junius gained a respected mentor for Pierpont, someone who could advise, encourage, and restrain him and smooth out his rough edges as no father could.

If anyone stood to suffer from Tony's proposed alliance with the Morgans, it was probably the Drexels' three other New York partners at Drexel, Winthrop & Co., which Tony now proposed to reorganize and rename. Robert Winthrop was a proud, wealthy man with many outside business interests. The other two resident partners were Tony's younger brother Joe, then forty, and J. Norris Robinson, also forty, an experienced and energetic banker who represented the house on the New York Stock Exchange but who was otherwise hesitant and indecisive. Under the new arrangement these three partners would find themselves working under a new chief, a driven, energetic, well-connected man younger than any of them.

Over the next three and a half months, through letters and visits to New York, Tony gently but forcefully steered Pierpont through the essential points that required their consideration before Drexel, Morgan & Co. could open for business on July 1. Within a week of their first meeting, Tony advised Pierpont that Robert Winthrop had withdrawn from their New York house to tend to his own affairs and assist his father-in-law at the National City Bank.

> I received yesterday a very kind letter from Mr. Winthrop in reference to the proposed change. He says, "As to myself, I will after all be relieved of my constant anxiety and worry about the foreign exchange businesses, which as you know I have always disliked from the beginning . . ."
> I am very glad that he is satisfied as we both felt alike on that subject.

The following day Pierpont wrote to Tony to say that Junius had approved Pierpont's new arrangement—which was no surprise to Tony, since Junius had suggested it in the first place—and that Pierpont's cousin James Goodwin had agreed to stay on to wind up the affairs of Dabney, Morgan & Co. On March 17 Tony replied:

> I am very glad to hear your father and Mr. Peabody both approve of the contemplated agreement. As to the time of its consummation, I leave that entirely to you. We will be quite ready by the first of July. . . .
> I am happy to hear you have arranged with Mr. Goodwin to extend his attendance and remain as his knowledge of your business will be very important. . . .
> I will be abroad from tomorrow. The second day I may go to New York . . . to spend a few days. I hope to see you there and we can have a full talk.

In the course of this correspondence it may have occurred to both Tony Drexel and Pierpont Morgan that they shared certain characteristics. Each had been dominated by a father who was often a continent away, and perhaps as a consequence each tended to worry excessively. Both were men of deeds rather than words. Neither was a man of introspection. Both were publicity-shy. The actions of both were driven by an informed skepticism, as opposed to the blind optimism that characterized many of their financial contemporaries.

Tony's letters to Pierpont during these months leading up to the opening of

Drexel, Morgan & Co. reflected his strengths as both facilitator and mentor. He politely deferred to the wishes of both Morgans and expressed his eagerness to accommodate them; at the same time, he gently pushed them to nail down necessary details. By April 7 he was addressing Pierpont in the more familiar "My dear Mr. Morgan," as opposed to the more distant "My dear Sir." In the process of discussing whether J. S. Morgan or the Drexel firm's existing European agents would handle letters of credit for Americans traveling in Europe, Tony mildly suggested, "Would it not be a good plan to write Mr. Harjes [Drexel's Paris manager] to see your father and talk these matters over with him. You might also write to him. . . . I could write Harjes by next mail if you approve of it." In a letter of April 13, Tony told Pierpont, "I will try to see you next week in New York, when we talk over matters. Please make a menu as points occur to you that ought to be discussed."

On May 17, six weeks before the new firm's contemplated opening, Tony sent Pierpont a copy of its proposed promotional circular for Pierpont's approval. "I will be very glad if you will alter it so as to meet the financial case and it ought to be placed into the hands of the lithographers as soon as possible so as to be ready to send out on the 1st of July." Tony proceeded to discuss details concerning the relationships of the four houses, suggested that Pierpont write his father about these matters, and concluded by reminding Pierpont, "As the time is getting short, we must go to work and fix matters up so as not to be too crowded when we commence."

At the same time that Tony was cultivating Pierpont's confidence, he was also assuming his new role as Pierpont's defender before his critical father. "Your son wishes to leave for a year and I think it is necessary for him to do so," Tony wrote Junius on March 10. "He has been overworked and ought to have relaxation and rest. I do not see why he could not leave, as I have full confidence that he could do so without serious injury to the business in case we carry out the arrangement."

Tony made the same point even more forcefully to Junius three weeks later: "I can see that your son has fully made up his mind to leave for Europe in July, and he talks in such a way about it that I feel it is but 'to accept the situation'." Tony assured Junius that the New York office could manage until Pierpont returned—and that Pierpont was well worth waiting for:

I think your son is just in that condition of mind that all overworked people get in occasionally and which I myself have experienced (and I have no doubt you have also) when business becomes such a load that it is necessary to throw it off at all hazards. . . . I feel that the arrangement *must* prove mutually advantageous in every way. From what I have seen of your son, I think he is a first-class businessman and that you have reason to be proud of him in many ways.

Under the partnership agreement of July 1, 1871, the six resident partners in Philadelphia and New York shared in the profits and losses of both houses. They also became partners in the Paris house (although the resident Paris partners enjoyed no such interest in the Philadelphia or New York houses). Drexel Morgan & Co. started out with $1 million in capital, of which $900,000 took the form of a "special bills payable" fund assembled by the three Drexel brothers. The remaining $100,000 was paid in by the firm's six partners, with most of that sum—$71,000—again contributed by the three Drexel brothers. J. Hood Wright, the other Philadelphia partner, put in $5,000, while J. Norris Robinson, who remained in New York, contributed $9,000. Pierpont Morgan's capital contribution was just $15,000, yet the agreement guaranteed him 50 percent of the New York profits or 15 percent of the two houses' combined houses' profits, whichever was higher, just as Tony had originally proposed.

Beyond the initial working capital, of course, lay the resources of the Drexel and Morgan families. Tony had told Junius in January 1871 that the three Drexel houses had "active means" of nearly $3 million, at least 90 percent of which belonged to the three Drexel brothers. All told, Tony estimated that he and his brothers were then worth about $7 million—$6 million for Tony and his brother Frank, and another $1 million for their younger brother Joe—which suggests that their greatest wealth was not in their banks but in their growing real estate investments. Junius Morgan at the time was worth more than $5 million, and Pierpont about $350,000.

But the capital assets were secondary to the new firm's mixture of expertise, contacts, and reputation. On Drexel, Morgan's first day in business, the *Commercial & Financial Chronicle* called this combination "one of the most important changes in banking circles announced at this time." It was a time when the nation's 1,900 private banks—unincorporated and therefore unregulated and unrestricted as to the services they could offer—accounted for slightly more than one-half of all the nation's banks. Of these banks, probably no more than a score—virtually all of them in New York, Boston and Philadelphia—belonged in the same class with Drexel, Morgan.

Tony Drexel, Junius Morgan, and Pierpont Morgan never did get around to formally defining the lines of authority among them. Over the next twenty years and more, each man functioned as the unquestioned boss of his own office. Tony (as principal capitalist) and Pierpont (as chief manager) between them determined the policies of the New York and Paris houses. Pierpont, because of his ties to his father, came to serve as the Drexels' principal link with J. S. Morgan & Co. in London. The underlying if unspoken principle shared by all three men was the need to protect their firms' credit by managing their affairs so as to keep them liquid at all times.

Countless business mergers before and since have collapsed over critical issues of ego, power, and control. The striking thing about the Drexel-Morgan alliance was the absence of these issues among the three principals. When disagreements arose, each seems instinctively to have deferred to the others in an atmosphere of mutual respect. This remarkable personal chemistry, far more than their capital or their experience, ultimately rendered the Drexel-Morgan alliance a force of influence and longevity unprecedented in the annals of banking. Years after Pierpont's first meeting with Tony, Pierpont's son Jack joked that Tony's old used envelope became "the first articles of partnership of Drexel, Morgan & Co." In fact it was the only partnership agreement they ever needed. The rest was mere commentary.

Since all four of the Drexel and Morgan banking houses were private partnerships, in theory the partners were risking all their personal assets on their new allies, and the Drexels were taking the greatest risk of all. In effect, the Drexels were staking Pierpont Morgan not merely to his own business but to a business that the *Financial & Commercial Chronicle* ranked "among the few leading banking houses of the world." It was a vote of confidence such as Pierpont Morgan had never received before from anyone, his father included.

Drexel, Morgan & Co. opened on July 1, 1871 in Pierpont's cramped old office at 53 Exchange Place. But Pierpont remained there only briefly. Two weeks later, as he and Tony Drexel had agreed, Pierpont left for an extended vacation in Europe with his wife and three young children. He would not return until late September 1872—an absence of nearly fifteen months. Meanwhile, Tony Drexel set out to provide the new firm with a suitable working environment for Pierpont's return.

In the fall of 1871, while Pierpont was in Europe, Wall Street denizens began to notice an unfamiliar figure poking about among the financial district's narrow streets and crowded little Dickensian countinghouses: a stocky, well-dressed man of middle years, mutton-chop sideburns, and respectable bearing. It was George W. Childs, running another errand for his friend Tony Drexel—in this case, investigating real estate locations. He had his eye on a jumble of two- and three-story houses at the corner of Broad and Wall, directly opposite Federal Hall, where George Washington had taken the oath as America's first president in 1789. Many of these hovels dated back almost to Washington's day; the building housing Delatour's soda-water shop at Numbers 3 and 5 Broad, for example, had gone up in 1808.

So the provincial New Yorkers who had frequented these streets for generations were astonished to discover one morning in February 1872 that Childs, acting on behalf of the three Drexel brothers of Philadelphia, had assembled and purchased the entire corner lot for $945,000 in gold. For one of these acquired properties, the cost of the land worked out to $21 million per acre—"the biggest transaction which has ever occurred in New York," said the broker who handled the sale. In fact, *Harper's Weekly* soon pointed out, it was "the highest price ever paid for land in the world, being about three times as much as the highest price ever paid for lots in the immediate vicinity of the Stock Exchange in London."

More daunting than the price was the complexity of assembling all the pieces. The small building on the exact corner of Broad and Wall, housing a soda fountain and a newsstand, was jointly owned by six siblings who had inherited it from their late father but could not agree among themselves on a cash price. The heirs were ardent Catholics, and the deadlock wasn't broken until Tony Drexel hit on the notion of bringing his Catholic brother Frank into the negotiations. The deal ultimately fashioned by Tony and Frank provided the heirs with six separate mortgages totaling $250,000 in gold, paying interest of 7 percent for the life of the mortgagees—in effect, an annuity for all six heirs.

This building predated indoor plumbing, but the property included an adjacent washroom and toilet that Tony now referred to as the world's costliest W.C. "But I shouldn't mind the cost," he jokingly added, "if I could only use it easily and regularly."

On this spot the Drexels proposed to erect what the broker called "a magnificent architectural temple": a massive brownish-gray six-story fireproof granite-and-iron building topped by a two-story cupola. Its sheer size would rank it as a companion to the elegant Stock Exchange Building, the broad Sub-Treasury building, and the spire of Trinity Church. Among structures owned by private businesses, nothing would compare to it, with the possible exception of the Equitable Life Insurance Society at the corner of Broadway and Cedar. The structure would cost $800,000, bringing the total cost of the ground and building to nearly $1.8 million.

To New Yorkers of 1872 this prospect was staggering. "The brokers in the street . . . were really astonished when the details of the purchase were known," wrote the *Journal of Commerce*. "Gentlemen would glance up at the old houses, whose many occupants they had known for years, and ask, 'Is it really possible that Drexel, Morgan & Co. have bought all that ground?'" Added the *National Republican* in Washington: "In New York, it is regarded as somewhat an affront that Philadelphians, and not New York [sic], should be the men to make this bold venture. The great banking house of Drexel & Co. that is to rise upon the newly purchased site is to be a monument of Philadelphia enterprise, which fairly throws New York enterprise into the shade, in this case at least."

This was the building Tony Drexel was erecting for his new partner Pierpont Morgan. It would offer the young banker space, light, comfort, and prestige among his fellows. Just as it would cause bankers to raise their perception of Pierpont Morgan, so it would cause Pierpont to raise his perception of himself. Tony Drexel had demonstrated more confidence in Pierpont's future than Pierpont himself; he had demonstrated more confidence in New York's future than New Yorkers themselves. From the time the new building opened at the end of April 1873, its address—23 Wall Street—would be as famous as the name of its principal tenant.

But Tony Drexel himself continued to transact business in the same twenty-foot-wide building on Philadelphia's Third Street that his family had erected in 1854. Tony had declined to expand his own offices for much the same reason that he had declined an offer from his friend, President Grant, to become secretary of the Treasury: He was leery of public attention and public life. But he would stake his fortune and a prime piece of New York real estate on the Morgans. Thanks to that confidence, Pierpont Morgan was about to become rich, famous, and powerful. And Tony Drexel would assume a new role as well. Up to this point he had been the driving force behind his family business, restrained occasionally by his more cautious older brother Frank. Now, at age forty-five, Tony would become the wise but cautious elder and teacher, restraining and checking the exuberant impulses of his more adventurous junior partner, Pierpont Morgan.

"No native banking house stands higher" than Drexel & Co., reported the R. G. Dun credit bureau in the fall of 1872, "and only Brown Brothers & Co. equals them in solidity." That same year a wedding announced that the Drexels had breached Philadelphia's most impenetrable social barrier as well. On March 7, 1872, in what was described as the Philadelphia social event of the year, Tony's twenty-year-old daughter Emilie married Edward Biddle, a scion of Philadelphia's most prominent family. President Grant attended the affair, and so did the business and social elite of the East Coast, from Boston to Baltimore.

On the surface, the wedding united America's reigning banking family with the nation's previous banking aristocracy. Edward Biddle was a grandson of the legendary Nicholas Biddle, whose Bank of the United States had closed just as Francis M. Drexel opened his currency exchange in 1837. Edward's father had been the only one of Nicholas Biddle's children to opt for a business career, first in banking and then in international trade in Europe. Edward, born (like his bride Emilie) in 1851, had received his first schooling in Europe—in Geneva, Dresden, and Paris—where his parents spent much of the 1850s. Upon their return home in 1861, young Edward's education was entrusted to tutors until his parents decided he was ready to enroll in private schools. But his formal schooling ended in 1868 when, at age seventeen, he was hired by Drexel & Co. as an office boy—then the conventional preparation for a business career.

But in fact Edward had no real interest in business, nor did his family hold real credentials as great bankers. Almost since their arrival in America in 1681 the Biddles—in their various roles as soldiers, statesmen, and connoisseurs of arts and letters—had constituted the social glue that held Philadelphia (and sometimes the nation) together. But for business they had demonstrated no aptitude or interest; they specialized in marrying fortunes, not making them.

Edward epitomized this tradition. He was a stunningly handsome young man, much taken with himself, who carried his topcoat over his shoulders like a cape. Like other upper class young men of his day, he indulged in strenuous sports like boxing and tennis. He walked with a firm, brisk step, held himself like a ramrod, and exuded the arrogant air of an educated buccaneer. He yearned not for a banking career but for the freedom to devote his time to fine arts, literature, and the company of fashionable gentlemen. For the first four years after he went to work at Drexel & Co., Edward was the prototypical proper Philadelphia bachelor whose life revolved around the teas, dinners, balls, and other parties of the city's upper class. It was at one such gathering that he met Emilie Drexel.

Like many another newly rich father of America's Gilded Age, Tony Drexel tended to equate love of family with material gifts, inundating his children with more wealth than was good for them. Although Tony asked little for himself in the way of creature comforts—as his modest Third Street office attested—he believed that no expense was too great for his immediate family. His gifts to his newly married daughter and son-in-law included a three-story red brick house across the street from the Drexel family compound, the first of five mansions he would build for his children within a block of his own home. Although Edward made little attempt to hide his contempt for business, Tony gave him a $150,000 interest in Drexel & Co. and a share in the bank's profits (although not yet a partnership).

It was almost as if Tony's hard-nosed commercial acumen had been counterbalanced by blind wishful thinking about his own family. He could mold grateful protégés like George Childs and John Harjes but not his own blood relations and in-laws. Edward Biddle as a young man possessed much the same raw material as Pierpont Morgan. But they would turn out very differently, and their proximity to Tony Drexel did much to determine the adults they subsequently became.

CHAPTER NINE

Panic and Progress

WHEN PIERPONT MORGAN returned from his long vacation in the fall of 1872, Wall Street had assumed many of the characteristics of a bordello. The infamous politician William M. "Boss" Tweed was swindling millions from New York City's treasury. Jay Gould's former henchman Jim Fisk had been shot to death by a pimp. Gould himself had finally lost control of the Erie Railroad, but not before making millions by watering the company's stock. The managers of the Union Pacific Railroad had drained millions from shareholders by setting up their own construction company, the Crédit Mobilier, which wildly overcharged the railroad for its services.

Jay Cooke, still America's most prestigious banker due to his Civil War heroics, had ensnared himself and his investors in a well-intended railroad disaster of his own making. Cooke had gained control of the Northern Pacific Railroad and sold $100 million in bonds to build it. He had planned to connect Minnesota with the Pacific Northwest by laying thousands of miles of railroad per year, much of it without any immediate hope of profitability—a project that was bound to tie up the country's available capital, not to mention much of Europe's. By 1872 the Northern Pacific had exhausted its funds before construction was finished, and now Cooke's attempts to peddle more bonds through public relations gimmickry (the capital of North Dakota was named Bismarck in the hope of attracting German investors to Cooke's railroad) fell on deaf ears. By the end of 1872 the Northern Pacific was paying its workers in scrip, bridges were collapsing, roadbeds were washing out, and George Childs's *Public Ledger* was comparing the Northern Pacific to eighteenth-century Britain's South Sea Bubble scandal, the notorious South Pacific trading scheme that ruined hundreds of investors.

Cooke had fallen into a common American business trap of the day: tying up his bank's deposits in the investment business. In effect he had crossed the line separating bankers from promoters. To remain solvent, Cooke was forced to turn to short-term loans at crippling interest rates. His one hope of paying off a massive bank overdraft was to secure the leading role in placing the new $300 million bond issue to refinance the federal government's Civil War debt. The underwriting fees for this job were minuscule, but the proceeds did not have to be turned over to the government until the end of 1873. If Cooke could sell the bonds quickly, he could have use of the funds for almost a year.

Cooke worked his connections with Treasury Secretary George Boutwell to try to get the business, but he faced stiff competition: August Belmont (the Rothschilds' American agent), the Seligmans, and Morton, Bliss & Co. were also competing. And so were the Drexels. During the Civil War Cooke had elbowed the Drexels out of the government bond business altogether; but now the Drexels enjoyed the weight of the Morgans on their side.

Tony Drexel had also become a minor national hero in May of 1872 when he and George Childs had spent several days in Washington as part of a four-man team negotiating the government's claims for damages done to the Union's merchant ships during the Civil War by British-built Confederate raiders. The settlement brought the United States a $15.5 million award from Britain and averted a possible break in relations between the two countries.

For the privilege of selling the government's bonds, Cooke would have to organize other major banks into a syndicate capable of outbidding potential rival syndicates. The maneuvering that followed was similar to the jockeying that occurs among U.S. presidential candidates during a primary campaign. Each candidate must decide whether to campaign vigorously for the White House and alienate his rivals, or throw his support behind the front runner and hope to be tapped for the vice-presidency or a cabinet post. The Drexels at first declined to join Cooke's syndicate, as did their friend Levi Morton at Morton, Bliss & Co. So did the Rothschilds, the Barings, and, of course, Junius Morgan in London.

These rejections exposed an open secret within the financial community: Cooke's credibility was limited almost entirely to smaller financiers—not to the titans of finance, who had little regard for him. But the most influential house of all—the Rothschilds in London—suffered from a similar perception gap: For all their well-earned prestige in Europe, the Rothschilds had never established a significant presence in America and remained unclear about how to go about it. Exploiting this weakness, Cooke won the Rothschilds' support as well as that of Kuhn Loeb, the new German-Jewish house in New York.

Tony Drexel and the Morgans now confronted the choice of joining Cooke's syndicate as minor players or continuing to fight him and thereby possibly shutting themselves out of the government loan altogether. Tony characteristically chose to swallow his pride but left the final decision to his new young partner in New York.

"As a business matter," Tony explained to Junius Morgan in January 1873, "I feel constrained to say that in order to get rid of J. Cooke & Co. & Rothschild's competition a combination with them should not be rejected provided it can be done in entire equity." The decision to join the opposition, Tony said, should be left "entirely with Morton & Pierpont as they being on the ground can better judge the success of it." But in any case, Tony added, no alliance with Cooke was "desirable" without the Rothschild firm's participation.

This arrangement was typical of Tony's method with Pierpont. On his weekly visits to New York (customarily on Mondays) he made recommendations and suggested guidelines but otherwise left thirty-five-year-old Pierpont to his own prerogatives on the bond issues under discussion, on the theory that Pierpont—not Tony or Junius—would be primarily responsible for selling them.

In this case Pierpont followed Tony's judgment (indeed, over the next twenty-two years he never rejected it). On the last day of January Secretary Boutwell announced that the $300 million loan would be sold by two syndicates: a European group headed by five English firms, including the Rothschilds, J. S. Morgan and Jay Cooke's London branch, and an American group jointly managed by three banks—Cooke & Co., Drexel Morgan, and Morton, Bliss & Co., the house of Drexel's ally Levi Morton.

This arrangement effectively forced Jay Cooke into an alliance with houses whose methods were very different from his own. Cooke was accustomed to doing a big job in a hurry. The other houses preferred to move slowly and cautiously, responding to market conditions or waiting until conditions improved. They had no need to rush—their option from the government was good until December 1, 1873. But Cooke needed the money desperately and immediately.

Despite the strength of the two syndicates, at first the government loan found few takers in America. Pierpont in February blamed the lack of subscribers on tight money, competition from higher-yielding securities of comparable quality, and the Treasury's failure to make the offering more attractive. In London, where investors were still shell-shocked from America's Erie Railroad and Crédit Mobilier scandals, the U.S. bonds moved even more slowly. (The loan wasn't entirely placed until early in 1876.)

Nevertheless, in April Pierpont confessed to his father that he was feeling "remarkably well . . . never better," and attributed his high spirits to his new partnership. He was beginning to attract favorable attention. "This young man is smart & is perhaps the most venturesome member of the firm," observed a Dun & Co. credit report on Pierpont, "but he is kept in check by the Drexels." (The railroad executive Archibald McLeod—no friend to either Tony or Pierpont—echoed a similar sentiment twenty years later: Tony Drexel, he said, "saved Morgan two or three times, for Morgan is a plunger.")

Pierpont himself readily acknowledged his dependence on Tony. After Tony left on a long vacation in March—in itself a remarkable expression of confidence in Pierpont—Pierpont wrote to his father that "the aspect of affairs at the moment is so threatening, that I do not like to leave, with Mr. A.J.D. on the other side of the Atlantic." When Tony returned to America early in June, Pierpont wrote to his father, "Mr. Drexel and family have arrived safely—and I cannot tell you how greatly relieved I am that he is back. It takes an immense responsibility off my shoulders, I can assure you, to have him here to consult and act with." In another letter six weeks later Pierpont contrasted his final years at Dabney, Morgan, with his current situation, in which he found "nothing harassing or disturbing." Although Junius urged his son to extend his country weekends to Mondays for the sake of his health, Pierpont replied that "Mr. Drexel is always in New York on that day," and "as it is generally desirable that I should see him at least once a week, I go down for that purpose."

Pierpont's candid letters to his father are notable for their tone of respect bordering on veneration whenever Tony Drexel (always referred to as "Mr. Drexel") is mentioned. The evidence suggests that Pierpont never opposed Tony's wishes, and in several cases Pierpont changed his position to suit Tony. When Tony in 1873 disapproved of establishing a direct representation in Boston, Pierpont wrote his father, "I would not for a moment set up my judgment in opposition."

Yet Pierpont's satisfaction with his new partnership arrangement did not blind him to the economic clouds he saw forming on the horizon early in 1873. Money seemed to be evaporating. The first signs of trouble appeared in April, when some businesses were forced to close and stock market prices dropped. As money grew increasingly scarce that summer, Pierpont attended a meeting one day where he learned, in confidence, the astonishing news that Jay Cooke was on the brink of failure.

On his way back to the office Pierpont decided to prepare for the inevitable impending panic by calling in all Drexel, Morgan's loans. That decision may have saved the firm, but it irrevocably split the Drexel family, for it forced Tony to choose between Pierpont Morgan and Tony's own devoted brother Joe.

. . .

Joseph Wilhelm Drexel was a big, bearded man with dark eyes, sensitive hands, and a low musical voice, whose jovial figure, with its unique stovepipe hat and pantaloons, was a colorful sight on Wall Street. Like his older brothers he was passionately fond of music. During his years at Drexel, Morgan he employed a German band by the year to perform symphonies and nocturnes in the street outside his office while he lunched, much to the annoyance of the neighbors and, one suspects, of Pierpont Morgan. "Only respect for Mr. Drexel," remarked a New York newspaper, "prevented the band being torn to pieces by its infuriated victims."

Since reaching adulthood Joe had faithfully served his older brothers, establishing connections in Germany and setting up their branch houses in Chicago, Paris, and now New York. But Joe's relations with Pierpont Morgan were difficult from the start. Pierpont was brilliant but rude, a genius who thrived on business pressures. Joe, six years older, was a refined and gentle soul who habitually came home from work "more exhausted than a field laborer," his daughter later recalled—so tired that he often fell suddenly asleep at dinner even "in the middle of a conversation that was obviously interesting him."

Although Pierpont was, in theory as well as practice, the dominant partner at the New York office, Joe Drexel was (again in theory) the New York representative of the Drexels, who owned the office. Thus Joe was in the difficult position of being Pierpont's subordinate and his superior simultaneously. This would have posed no problem had the two men respected each other. But Pierpont had little use for Joe; by his standards Joe was neither a good banker nor an astute businessman, and Pierpont rarely consulted him.

"You will find him very different from his brother," Pierpont warned Junius when Joe Drexel traveled to London in June 1873. In the office Pierpont did not hesitate to disparage Joe's capacities, treating him "rather roughly at times," another partner reported. The banker Joseph Seligman, who visited Drexel, Morgan regularly, told his brother that Pierpont was "a rough, uncouth fellow, continually quarreling with Drexel in the office." Once when Joe left his cherished hat on a desk rather than on its accustomed peg, Pierpont knocked it to the floor with his cane.

Joe Drexel's primary function was to lend out the firm's money at the highest possible rate on call loans—that is, loans that Drexel, Morgan had the right to recall at its discretion—and to monitor the loan payments. He spent most of his time sitting in a small corner room in the Drexel Building, next to a safe in which he kept the securities on these loans. From Joe Drexel's narrow perspective in the summer of 1873, this business seemed immensely satisfying. The loans were earning high interest, and the debtors seemed to be meeting their payments. So Joe was flabbergasted when Pierpont Morgan walked into his little room that day and announced, without explanation, "Call all loans."

"But Mr. Morgan," Joe replied, "I am getting 6 percent for the money."

"*You do what I say*," Morgan barked. "Call the loans." When Tony declined to overrule that order, the humiliated Joe had no choice but to comply.

Whatever effectiveness Joe exercised as a partner was largely undermined by this incident, and thereafter it became increasingly difficult for him to work with Pierpont. But Pierpont's decision to call the loans proved brilliantly prescient. By September money was tighter than ever, more railroads were in trouble, and America's credit abroad had been further undercut by revelations of scandals within the Grant administration—including bribery of cabinet members (and even Grant's private secretary) by railroads and the notorious "whiskey ring."

On Saturday September 13, Daniel Drew's old Wall Street firm of Kenyon, Cox & Co. declared itself insolvent and shut its doors. The following Wednesday, stocks began declining amid increasing trading volume. That night President Grant—in Philadelphia to enroll his son in a private school—spent the night at Ogontz, Jay Cooke's mansion. The next morning, while Grant took a carriage to the train station and Cooke headed for his Third Street office, Cooke's New York partner Harris C. Fahnestock met with the presidents of several major banks. When Cooke arrived at his office shortly before 11 A.M. he was greeted by a telegram informing him that Fahnestock had closed the doors of Cooke's New York office and announced its suspension. Since Cooke's New York house was doing ten times the business of his Philadelphia office, Cooke had no choice but to cease operations as well.

For a moment tears streamed from his eyes. Then, at about 11 A.M. the doors of Cooke's Third Street bank swung shut, never to open again. By 12:15 Cooke's Washington house and the First National Bank of Washington, which he controlled, had followed as well. After twelve tumultuous years in business, America's most famous banker was bankrupt.

When the news of Cooke's failure reached the floor of the New York Stock Exchange, according to the *New York Tribune*, "a monstrous yell went up and seemed to literally shake the building in which all these mad brokers were confined." Outside on Wall Street, "dread seemed to take possession of the multitude." A similar scene unfolded in Philadelphia, where panicked brokers and investors milled about in Third Street.

Tony Drexel was as concerned about this disaster as anyone: If Jay Cooke could fail, no banker was safe. But at this extraordinary moment he chose to do a very ordinary thing. At noon he made a point of emerging from his building and strolling calmly through the Third Street crowds, then around the corner and up Chestnut Street for his customary lunch date with George Childs—looking, according to one report, "as cheerful as if there was not a woe in the world." In the words of one witness, "Many people, seeing him looking so serene," felt that "that things could not be so bad after all, and thus to that degree confidence was improved."

But no symbolic act could stem what now became the Panic of 1873. It brought down scores of banks and brokerage houses, damaged many more, and threatened to destroy still others. On Saturday morning, September 20, the New York Stock Exchange suspended trading for the first time in its history. It remained shut for ten days, and when it reopened the country quickly lapsed into a depression that persisted for five and a half years.

Yet the Drexel and Morgan houses not only survived the panic but emerged from it stronger than ever, thanks to Pierpont's foresight. "Impossible foresee future," Pierpont telegraphed his father the day after Cooke failed. "Affairs continue unprecedentedly bad—large failures Phila. and N.Y." Then he added: "Everything satisfactory with us with ample margin."

Pierpont's demonstrated prescience in calling in the firm's loans should have bolstered his self-confidence, yet he continued to lean almost slavishly on Tony Drexel's judgment. Writing to Junius late in 1873 about the Drexel and Morgan houses' involvement with the troubled Cairo & Vincennes Railroad, Pierpont simply forwarded "a letter from Mr. Drexel to me on the subject, also his private letter to me, which gives more clearly his views as to continuing to advance money to the road, all of which I think merits your consideration. . . . As to the reorganization, I scarcely know what to say—Mr. Drexel will be over here on Monday next week and we will talk the matter over." In one letter Pierpont even upbraided Junius for failing to be more supportive of Tony.

> I think you make a mistake in not appreciating the strength of the organization on this side [of the Atlantic], whose influence is most cheerfully thrown in your favor at all times and who are always wishing to protect your interests in every way. . . . I don't believe there is any one man in financial circles who has the influence today that Mr. Drexel has, and of course his power and control is equally great, and they are naturally bent to protect and promote your interests.

Jay Cooke's failure removed a major competitor for the U.S. Treasury's business, leaving it to be divided among Cooke's former rivals. The leaders included two Yankee houses—Drexel, Morgan and Morton, Bliss—and two German-Jewish firms, August Belmont (the U.S. agent of the Rothschilds' London bank) and J. & W. Seligman.

To the U.S. Treasury, Pierpont Morgan now could offer distribution facilities of demonstrated effectiveness, represented by a combination of Drexel-Morgan capital plus the machinery of J. S. Morgan & Co. in London and Drexel Harjes & Co. in Paris. He could also offer international distribution through Levi Morton and the Rothschild firm. Before the Panic, the Drexel and Morgan houses had been merchant banks that incidentally also negotiated and distributed government and corporate loans. After that crisis, lending to governments and large businesses became their primary activity.

Despite the depression, all Cooke's former rivals ended the year 1873 showing a profit, but none seems to have fared better than the Drexels' New York and Philadelphia houses. The two firms' combined year-end profits exceeded $1 million—$584,191 for the Philadelphia partnership and $459,890 for Pierpont's operation in New York—and these figures did not include nearly $200,000 that Tony and Pierpont had prudently set aside to cover probable losses from bad debts. If Tony appeared serene on the day of his symbolic September 18 stroll up Chestnut Street, perhaps he had good reason.

About one issue Joe Drexel was keenly astute: Among the three Drexel brothers, he was the odd man out. By the panic of 1873, Frank and Tony Drexel had worked together for thirty-four years. Their divergent temperaments, far from conflicting, had complemented each other brilliantly. Within their Third Street office Frank was the cautious and conservative inside man, Tony the energetic and visionary outside man. Frank was nominally the head of Drexel & Co., but Tony was recognized by everyone, including Frank, as the firm's true driving force. Frank had remained a devout but socially conscious Catholic, donating some $1.5 million in the post-Civil War years to church-related institutions; Tony, with equal devotion, had embraced the Episcopal church, the more liberal denomination preferred by Philadelphia's assertive upper classes. Yet neither man ever questioned the other's function or faith; the brothers' unspoken acceptance of their differences in fact laid the groundwork for the chemistry that developed between Tony and the Morgans.

The brothers' divergences, after all, were merely a matter of degree. Compared to Pierpont Morgan, Tony was himself the soul of cautious conservatism. And compared to his footloose father, Francis M. Drexel, Tony was a pillar of dull predictability. In his office he worked at a plain, flat-topped leather table. When he traveled to Europe—as he did at least once year, both on business and to take the waters at the spa resort of Carlsbad, Bohemia—he always made out in advance a map of his route and an itinerary specifying precisely the time to be spent at each place, so his office could reach him by cable wherever he happened to be.

The need to impose order on his day was a constant preoccupation. "I always write under difficulties as I am interrupted every minute and it takes me all day to write every letter," Tony once apologized to his nieces—Frank's daughters. In another personal letter written from the office, Tony complained, "I don't know whether you will be able to read this disconnected scrawl but I write under difficulties as I no sooner start a line than someone comes in and interrupts me."

His punctuality was legendary, too. One morning, having made an appointment to receive a caller at 11 o'clock, Tony was seated with his secretary, E. T. Stotesbury. Glancing at the clock, he remarked, "Ed, it is three minutes after 11. We will go ahead with the mortgages." At 11:20 an office boy brought in the visitor's card. Glancing at it, Tony said, "Tell the gentleman my next free hour is at 12. He may wait in the outer office." The visitor, as the story is told, was President Ulysses S. Grant.

It may seem incredible that the same Tony Drexel who so readily accommodated the little-known Pierpont Morgan's travel schedule in 1871 would have kept the president of the United States waiting in an anteroom. But this incident reflected not only Tony's punctual nature but also Grant's subservient relationship with Tony and the business community. As a soldier Grant had introduced the concept of delegating authority to experts and specialists; now he applied the same concept in politics—an approach that was too far ahead of its time, as the scandals of Grant's administration soon demonstrated. When Grant sought out business leaders for advice, he often did so on their turf—New York, say, or Philadelphia—rather than his own, a tacit acknowledgment that his government needed their support more than they needed his.

Some sense of the relationship between government and business during the Gilded Age can be derived from Tony's response in early 1874 to a request that he appear before a Congressional committee: "I regret very much that important business calls me away next week, and I therefore cannot visit Washington for the purpose of meeting your committee, nor can I name a time when I will be able to do so."

Although Tony had declined Grant's offer to become Secretary of the Treasury, Grant often sought Tony's advice, especially on Grant's occasional visits to

Philadelphia. But the general appears to have had closer camaraderie with George Childs as well as some of Tony's rival bankers, such as Joseph Seligman and even Jay Cooke, most of whom were eager to encourage Grant's friendship.

Tony, by contrast, appears to have kept Grant at a respectful arm's length. When Grant came to Philadelphia, he usually stayed overnight with Childs or Cooke, not with the Drexels. Although Tony was keenly interested in public issues, he was leery of partisan politics. He supported Lincoln during the Civil War and Lincoln's fellow Republican Grant after the war, but in 1884 he would support the Democrat Grover Cleveland because of his faith in Cleveland's integrity. As one newspaper put it, Tony was "simply a liberal, conscientious citizen and held his own judgment above all party obligations."

Grant demonstrated his respect for Tony's judgment in the fall of 1873, when Congress was considering the so-called "Greenback Bill" to expand the nation's currency by issuing the $44 million of greenbacks then in the U.S. Treasury. Grant (like Drexel) opposed the measure as inflationary, but in September he spent a night and day in New York listening to businessmen, most of whom appealed to him to release the currency in order to stimulate the economy and combat unemployment. Their arguments so dazzled the economically naive Grant that he turned to Tony Drexel as a sounding board.

Tony, according to one account, refuted the inflationists' views so persuasively that Grant vetoed the bill in April 1874. His veto message, which largely echoed Tony's reasoning, was subsequently acknowledged as sound even by the bill's leading advocates. To George Childs, the incident was a tribute to Grant's openmindedness and quick perception in financial matters: "Here was a subject he had considered, as he had thought, fully, but when new light was given to him by A. J. Drexel, whom he knew to be a well-informed, conservative, unselfish, and reliable man, and an experienced and able financier, and who possessed the public confidence, he changed his opinions and wrote the veto message."

In the winter of 1875 Grant and several of his cabinet members—including Treasury Secretary Hugh McCulloch—gathered at Tony's home in West Philadelphia to consult with him about financial issues. While they were meeting, a young physician rang the front doorbell. At the time, Tony was a trustee of Jefferson Medical College, and the young man had taken the Chestnut Street horse car out to seek advice about his career. A servant answered and took the young physician's calling card. A few minutes later Tony Drexel himself came downstairs to the front door and extended his hand.

When the physician apologized for intruding, Tony replied that he was "always ready to be of service to any person who needs it or to spare a few minutes for the sake of another, no matter whether I am busy." He talked with the young doctor for ten minutes while Grant and his cabinet members waited inside.

On Grant's last morning in office—March 4, 1877—Childs was with him in Washington as the general anxiously awaited news of the passage of a retirement bill stipulating his pension. Childs sought to reassure him that the bill would pass, but Grant replied, "Mr. Childs, you know that during the last day of a session everything is in turmoil. Such a bill cannot possibly be passed." As they were talking, Childs later recalled, "I got a telegram from Mr. A. J. Drexel, saying that the bill had passed, and the general seemed exceedingly gratified." The anecdote is a telling one: Tony Drexel's sources of information were superior to those of the President himself.

Grant's dependence on Tony increased after he left office. In May 1877 Grant and his wife left on a global cruise, relying on Tony's correspondent bankers around the world to handle his finances while he traveled. Days before they departed, Grant spent a few days in Philadelphia with Childs, who hosted an intimate farewell luncheon with Tony and one other local businessman. By Christmas the former president had been abroad so long that American newspapers began conjecturing that the money he was spending was not his own. Not so, reported John Russell Young of the *New York Herald*, who was part of Grant's entourage: The general was living and traveling on the income from the gifts he had received twelve years earlier, at the end of the Civil War, invested since that time by A. J. Drexel.

In December 1879 Tony and Ellen Drexel threw an enormous reception for Grant at their home, attended by some 700 prominent guests. In 1881 Childs and Drexel successfully raised still another house fund for Grant, with which the general bought an unpretentious home at 3 East 66th Street in New York.

None of this support prevented Grant from going bankrupt on Wall Street in 1884. When he died of throat cancer the following year (expiring at Joseph Drexel's cottage in upstate New York), Tony was one of his pallbearers. But in retrospect Tony's friendship with Grant was largely a byproduct of Tony's friendship with George Childs. Tony was, after all, a private man, reluctant to pursue public figures. Instead he cultivated private allies, like Junius and Pierpont Morgan. He could hardly be blamed for failing to see that, in the process of this cultivation, Pierpont Morgan would become a more visible public figure than any American president of his epoch.

Yet Pierpont's future was hardly assured in the fall of 1873. His victory over Jay Cooke had come at a stiff price: the end of his relationship with Joseph Drexel and, Pierpont therefore assumed, with Tony Drexel as well. Once the worst of the panic of 1873 had subsided, Joseph appeared at the office less and less frequently—and when he did show up, the tension between him and Pierpont was palpable. Drexel, Morgan's third resident partner, J. Norris Robinson, was in poor health and increasingly absent as well. When Robinson retired at the end of 1874, Tony Drexel sent his partner J. Hood Wright up to New York from Philadelphia as a replacement. Still, the net effect was an increased burden on Pierpont, and what he perceived as an unresolvable situation.

Unwilling to provoke a confrontation with his father or Tony Drexel, Pierpont reacted as he had with his previous partnership: by assuming he had no alternative but to quit. "I note carefully what you say about the necessity for another partner," Pierpont wrote to his father in March 1875, unburdening himself for the first time about his irritation with Joe Drexel.

> Of course as long as Mr. J.W.D. continues in business, any such arrangement is out of the question. Between ourselves, every day convinces me more than ever of his not being capable of filling his place, and it would be impossible to get anyone else in who would take precedence of him. He is *very* sensitive and I have to study his whims constantly to avoid any questions.
>
> If I could have Mr. Wright with me alone it would be all I could ask. He is entirely competent in all respects, very quick, a capital negotiator besides very accurate and good bookkeeper.
>
> However, I don't see any prospect of change at present. I feel as though perhaps the best thing would be for me to give up myself. I don't feel good for much anyway.

Once again it was Tony Drexel who took the initiative, as he had in 1871, to steer the indecisive Pierpont in a productive direction. "Never mix business with friendship" had long been one of Tony's favorite maxims; now he applied the same principle to his family as well. On September 14, 1875, Pierpont advised his father of a new development that Pierpont could not have imagined six months earlier:

> Mr. Joseph Drexel told me, a day or two ago, that he had made up his mind to withdraw on the 1st of January. I have noticed for some time the feeling growing up between him and his two brothers, and was not surprised at his decision. I have not discussed the matter as yet with Mr. A.J.D. I do not know what his views or plans may be arising from this change; and I mention it to you now in confidence, and would ask that no allusion be made to it in your letters to Mr. A.J.D. at present until after I have had a talk with him upon the

subject. I do not feel at all sure as to what I had better do. As I have before written you, I feel, so far as I myself am concerned, strongly disposed to give up; but that must depend in a great measure upon what your plans may be for next year. But I can write more fully after seeing Mr. Drexel.

Without Pierpont's ever raising the issue of his relations with Joe Drexel, Tony had perceived the problem and had dealt with it. Pierpont had felt "strongly disposed to give up"; Tony refused to let him. He had sided with Pierpont rather than Joe, with the business over the family, with cold logic over blood loyalty. His refusal to side with a relative whose advice struck him as wrong or risky anticipated a notion that would not receive wide acceptance until the twentieth century: that in business practices, merit should take priority over bloodlines.

With Joe Drexel's departure, a freshly energized and confident Pierpont Morgan now assumed clear and unquestioned command of the Drexels' New York house. That decision to side with Pierpont over Joe would generate millions of dollars for Tony over the next generation; it would also play a major part in stabilizing the chaotic U.S. economy. The price Tony paid was the end of his relationship with his brother Joe.

"My grandfather, Joseph Drexel," wrote the historian Boies Penrose in a private letter years later, "had a furious row with old Morgan: No one knows exactly what happened, but he never went back to his office and never spoke to either of his brothers (or old Morgan) as long as he lived. He was obviously eased out of the firm in a far from gentle manner."

CHAPTER TEN

The Perils of Partnership

LIKE A MODERN HIGHWAY SYSTEM that compounds traffic problems by encouraging more people to drive automobiles, the effectiveness of the Drexels' financial network stoked the appetites of governments and business for ever greater quantities of capital. Clerks, bookkeepers, and office boys now seemed to multiply like rabbits in the halls of the Drexels' two U.S. houses. When the new Drexel Building at Broad and Wall Streets opened in April 1873, Drexel, Morgan shared the ground floor with Morton, Bliss & Co., but within two months the firm was cramped for space, and by February 1878 Drexel, Morgan had taken over the entire first floor.

But neither support troops nor additional square footage could solve the conundrum of a growing partnership. By legal definition, a partnership consisted only of its partners; anyone else on the payroll was merely a supplier of services. Only the partners could sign checks, approve loans, and negotiate securities offerings. Even the mail—since it was addressed to the partnership—could be opened and read only by the partners.

These precautions were taken for granted because a partnership was much like a marriage. Whereas shareholders in a corporation stood to lose no more than the amount they had invested, in a partnership each of the partners could be held personally liable for the partnership's debts. Like a drop of ink in a glass of water, a single rogue partner could ruin not only the business but his individual partners as well. This unlimited liability explained why most partnerships consisted either of blood relatives or of close friends. Yet by its very inbred nature this requirement usually prevented partnerships from expanding to meet their customers' growing needs.

Joseph Drexel's retirement in the fall of 1875 reduced the Drexels' New York and Philadelphia houses to five partners between them—Tony and Frank Drexel and their recently promoted clerk Charles Godfrey in Philadelphia, and Pierpont Morgan and J. Hood Wright in New York. The burden on these five partners was heavy; yet the prospect of adding new partners was as momentous as the thought of changing spouses might be. More so than most senior partners of their day, Tony, Pierpont, and Junius recognized that they must admit more partners, whatever the risk.

The task, as Tony put it to Junius, "must be done with the greatest caution in every way." Few issues were more important: No one became a partner at any of the Drexel or Morgan houses without the approval of the three seniors. But the choices in New York and Philadelphia appear to have been largely left to Tony's initiative, at least at first.

The ground rules Tony established and impressed on Pierpont were a model for their day. He was not looking for technical training in banking or finance, which could be learned on the job. His first priority was integrity, followed by general business competence. Nor would Tony admit anyone to partnership solely for his business connections. The senior at each house, not the junior partners, was responsible for developing new business.

The admissions process was wealth-blind as well. All partners, including Pierpont and Tony, were required to leave half their assigned percentages of the partnership's annual earnings on deposit at the firms where they worked. Consequently, the houses had no need to recruit wealthy partners solely for their money.

Pierpont sometimes questioned Tony's partnership choices but always acceded to them. When Tony suggested replacing Joe Drexel in New York with the Philadelphia banker J. Lowber Welsh, Pierpont was dubious but assented, as he explained to his father:

> When Mr. A.J.D. was here on Monday he suggested taking J. Lowber Welsh into the firm here instead of J.W.D. who withdraws. He thinks he knows him well, his faults as well as his virtues, and that he thought he was one of the ablest young men he knew of. I told him I had my doubts whether our business would be improved by the connection but that I would think it over and let him know within a few days. . . . I think I can get along smoothly with anyone who is capable, clear headed and industrious. . . . I have therefore pretty much made up my mind after getting your favorable opinion to accept Mr. D.'s proposition. If it should happen that it proves unsatisfactory, I have the option of going out myself at any time. . . . However, as Mr. AJD is anxious to have my reply without much delay I shall give it in the affirmative, and hope all for the best.

Pierpont was relieved when, shortly afterward, Welsh declined the offer after all. The partnership instead went to Pierpont's preferred choice, the Italian-born merchant Egisto Fabbri, an old business friend of Junius Morgan. Tony next suggested, in keeping with his customary practice, that Pierpont and the Drexels reduce their share of the New York profits in order to give Fabbri a percentage. Pierpont was dismayed but, characteristically, acquiesced. He wrote to his father:

> When we were discussing Fabbri, AJD said he thought there should be a new deal all around. He said that he had felt for some time that the original arrangement of 50% to me and 50% to D & Co. who were to supply two partners was not an equitable arrangement in view of the larger money investment they had in the N.Y. business, and that he thought we ought to divide the 15% of N.Y. which it was then proposed to give to Fabbri. I did not like the proposition being made but I did not want to take any stand. . . . I again suggested my own preference that he should come to some equitable and satisfactory basis and divide both houses to all, but Mr. D. would not listen to that so it was dropped.

Yet in fact Tony did listen: He wound up giving Pierpont a larger share of the New York profits than he took for himself and his brother. Beginning January 1, 1876, Pierpont got 42.5 percent of the New York profits, Fabbri 20 percent, and the Philadelphia partners—including both Drexel brothers and J. Hood Wright, who had actually moved to New York—just 37.5 percent.

Through the 1870s and 1880s the Drexel and Morgan partnerships added twelve new partners—seven in London and five in New York and Philadelphia. But the first new partners were added only to replace those who departed; not until 1883 would the New York and Philadelphia houses have more than three partners each.

Like other private banks in Europe and the United States, the Drexel and Morgan houses recruited their partners from a small circle of family, friends, and close business associates. Junius Morgan's son-in-law Walter Burns joined the London house in 1879, and for the next five years he and Junius were the sole partners there. Tony's son-in-law James Paul, Jr., husband of Tony's daughter Frances, joined the Philadelphia house in 1883.

Tony also followed the rare practice of cultivating partners from the ranks of his employees. His philosophy held that no one at the firm could stand still. For many years he applied the unique rule that an employee who did not become more valuable to the firm every year ought to be dismissed. This meant that each New Year's Day, everyone at Drexel & Co., from department heads down to office boys, received either a pay raise or a letter urging him to seek other employment—a forerunner of the annual performance evaluations that became common in the late twentieth century. (In practice, Tony's firm was so careful about its hiring that dismissals were almost unheard of; slow promotion was the rule for most employees.)

Sometimes Tony encouraged the most promising clerks by giving them a small percentage of the profits even before they became partners. The original Drexel-Morgan partnership agreement of July 1, 1871 assigned 2 percent of the joint houses' profits to the Drexels' long-time employee Charles Godfrey. By 1875 Godfrey was himself a partner and two other clerks—Edward T. Stotesbury, then twenty-five, and Tony's son-in-law Edward Biddle, then twenty-three—were each assigned 2 percent of the joint profits "for their services." Stotesbury, who had joined Drexel & Co. as a seventeen-year-old in 1866, would remain there for seventy-two years and eventually become the senior himself. The hot-headed Edward Biddle, on the other hand, would live almost as long as Stotesbury but would be gone from the firm by the end of the 1870s, a jarring reminder of Tony's inability to transfer his patience, endurance and judgment to his own relatives.

The opulence of Emilie Drexel's 1872 wedding to Edward Biddle, like that of many another society marriage of the Gilded Age, soon proved inversely proportional to the rapture of the couple involved. Within a few years of their marriage Edward had abandoned any pretense of regard for business in general or for his *arriviste* in-laws in particular. The mere acquisition of wealth—especially by men like Tony Drexel, who already had far more money than they needed—was genuinely repugnant to a Philadelphia gentleman of taste and breeding, as Edward fancied himself. The fact that Edward was financially dependent on the Drexels merely compounded his resentment.

Although the Biddles' house at 3915 Locust Street (which Tony and Ellen had given them as a wedding present) was just a block from Tony's, Edward made a point of closing his house to Drexel influences. Here Edward reigned like a martinet over his forlorn wife and their three small sons. At dinner, when the conversation displeased him, he peremptorily ordered the subject dropped. He arranged all the parties and played the imperturbable host. He even performed the family's marketing, on the theory that only a superior man could thwart the swindling grocer and butcher.

Tony and Ellen Drexel were not amused. Although they were cultured people themselves, they believed that Edward's intellectual and social interests should not be ends in themselves but accouterments of business success. Tony had worked long, tedious hours at the bank in his youth without sacrificing his artistic education, and he couldn't imagine why Edward would not embrace the same career path. Although Tony harbored hopes that Edward would become a partner, thus assuring the family's business continuity for a third generation, Edward instead became a negative influence within the firm. He made no secret of his contempt for his colleagues at Drexel & Co., and they responded in kind.

One day early in 1878, by which time Edward had worked at Drexel & Co. for nearly ten years, a junior clerk bumped into Edward within the narrow confines of the bank's vault. "Look where you're going, you clumsy ox," the clerk muttered. Edward, who prided himself on his boxing skills, promptly knocked the clerk down and strode, unruffled, back to his desk, leaving others to pick up their dazed colleague.

Such behavior, Edward well knew, was anathema to Tony. From Tony's earliest days as an apprentice, the Drexels had always demanded more from themselves and their family than from other employees. Edward waited until Tony had received a full account of the fight. Then he strode into Tony's office, where, according to the surviving accounts, he was received solemnly.

"Are you here to give me a report of the incident, Edward?" Tony asked.

"I have no report to make," Edward replied unapologetically. "The man offended me and I knocked him down. I think now it is a question of his going or my going."

"Edward," Tony replied, "I think you had better leave. I'm afraid you're not cut out for a banker."

"I'm certain I'm not," Edward agreed. The two men stared at each other for a few moments more until Tony suggested that he could arrange for Edward to study law with Logan Bullitt, Tony's lawyer.

This was fine with Edward. The law—at least as practiced in the nineteenth century—offered Edward the leisure time he needed to pursue his true calling as a gentleman of letters. Tony further eased the transition by purchasing Edward's $150,000 interest in Drexel & Co., which Tony had given him as a wedding present. At the same time, Tony furnished Emilie with an allowance of her own.

Edward promptly took Emilie and their three sons to Europe for a long trip. The year 1880 found him studying law at 32 South Third Street, next door to Drexel & Co. In 1881 he was admitted to the Philadelphia bar. In this manner Tony eased his obstreperous son-in-law out of Drexel & Co.

Other family firms, embracing the ancient maxim that blood is thicker than water, routinely turned a blind eye to the failings of family members. Tony was unusual for his day in his refusal to practice this kind of nepotism. As he had done in the conflict between his brother Joe and Pierpont Morgan, Tony refused to side with his relatives when they were wrong. For better or worse, he was creating the outlines of a modern American business—one based not on bloodlines but on merit.

Tony's truce with his son-in-law did not last long. Edward's despotic treatment of Emilie continued. She was a fine pianist, and in a household where she seems to have known little pleasure, she lost no chance to invite her friends over for the afternoon: With Edward away, the mice could play. On one such occasion in January 1883 they played too hard. Emilie had been something of a tomboy in her youth and prided herself on her physical strength. On a dare from one of her friends, she proceeded to lift up the end of her grand piano. The strain was too much for her heart: She died shortly afterward, at the age of 31.

Emilie's death was devastating emotionally to her father and financially to her husband. Nine days after she died, Tony and Edward sat down to review their relationship.

"If my daughter hadn't died," Tony said, as the conversation was later reconstructed, "you would probably have had seven million dollars. But she did die, and I know you're too much of a gentleman to expect anything further."

Edward agreed that he wanted no part of the Drexel fortune.

"You are still young and will probably marry again," Tony told him. "But with three boys, it will be difficult for you and difficult for them." The oldest son, Anthony, was eight—"old enough to know you and love you," Tony reasoned. Livingston and Craig, on the other hand, were only five and three. "Let them come to live with me," Tony suggested. Tony promised to create three trusts of $1 million each that would generate income for Edward's three sons when they reached the age of 21.

Edward had little choice but to acquiesce. But since the Drexels' allowance to Emilie had stopped with her death, Edward found himself with no income other than his earnings from his law practice. His house technically belonged to Emilie's estate (although he retained a life interest in it)—a precaution Tony had taken precisely to guard against a gold-digging son-in-law—so Edward could live in it but not sell it. Small wonder that, within the droll circles of the Biddle family, the blow Edward had so impulsively administered to his fellow clerk subsequently became known as the "million-dollar punch."

Tony took the break with Edward very seriously. Although Edward was living almost next door to his younger sons Livingston and Craig, they were not allowed to visit him. When Edward wanted to see them, he had to go to their school or arrange to meet them at the zoo. This bizarre arrangement, which effectively split Edward's family in half, suggests a sincere if misguided attempt on Tony's part to impose a rational solution on an emotional problem—an approach that was not uncommon in Victorian society. When Frank Drexel's wife Hannah had died following childbirth in 1858, Tony and Ellen had unhesitatingly taken Frank's two infant daughters into their own home until Frank remarried two years later. To Tony, it seemed logical that he and Ellen should now perform the same service for Edward and Emilie's children, generously granting Edward the companionship of his oldest son. This seemed healthier than keeping the three boys together and shuttling them back and forth between two homes, one of which lacked a mother. And given the frosty relations between the two households, perhaps it was.

Tony was fond of Edward's oldest son—Tony's namesake, Anthony J. D. Biddle—and often took him to lunch with George Childs in the financial district. But young Tony Biddle and his descendants—some of whom had to suffer such indignities as attending public schools—grew up considering themselves the Drexel family's poor relations. Unlike King Solomon, who perceived the inequity of cutting a baby in half, Tony failed to see the psychological damage that would be rendered by the family's rejection of Edward's oldest son. And when Edward in 1889 married a woman of whom the Drexels disapproved and who, in turn, disapproved of Edward's sons (she felt they should have been more supportive of their father financially), Tony's temporary custody arrangement of six years earlier became more or less permanent.

Things were less rigid in the summer, when Edward—who never allowed his finances to restrict his lifestyle—traveled to Europe. At these times his three sons were usually reunited at Runnemede, the Drexels' sprawling summer estate in Lansdowne, west of Philadelphia, which Tony had bought in 1881. From Runnemede's veranda, Tony and Ellen could see both the Delaware River and Philadelphia's distant City Hall tower, then under construction. Tony hired what his great-granddaughter called "a small infantry division of gardeners" to tend the surrounding groves, orchards, walks, flower beds, hedges and the imported grapevines.

Tony would typically rustle his grandsons out of bed at 6 A.M., lead them in extended prayers, then pace them on a brisk mile walk, and bring them back famished for breakfast. "It was a Spartan regime, but I suppose good for our health," Tony's grandson Livingston Biddle later recalled. Near the carriage entrance was a fountain made of sea shells; in its center stood a marble figure representing Hospitality. The Biddle boys later remarked that, while their Drexel grandparents were kind at heart, outwardly they resembled the statuary: cold, stern and relentlessly formal.

After six years as a fugitive from the Napoleonic wars, young Francis M. Drexel returned home to Dornbirn, Austria in 1815 and painted this portrait of his family. His parents, Francis J. and Magdalena Wilhelm Drexel, are seated at left. Their three children at right are Susanna, then 26; Anton, then 19; and Francis M. himself, then 23. Drexel University.

Self-portrait of the artist as a young man: Francis M. Drexel after his arrival in Philadelphia, about 1820. Drexel University.

Catherine Hookey Drexel, whom Francis married in 1821, was a grocer's daughter with prestigious connections. Francis was soon embroiled in a libel suit against her brother-in-law. Drexel University.

The forty-year friendship of Anthony Drexel and the publisher George W. Childs might cause raised eyebrows today but was esteemed in Victorian society. In this photo, taken about 1855, Drexel (left) is about 29 and Childs about 26. Drexel University.

A struggling artist and adventurer no more, by the mid-1850s Francis M. Drexel had found wealth and respectability as a Philadelphia banker and philanthropist. But his social position didn't prevent him from rushing off to California in 1851 to capitalize on the Gold Rush. Drexel University.

Philadelphia's Third Street financial district, looking north from Chestnut Street, 1859. The curved rooftop dormer at left (arrow) marks the building where Francis M. Drexel opened his currency exchange in 1838. Six doors to the right is the showcase white Grecian marble four-story building which the Drexels put up as their new office in 1854. Remove the telegraph poles, trolley tracks, and cobblestones from this picture and Third Street looks much the same today as it did then. *Philadelphia City Archives.*

The original 1838 home of Drexel & Co., now 48 South Third Street, in a photo taken about 1950. The building still stands just north of Chestnut Street, but the exterior and interior were gutted and renovated in the 1870s and again in the 1970s. The dormer barely visible at the top is the only surviving remnant from Francis M. Drexel's day. Philadelphia City Archives.

The Drexels' state-of-the-art building at 34 South Third Street was the talk of the financial district when it opened in 1854, but it had decayed by the time this picture was taken, about 1950.
It was torn down for a parking lot in 1976, much to the chagrin of preservationists and nuns
from Katharine Drexel's order, who picketed the demolition. Philadelphia City Archives.

Anthony Drexel was only 36 when his father was killed in 1863, but he had effectively been running Drexel & Co. for at least a dozen years. This portrait of Anthony was probably painted in the mid-1860s. Drexel University.

Francis A. Drexel, two years older than Anthony, deferred to his younger brother's leadership during their forty years as equal partners in charge of Drexel & Co. Archives, Sisters of the Blessed Sacrament.

Joseph W. Drexel, the sensitive youngest of the three Drexel brothers, served his brothers faithfully. But he clashed with Pierpont Morgan and left the firm when Anthony took Morgan's side of the dispute. Free Library of Philadelphia.

With Tony Drexel's support, the garrulous Jay Cooke raised prodigious sums for the Union cause during the Civil War. But Cooke closed his bank's doors in 1873, blaming Tony for his failure. Free Library of Philadelphia.

Tony's niece Katharine Drexel, shortly before she took the veil in 1889. She was Tony's aptest pupil and the only entrepreneur among the family's third generation. Lacking an opportunity in banking, she founded a religious order and ultimately achieved sainthood. Archives, Sisters of the Blessed Sacrament.

Ellen Rosét, whom Tony married in 1850, was refined, quiet, and cosmopolitan, much like her husband. Her father, a prominent dry goods merchant, boasted that he had imported window glasses for customers like Thomas Jefferson and Benjamin Rush. Drexel University.

Facing page: Like the house itself, the interior furnishings reflected the judgment of an owner whose interest in art and beauty was genuine but hardly daring or unconventional. Drexel University.

Shunning polite Philadelphia society, Anthony and Ellen Drexel moved in 1856 to the far reaches of West Philadelphia. A few years later they built this Italianate villa at 39th and Walnut Streets, where they spent the rest of their lives. Drexel University.

Junius Morgan (inset), a prominent American banker in London, needed Paris connections as well as a mentor for his troubled son Pierpont, shown here at age 31 in 1868. Anthony Drexel filled both needs. Pierpont Morgan Library, New York.

The Drexel Building, which Anthony Drexel built for Pierpont Morgan in 1873, reshaped Wall Street's physical and psychological landscape. In this rare woodcut made shortly after it opened, the Drexel Building towers over its neighbors.

By 1900 the Drexel Building had been surpassed by its neighbors, but its corner at Broad and Wall Streets remained the world's financial crossroads. J. P. Morgan & Co., Inc.

When Drexel & Co.'s white marble building opened at Fifth and Chestnut Streets in Philadelphia in 1885, it was widely considered the handsomest private bank in the world. But it represented merely the beginning of Tony's vision.

Within three years, Anthony had built, above and around his new bank, Philadelphia's first large office building: an eleven-story structure, the city's tallest. The building was designed in the shape of an H to avoid the Independence Bank (the small dark building at left), which refused to sell to him. Free Library of Philadelphia.

Tony (seated) and his lifelong friend George Childs, probably in the late 1880s. Tony holds a copy of Childs's famous newspaper, the Philadelphia Public Ledger. *Drexel University.*

Tony's lifelong dream, the Drexel Institute, opened in 1891. But despite a guest list of world notables and an audience of 2,000, its shy creator found an excuse to avoid the opening ceremony. Drexel University.

The interior court of the Drexel Institute, 1893. Aside from a bust of Anthony Drexel at the top of the main stairs, the interior looks much the same today. Drexel University.

A rare candid shot of Anthony Drexel, not long before his death in 1893. In his quest for obscurity he rarely posed for pictures, never gave interviews to newspapers, declined public offices, and destroyed his personal papers. Drexel University.

Railroad Boom

FOLLOWING JAY COOKE'S failure in 1873, Pierpont Morgan, with Tony's approval, steered the New York house into ever larger securities operations. In 1877 Pierpont organized the syndicate to market $260 million in U.S. Treasury bonds. That same year Drexel, Morgan underwrote the pay of the entire U.S. Army when Congress briefly balked at authorizing the funds. In 1878 the Drexel and Morgan partners put up the initial capital for Thomas Edison's Edison Electric Light Company. In 1880 Drexel, Morgan led the syndicate formed in Paris for construction of the Panama Canal. In the process, the New York house now became the guiding force behind the evolution of a new American industrial society.

But the most explosive force in America's post-Civil War economy remained the railroads. Between 1870 and 1890 U.S. railroad mileage more than tripled and the railroads' appetite for capital quadrupled. The total combined outstanding shares of railroad stocks and bonds grew from $2.5 billion in 1870 to $10 billion in 1890. By linking together vast and distant reaches of previously inaccessible land, the railroads revolutionized Americans' habits as consumers and investors in much the same way that the Internet did more than a century later.

No other industry relied so heavily on international banking houses. In good times, railroads turned to bankers for funds to extend and improve their lines; in bad times, they turned to bankers to help save their companies from default, or to reorganize and rehabilitate the enterprises.

The Drexel-Morgan combination was uniquely suited to serve these needs. Much of the European capital invested in American railroads passed through London, where Junius Morgan's knowledge and experience stretched back to the 1850s, when he and George Peabody had helped finance the first great construction boom. But on the subject of railroads even Junius deferred to Tony Drexel, whose close relationship with the Pennsylvania Railroad—the world's largest railroad, and indeed the world's largest corporation—similarly extended back to the early 1850s. During one loan negotiation with the Pennsylvania in 1873, for example, J. S. Morgan & Co. sent a frantic letter to Drexel, Morgan & Co.

> We quite realise the trouble Mr. Anthony Drexel has had in this negotiation and regret being compelled to ask him to attend to it at a time when all his time must have been fully occupied. We were unwilling however to enter upon so important a matter, in which our friends too would be interested, unless we had the aid of one in whose discretion and judgment we had so much reliance, and feel greatly indebted to him for the thorough manner in which he has managed the affair.

On the subject of transportation companies Tony likewise played teacher to his star pupil, Pierpont Morgan. When in 1877 the New York and Philadelphia houses took a $1.2 million interest in an offering of the Delaware & Hudson Canal Co., Pierpont wrote his father, "I felt disposed to do somewhat more, but Mr. Drexel thought it best not to take too large amounts in any one thing, and I have no doubt he was right." A letter from Pierpont that December, discussing the behavior of the Baltimore & Ohio Railroad's president John Garrett, suggests that Tony had even made inroads with Pierpont concerning business etiquette, a subject in which Pierpont had been somewhat deficient:

> both Mr. Drexel and myself felt as we feel every time we have anything to do with him, that we will never undertake another negotiation. . . . You will remember when you were here, we made the proposal to Mr. G. to give him the credit—and he had let the matter run along in its present unsatisfactory shape without either accepting or declining it. That had annoyed Mr. Drexel particularly—more than anything that had happened—as though the whole world revolved around Mr. Garrett, to obey his beck and call, without any regard to the usual courtesies of business, or any appreciation of the efforts made in his behalf.

Because of J. S. Morgan's connection with the Drexels, no other London house enjoyed such contacts or expertise or synergy concerning American railroads. Thus it was not the Rothschilds or Barings of London but Pierpont Morgan of New York whom the New York Central heir William Vanderbilt approached with a sticky challenge in 1879. Vanderbilt—who had famously committed the egregious error of blurting, "The public be damned!" to a newspaper reporter—was weary of criticism and eager to diversify his holdings. He sought to unload about 250,000 of his New York Central shares without depressing the price of the rest of his shares. Pierpont, utilizing his new Drexel, Morgan connections, disposed of Vanderbilt's shares privately in England for $25 million, and he executed the sale so discreetly that it caused no stir on the New York Stock Exchange. When word of the sale reached the public, the *Commercial & Financial Chronicle* called it "a grand financial operation" and proclaimed Pierpont, then forty-two, the leading American railroad banker.

Yet Pierpont continued to rely on Tony Drexel's judgment, even over his own father's. When Junius, from London, suggested that Drexel, Morgan should join in leasing rolling stock to the struggling Cairo & Vincennes Railroad, Pierpont replied, "I thought I would wait and sound Mr. A. J. Drexel, without actually putting the question to him point blank, and I soon detected from the conversation I had with him today, that it was not a business which would meet his approval. . . . In the meantime it seems to me to be wisest to let the thing stand as at present."

In fact Pierpont was the point man for his father, Junius, and for his patron, Tony Drexel. In tandem they constituted a combination that railroads would find indispensable in good times and bad. Given the volatile nature of railroads during this period, it was usually only a matter of time before the railroad builders turned to bankers to bail them out of the morasses they created. In some cases, as with the Philadelphia & Reading Railroad, their dependence on bankers became constant and perpetual.

When the wheels of a Reading Railroad train crushed Francis M. Drexel to death in 1863, the Reading had been merely one link in a chain of many small rail and barge lines delivering anthracite coal from Pennsylvania's Schuylkill Valley to Philadelphia. But Franklin B. Gowen had bigger ideas. Gowen was the son of middle class Irish immigrants to Philadelphia; he was not an engineer but a lawyer who became the Reading's legal counsel and then its president in 1869. Confronted simultaneously with competition from other railroads as well as coal strikes by the labor activists known as the Molly Maguires, in the 1870s Gowen sought to convert the Reading into a road that, in his words, "owns its own traffic, is not dependent upon the public and is absolutely free from the danger of the competition of other lines."

In practice this meant buying up coal properties all along the Reading's lines in the Schuylkill Valley. It also meant breaking the Molly Maguires by hiring the Pinkerton detective James McParlan, who joined the Maguires' inner circle under an assumed name. In a blatant conflict of interest, Gowen himself served as prosecutor in the famous 1875 trial at which McParlan identified the ringleaders and testified as to the group's inner workings. By 1880, nineteen men had been hanged and others imprisoned.

The Molly Maguires were finished, and by this time the Reading had grown into a large regional network that controlled not only the delivery of anthracite coal but much of the industry itself, owning 150,000 acres of coal estates—more than 60 percent of the total in the region. In the process, the Reading's activities came to affect not only its own stock price but hundreds of millions of dollars' worth of stocks and bonds of dependent trunk line systems and coal companies —the engines of the U.S. economy. "Directly or indirectly," noted the Philadelphia *Public Ledger*'s financial columnist in 1886, "the welfare of almost the entire railway system of the country depends upon it . . . and the ups and downs of almost all prices move with Reading pulsations."

To finance these ventures, the Reading engaged in what one historian called "an orgy of borrowing." During the 1870s Gowen spent more than $73 million to acquire coal properties, mostly with borrowed funds secured by issuing mortgage bonds. By his own admission, the Reading also invested $4 million to break the miners' unions during the late 1870s.

Nevertheless, Gowen's gamble for control of the anthracite trade failed to pay off. In the deflationary U.S. economy of the 1870s and 1880s, coal prices fell sharply along with everything else. By May 1880 the Reading's total bonded debt exceeded $95 million, plus floating debt of another $13 million; and in July of that year the Reading's managers were forced to default on the payments and seek receivership. Since more than 50 percent of the Reading's stock was then held by the McAlmont family of London, in 1882 Gowen asked Junius Morgan in London to reorganize the Reading. Junius promptly turned for advice to Tony Drexel, who had helped finance the Reading's growth.

Then as now, the reorganization of a railroad was an incredibly complex task. It required not only access to financing and the ability to command public confidence, but also the ability to master endless amounts of detail about the company's legal and financial structure. In the Reading's case, Tony advised Junius, it would be a thankless task for one overriding reason: Tony didn't trust Gowen.

"We do not consider the proposed business desirable and do not feel disposed to take any interest in it," Tony cabled Junius on September 29, 1882. When Junius asked Tony to suggest terms that could make the Reading business desirable, Tony replied, more emphatically:

> F. B. Gowen has always understated his fixed charges and his statements have been systematically unreliable. If he will obtain money enough now to pay all

floating debt he would have another [debt] in a year. The bond is not the kind I would care to buy or recommend and therefore proposed business cannot be made attractive to me.

Nevertheless, Tony pledged his cooperation should Junius proceed despite Tony's objections. In such a case, Tony added, Junius should make certain to keep complete control of the transaction.

This exchange was typical of the relationship between Tony and Junius in the 1870s and 1880s. Each sought the other's advice respectfully and delivered it incisively; each deferred to the other's judgment; but each committed himself to assist the other even on the rare occasions when their judgments conflicted. This was not such an occasion. Two days later Junius cabled back: "Being unable to secure your cooperation we have declined Philadelphia & Reading business."

As events developed, that was a wise decision. When the Reading emerged from receivership in May 1884, Gowen—none the wiser for his brush with bankruptcy—resumed his grandiose expansion plans. This time he sought to construct several new railroad lines to link up with William Vanderbilt's New York Central in order to defeat their arch-rival, the Pennsylvania Railroad. But the much larger Pennsylvania promptly retaliated by building a railroad in the Schuylkill Valley to compete with the Reading. The new floating debt arising from the Reading's construction program forced Gowen's company into a second receivership.

In October 1885 the Reading approached Drexel, Morgan in New York for help in rehabilitating the railroad. This time Drexel, Morgan was equal to the task. The previous year the New York house had added two partners—Charles Coster and George Bowdoin—whose grasp of detail and capacity for hard work made them masters of reorganization technique. "Men saw him day by day," it was said of Coster, "a white-faced, nervous figure, hurrying from directors' meeting to directors' meeting; at evening carrying home his portfolio of problems for the night." (When Coster died March 13, 1900 at the age of 47—one of a long line of Pierpont Morgan colleagues who died prematurely from overwork—he was a director of fifty-nine corporations.)

Heeding Tony's principle—keep control of the transaction—Coster and Bowdoin swung into action. They assembled a team of lawyers, independent accountants, and outside railroad experts and produced a reorganization plan that was notable for its ingenuity. Instead of leaving the Reading's executives in control, as usually happened during a reorganization, the railroad's management was entrusted to a three-man committee chosen from among the members of the reorganization syndicate. This committee consisted of Pierpont Morgan and two Philadelphians close to Tony Drexel: Tony's lawyer, John C. Bullitt, and Tony's fellow banker J. Lowber Welsh. In this manner Pierpont found himself working side by side with the very same Lowber Welsh whom Pierpont had opposed as a Drexel, Morgan partner ten years earlier. Welsh, the committee's official chairman, had been intimately involved with the Reading's finances since 1870, when he had helped place the company's first European loan. Pierpont and Welsh—both protégés of Tony Drexel—seem to have coexisted smoothly: The committee remained in effect for some twenty-two months, from March 1886 through December 1887.

At the same time, Pierpont headed a syndicate that raised $20 million for the Reading, but only under condition "that the railroad should be worked in harmony with other coal-carrying roads." When the second receivership ended in 1888, the Reading emerged a much healthier road. Gowen was replaced as president with the Morgan syndicate's hand-picked choice, Austin Corbin, a former banker in Iowa and New York, who pursued a conservation program designed to improve the system's physical condition and efficiency. A voting trust created by Pierpont supervised the railroad's management in order to prevent any resumption of Gowen's free-wheeling speculations. And Drexel, Morgan maintained its leading role in the Reading's subsequent financings well into the 1890s.

The only real loser in the process was Franklin Gowen, who was forced from the Reading's presidency after seventeen years (with a few interruptions) in office. But like Jay Cooke—another flamboyant figure brought to earth by Tony Drexel—Gowen maintained his popularity among many Philadelphia investors. As a result, the Reading Railroad would haunt Tony for the rest of his life and would, indeed, be instrumental in ending it.

As the Reading reorganization demonstrated, Pierpont's influence with railroads through the 1880s and '90s extended beyond the banker's customary functions—providing financing and advice—into the actual creation and management of trusts and holding companies. Drexel's New York and Philadelphia firms headed or coheaded nationwide and international syndicates that financed some of the country's largest carriers. In 1880 Pierpont organized the largest offering of railroad bonds up to that time for the Northern Pacific, pointedly succeeding where Jay Cooke had failed. In 1885 Pierpont negotiated the famous New York Central-Pennsylvania peace pact that ended the prospect of a major railroad war between those two giant trunk lines.

These feats brought the Drexel banks an endless stream of clients and large profits. Precisely how large can only be inferred from the few fragments of partnership records that survive from those years. One such record—a table of the firm's combined reserves for the New York and Philadelphia houses between 1874 and 1883—provides some clue. In 1874 both Tony and Frank Drexel contributed reserves of $438,852; Pierpont Morgan was credited with none. But in 1875 Morgan's reserve was credited with $433,227 while the two Drexel brothers each got $137,613, and the total reserve for the year was $866,454. Thereafter Pierpont's reserve credit consistently ran about 50 percent higher than the sums credited to Tony and Frank Drexel, reflecting the ascendance of the New York house and Pierpont's guarantee of 50 percent of New York's profits.

Since each partner was supposed to leave 50 percent of his share of the earnings in the partnership as a reserve, the firms' actual earnings are probably double the figures provided. By 1879 the combined houses' additional reserve for that year exceeded $1,777,890, which suggests a profit of about $3.5 million. In 1881 and 1882 the total new reserve exceeded $2 million.

By the end of 1883 the firms' total cumulative reserves exceeded $20 million, of which Tony Drexel's share was $6,457,813 and that of Frank Drexel (who reduced his share after 1879) $5,026,408. At the same time, Pierpont's total reserve by 1884 exceeded $4.5 million. Two other partners—Egisto Fabbri and J. Hood Wright—also had reserves exceeding $1 million.

By the mid-1880s Junius and Pierpont Morgan between them were probably worth more than $20 million. But the three Drexel brothers at that point were worth more than twice that amount. (Frank Drexel alone left an estate worth $15.5 million when he died in 1885.) At a time when 80 percent of American families earned less than $500 a year, these were awesome amounts. Tony's investment in Pierpont—psychic as well as fiscal—had created a wealth machine that would continue generating riches for the Drexels for years to come. And by thrusting Pierpont into the limelight, it had enabled Tony Drexel to slip back into the shadows, as he preferred.

Despite their spectacular railroad successes, the Drexels and Morgans were unable to monopolize the railroad banking business, due to a basic self-correcting law of economics. The largest railroads, as they flourished and expanded, balked at committing themselves to a single banker, no matter how loyal or proficient. Despite Pierpont's expertise and Tony's long relationship with the mighty Pennsylvania Railroad, in the mid-1880s the Pennsylvania began to encourage other bankers to bid for its securities offerings, in order to obtain the best possible prices. To encourage competition among railroad bankers, in 1885 the Pennsylvania sold the balance of a bond offering through Speyer & Co., a German-Jewish banking house with offices in New York and London, and it did so without Tony's knowledge, even though the Drexels and Morgans had taken all the trouble of marketing the bond issue originally.

"The more we reflect upon this matter," Tony wrote angrily to Junius, "the less we are able to understand it." Drexel & Co.'s relations with the Pennsylvania

> have been of the most friendly character. . . . We had of course no agreement with them that the bonds must not be sold except to us, or without our consent, but every principle of fair dealing and honor required that they should have notified us when they determined to sell, and at least give us the opportunity of competing. . . . It would appear that from some cause or other, now not known to us, we and also yourselves have not been treated with, to characterize it in the mildest terms possible, a proper consideration of what any fair-minded person would say was our right in the matter.

When Tony remonstrated with George Roberts, the Pennsylvania's president, Roberts claimed ignorance of the transaction and blamed it on the railroad's finance committee. While Roberts invoked the railroad's right to sell its bonds to whomever it chose, Tony wrote to Junius, "he did think an opportunity should have been offered us, and that nobody could have been more surprised than he was when informed of the negotiations."

In this case Roberts, like many a corporate chief executive after him, used his power to delegate authority within his company as a means of insulating himself from personal blame. By contrast, in a partnership like Drexel & Co. there could be no delegation: The senior partner was responsible for all decisions, in practice as well as theory. Because of this disadvantage, over the next few years the Drexel-Morgan alliance was forced to share the Pennsylvania's bond business with competing banks, notwithstanding Drexel's and Morgan's superior expertise and experience.

This situation exposed Tony's greatest weakness as a negotiator, which was also the greatest source of his appeal: He was all carrot and no stick. In his dealings with clients he shrank from coercion, relying instead on moral suasion, on "fair dealing and honor," to bring clients to his way of thinking. He refused as a matter of principle to take stock or directorships in the companies he financed. Clients were trusted to fulfill a contract (or, in the Pennsylvania's case, an implied contract); the only deterrent was the likelihood that, if they violated Tony's trust, he would withhold his services in the future. Such moral leverage, to be sure, was substantial: Tony's unwillingness to fund the Northern Pacific Railroad had caused Jay Cooke's failure in 1873. But when the offending client was the Pennsylvania Railroad, Tony had no recourse but to swallow the affront and hope for a bigger piece of the next financing.

In this important respect, Pierpont Morgan differed from Tony. Pierpont did not hesitate to impose his will on railroads through his power as a potential lender, as a creditor, as a stockholder and as a director. Where Tony Drexel preferred to invest his excess personal funds in real estate, Pierpont made a practice of holding stock in his client companies not only as a means of exercising control but as a public demonstration of his faith in those companies (much like, say, a professional philanthropic fundraiser who puts his money where his mouth is by making a sizeable donation himself).

In the absence of a central national bank or a forceful federal government, Pierpont increasingly cast himself as the stabilizing force that imposed order out of the railroads' chaos. In the process he spread confidence among investors (especially those in Europe) that the money they put into American companies would be relatively safe. Yet Pierpont too recognized the lesson he had learned from both his father and Tony: that the most effective tool at their disposal was the moral capital they enjoyed from their reputations as honest men in a den of thieves. In the 1860s Pierpont had succumbed to the temptation to make quick killings by manipulating the wartime gold markets; in the 1880s he pointedly avoided speculation of any kind.

During a bank panic early in 1881, he wrote his father, "As I telegraphed Mr. Drexel, I saw but one thing to do, and that was to haul in sail and await developments. . . . We could, probably, have made a good deal of money by buying stocks and Exchange, but I think you will agree with me that in such times, no profit pays for the anxiety and uncertainty attending all such transactions." Pierpont's character had indeed undergone a radical change since his alliance with Tony Drexel.

Anthony Drexel and Pierpont Morgan left little evidence of their day-to-day interactions. Until the late 1880s, when the first telephones were installed in their offices, the two men communicated mostly in person (one visited the other's office usually once a week) or by telegraph (a private line connected the New York and Philadelphia houses), and letters between them were infrequent and more formal. But one surviving exchange of cables between New York and Philadelphia provides the closest thing to an overheard conversation between the two partners.

The transcriptions of these messages bear dates—late December—but no year, although they appear to be from 1885 or possibly 1886, when their combined houses were at the peak of their prestige. In this exchange Tony and Pierpont discussed division of profits and bonuses under a revised partnership agreement to take effect the following year. More than a century later, what emerges most forcefully from the exchange is the manner in which each man respectfully defers to the other, and the unselfish manner in which each places the welfare of their two houses ahead of his immediate profits.

A. J. Drexel to J. P. Morgan, Dec. 26:
The new articles provide a fixed amount as capital. Don't you propose dividing up the old reserves to pay for this capital? Any new reserve will be dealt with hereafter as specified in new articles.

J. P. Morgan to A. J. Drexel, Dec. 26:
Oh yes. I propose to divide up the reserves & start anew. That is not the question I was bringing up. What I proposed was that the new capitals should be treated as the new reserve funds and accumulate by credit of interest until you and I choose to divide any part. This in view of the fact that each year we shall hereafter divide half the profits & it seems to me and to all of us that that is enough to divide. I am sorry that my last dispatch was not clear but as I said then I thought that I was carrying out your views but am quite willing to follow your wishes if I am wrong.

A. J. Drexel to J. P. Morgan, Dec. 26:
That is all right and we so understand it. The only question was as to the amount of our Phila. capital & whether you are satisfied it shall be made [illegible word] and anything in addition belonging to any of the partners will be kept as balances in our private ledgers and considered reserve.

J. P. Morgan to A. J. Drexel, Dec. 30:
If agreeable to you I think we will divide the balance of P&L 1886 on our bonus. The amount is minimal so I think it desirable. We shall have our 16,000,000 as capital, & that is I think sufficient credit reserve. How do you feel about it?

A. J. Drexel to J. P. Morgan, Dec. 30:
Perfectly agreeable.

PART V

SALVATION

Reluctant Titan

VICTORIAN TRADITION SHIELDED WOMEN from worldly concerns, the better to enable them to focus on their families' spiritual needs. This sheltered treatment often infantilized women, rendering them helpless to deal with financial or civic issues and vulnerable to petty jealousies. Tony's mother, Catherine Hookey Drexel, had died in September 1870 at the age of 75, leaving bequests totaling $19,000 to seven Philadelphia institutions, all but one of them Catholic hospitals and orphans' asylums. These were sizable gifts for their day but minuscule next to the multimillion-dollar fortunes Catherine's sons were accumulating. Her will bypassed the customary choice as executor—her eldest son Frank—in favor of her second son, Tony, perhaps because of Catherine's animus toward Frank's reclusive (and, Catherine felt, standoffish) second wife, Emma Bouvier Drexel. The bulk of Catherine's estate was divided equally among Catherine's eleven grandchildren then living, with one glaring exception: Emma's only daughter, Louise, then seven years old, was conspicuous by her omission.

Like Catherine, the women of the next Drexel generation tended to be even more modest and self-effacing than their husbands. Tony's wife Ellen rarely attracted attention as anything other than her spouse's charming and gracious consort. But no one was more retiring than Frank's ascetic wife Emma, whose self-sacrificing instincts inadvertently set in motion a chain of events that terminated the long business partnership between Frank and Tony.

When, late in 1879, Emma found herself feeling increasingly exhausted, she took care to conceal her condition from her family. A doctor suggested a minor surgical procedure, which for the sake of secrecy she arranged to have performed not at a hospital or the doctor's office but at her city home while her husband and daughters were at their country estate in Torresdale. (She told the family that she was going to town to rearrange some furniture.) The surgery failed; the ailment was diagnosed as cancer; and Frank Drexel, when he learned of it, was beside himself. "Emma, Emma," his daughters heard him cry, "oh why did you let anyone do this?"

To devote his attention to his ailing wife, Frank voluntarily cut back his activity at Drexel & Co. as well as his share of the firm's profits. For forty years Frank and Tony had taken equal shares of every partnership, down to the penny, and had maintained at least the formal illusion of being equal contributors to the firm's success. Now, for all practical purposes, Frank would withdraw from the firm.

He hired the best doctors to attend to Emma and arranged family trips to the most invigorating climates. A vacation in Colorado in 1880 failed to improve Emma's condition, nor did a sojourn in Sharon Springs, New York, in 1882. After Emma died in January 1883, Frank—a widower for the second time—now devoted himself to his three unwed daughters, aged twenty to twenty-eight. That fall he took them on a seven-month tour of Europe, and the following fall on another trip, this one by private railroad car to the Great Northwest and Yellowstone Park. His ostensible purpose for this journey was to investigate whether the bonds of Jay Cooke's creation, the Northern Pacific Railroad, would be a good investment for Drexel & Co. But in fact Frank Drexel's business career was finished. Early in February 1885 he caught a cold that developed into pleurisy, an inflammation of the lungs. By February 15 he was dead, at the age of sixty-one.

Tony and Ellen had taken charge of Frank's and Hannah's two small daughters, Elizabeth and Katharine, until Frank remarried in 1860. Now, with Frank gone, Tony and Ellen again became unofficial guardians of Frank's children as well as their own offspring, six of whom were living at this point. After Frank's death, his daughters Elizabeth, Kate, and Louise moved in at Tony and Ellen's summer estate, Runnemede, for several months before returning to their father's downtown house at 1503 Walnut Street.

Frank's serious, devoutly Catholic daughters proved quite different from Tony's own pleasure-oriented children. The three orphaned sisters were unmarried and in no hurry to find husbands. None of them had attended school (in keeping with the fashion of the day for girls); since early childhood they had grown up under the forceful influence of their governess, Mary Cassidy, the well-educated daughter of an impoverished Dublin family. Miss Cassidy, as she was called, was a devout Catholic who instilled in her charges a well-rounded classical education that included music and the arts, Latin, and French. With her encouragement, the girls had developed the practice of keeping personal journals—the sort of introspective exercise that would have struck Tony and Ellen as wastefully self-indulgent.

By contrast, Tony's six children still living after 1885 were for the most part grown and married adults, ranging in age from thirty-three-year-old Frances Paul to seventeen-year-old George Childs Drexel. Some of them were already parents themselves. Tony's three sons—John, Anthony, Jr., and George—all went through the motions of apprenticeship at Drexel & Co., and Anthony was actually made a partner in 1890. Yet Tony's sons, like his daughters, seem to have remained in a state of perpetually dependent and sheltered childhood.

Tony's greatest pleasure came from presiding at the family dinner table each evening and afterward playing duets, quartets, and operatic arias with his daughters on the two pianos he kept in his music room. To extend this pleasure as they grew older, in the 1870s and 1880s, Tony built homes on or adjacent to his Walnut Street lot for his daughter Emilie (who married Edward Biddle), for Frances (who in 1877 married James Paul, Jr., later a Drexel & Co. partner), and, as they married, for his sons Anthony, Jr., John, and George. The unhappy Emilie Biddle was dead by 1883, and with the death of Tony's daughter, Mae Stewart, in January 1886 at age twenty-eight, only Sarah ("Sallie") Fell, then twenty-five, lived beyond a two-block walk from her parents. Perhaps not coincidentally, Sallie developed into the most confident and forceful of Tony Drexel's children. In his independent and altruistic nieces, Tony found something that his own self-absorbed children seemed to lack, with the result that Tony may have lavished more attention on his orphaned nieces than on his own children.

"I have always felt towards you three girls as towards my own daughters," Tony wrote to Katharine, Frank's middle child, in 1891. Where Tony's own grandchildren found him formal and distant, his letters to his nieces were punctuated with "lots of love and kisses"; his letters to Katharine are addressed to "My dear Kate," "My dearest Kate," and even "My darling Kate."

The three sisters responded in kind. When they joined "Uncle Anthony" at the spa resort of Carlsbad, Bohemia, as he took "the cure" for his recurring rheumatic gout, Elizabeth wrote to her sister-in-law, "His companionship has been the seasoning of our pleasure here; you can form no idea how sweet and fatherly he has been. To have had him for a whole month with no screen of business thrown in between us, has been more delightful than I can express."

Like his brothers Frank (an accomplished organist) and Joe (a founder of the New York Philharmonic Orchestra), Tony took music seriously; he could sight-read the most difficult pieces, and his daughters Emilie and Frances were said to rank among Philadelphia's finest amateur pianists—no small compliment at a time when pianos were as ubiquitous as television sets today. But Tony's tastes in music, like his tastes in art, were narrowly conventional. The banker who risked a million dollars on a parcel of Wall Street real estate would not risk an evening on an unpredictable opera. "I went on Monday night and found it unsatisfactory and will therefore not go again," he wrote to his niece after attending a performance by the Boston Ideal Company at the Academy of Music. At a dinner party at his home in the late 1880s Tony attacked the music of Wagner as well as that composer's leading American advocate, assistant conductor Walter Damrosch of the Metropolitan Opera.

"There's going to be a concert next week," his voice boomed through the room, "and I want no child of mine to go to it. Some fool whose name is Dam —Dam—some kind of bug or other—roach, that's what it is, Walter Damroach, and he's going to play the music of that miserable Wagner! None of you go to it, you understand."

Like his brother in 1879, Tony himself might logically have reduced his activity at Drexel & Co. now that his business was well established. With Pierpont Morgan confidently in control in New York, funneling capital from London and overseeing the Paris office as well, Tony's role as he approached sixty was largely advisory. He still ran the Philadelphia house, but its day-to-day activities—dealings in foreign exchange, sale of letters of credit, loans, and execution of orders for the sale and purchase of securities—paled in comparison to the volume Pierpont Morgan was handling in New York. Increasingly in the 1880s the Philadelphia house owed its prominence to Pierpont. What Frank Drexel had been to Tony—the titular senior to the de facto star performer—Tony now became to Pierpont Morgan.

And much of Tony's wealth was no longer invested in Drexel & Co. Just as a doctor knows better than to trust hospitals implicitly, Tony was keenly aware of the fragile nature of banks. "I believe there is no more certain or reliable property to be held than real estate," he declared in his will. In addition to his homes in West Philadelphia, Lansdowne, and Long Branch, New Jersey, by the mid-1880s Tony also owned ten lots in South Philadelphia, a share of the Public Ledger Building (as well as his majority share of the *Ledger* itself), a share of the Drexel Building in New York, and large tracts worth several million dollars on Chicago's south side. West of Philadelphia, on 600 acres along the Pennsylvania Railroad's Main Line extension, Tony and George Childs in the late 1870s developed an idealized suburban community of fifty modern homes featuring spacious lawns, ample shade trees, and conveniences then known only in cities, such as water, sewer, and gas mains; out of this development grew the suburb of Wayne. (When asked why they built this new development so far out in the country, Childs replied, only half in jest, that the train ride into the city would give the residents more time to read the *Ledger.*)

Between his real estate and Pierpont Morgan, Tony at this point had little incentive to remain at the bank and every incentive to coast. But as someone who had worked from the age of thirteen, the concept of leisure was foreign to him.

"Loafing is, they say (I have never had a chance to try it), a bad business for any man," Tony once wrote his nieces. He spent a month or two each summer at his seaside villa in Long Branch, next door to his friends Childs and Grant, and early summer and early fall at Runnemede, his suburban Lansdowne estate. But when his wife, children, in-laws, grandchildren, and servants bundled off on pleasure trips to Europe in the fall—often in groups of twenty or more— Tony remained in Philadelphia by himself, the better to focus on business.

"I think your Aunt Ellen requires a good rest and change and I will do all I can to have her go," he wrote to his nieces in Europe in September 1886. "She doesn't want to leave me but I tell her I can get along very nicely and join her in the spring." Later that fall he told his nieces, "I am quite content to stay home and not go abroad even if I were able to leave, which I am not." In another letter while his family was away, he wrote, "I don't go out any but go to bed early and enjoy myself that way."

What relaxation he knew was a kind of enforced leisure, which he experienced on his annual visit to the curative springs of Carlsbad. This celebrated Bohemian spa was nestled in a narrow, winding valley surrounded by thick woods, some seventy miles west of Prague. The boiling waters from its volcanic springs had been valued for their medicinal properties at least since the fourteenth century. By the mid-nineteenth century it had become a gathering place for Europe's wealthy invalids and their fashionable families, an eclectic mix of Germans, Jews, tycoons, handsome matrons, and pretty girls. But even here Tony followed a strict regimen.

"Almost everyone who comes here, at least one member of every party, is here for serious business," wrote Tony's niece, Elizabeth Drexel, during a visit with him at Carlsbad in June 1889. Even at 6 A.M., she noted, "The jostle of the quiet, solemn water-sipping crowd around the Sprudel is something amazing at that hour of the morning. It sometimes takes as much as eight or ten minutes to reach one of the more popular springs in line. . . . From two to three hours are given up to water imbibing after which the crowd disperses." After dinner, she said, "Uncle Anthony dozes off, senses immersed in a flood of news poured in upon him from papers, English, French, American."

He traveled often to Europe on business, but rarely for pleasure. On the Continent, as in the office, his greatest concern was to eliminate uncertainty. His travel advice to his nieces—Frank's daughters—as they embarked on a grand tour of Europe in 1886 captured the essence of his philosophy:

My dear children,

I send you these few lines to bid you goodbye and to beg of you to follow my advice in these particulars.

Don't travel too much in one day. I think six hours ought to be the outside limit. Don't travel at night. You must not go to any northern country in the winter. Remember, the days are short, the skies gray and dark and the weather generally bad. Try to spend the winter where there is sunshine and warmth, where you can be in the open air.

I don't want you to go Egypt, for various reasons. In Rome avoid being out about *sunset*, as that is the danger time, and while there always eat a hearty breakfast and lunch. Never have empty stomachs. I think this very important. Drink good wine at meals. Avoid staying too long in damp and cold churches. Going from the warm sunshine into a cold church is often very dangerous . . . have warm covering to put on while in the church. Your man can always carry a lot of wraps with him so as to have them ready for use.

Don't let exorbitant bills . . . worry you. That is one of the expenses of travelling. Avoid any places where there is a suspicion of cholera or any other disease. Naples is unhealthy on account of bad drainage. Sorrento is much the best place to stay if you want to go to Naples.

You must not go to the Holy Land or any similar long journey out of the reach of railways.

In case of need telegraph "Drexel" Paris. That is the telegraphic address. I have no doubt Mr. Harjes would come at once if it should be necessary.

If you want advice or aid in any strange place where you have no acquaintances or friends, send for the Banker indicated on the letter of credit. If you should require a doctor, if the hotel you are stopping at is a first-class one, apply to the manager for the best doctor in town. I would give a homeopathic doctor the preference if there is one in the town.

Now goodbye. May God have you in His holy keeping and bring you back in good health to your loving uncle,

A. J. Drexel

These words may seem ridiculously cautious in retrospect, but they constituted reasonable advice in an age devoid of antibiotics. Tony was simply offering the sort of guidance that a seasoned traveler today would provide to someone visiting, say, sub-Saharan Africa or Mongolia. Tony never shrank from traveling abroad, nor did he discourage his nieces from doing so. In travel as in business, he simply believed in gathering as much information as possible in order to eliminate risk.

Six months after writing the above letter, with his nieces still in Europe, Tony told them that "I have felt anxious all the time you have been in Spain, fearing one of you might have been taken ill in which case you might have fallen into the hands of a Spanish doctor. I must confess having a prejudice against the practice of medicine in Spain coming from my reading so often *Gil Blas*"—a reference to the picaresque eighteenth-century French novel about a Spanish adventurer.

Although Tony and Ellen hosted one of the most notable parties of Philadelphia's Gilded Age—their reception in December 1879 for General Grant at their West Philadelphia home, attended by some 700 prominent guests—Tony appears to have viewed such lavish affairs as more duty than pleasure. After his son Anthony, Jr.'s marriage in 1886, Tony wrote, "The wedding passed off nicely and I am glad it is over as I get tired of such excitements," although he expressed satisfaction that "everything was done very quietly and in good taste."

Public attention made him uncomfortable. He gave no speeches, granted no interviews to reporters, rarely posed for photographs, made his charitable gifts anonymously and generally tried to discourage interest in himself. He was willing to lend his name and resources to civic and political reform movements but rarely took the lead role. Confronted with the rise of Philadelphia's Gas Trust, the infamous political ring run by an Irish immigrant boss named James McManes, Tony joined with George Childs and the scholar Henry Charles Lea in the early 1870s to create the Reform Club, a vehicle for municipal reform. He served quietly as president of the Fairmount Park Art Commission, which approved statues and other permanent art works for installation in the city's huge public park. Yet, as for many another well-intentioned Philadelphia civic leader of the post-Civil War era, his distaste for politics rendered him an ineffective champion of municipal reform, as his struggle with the Gas Trust demonstrated.

In 1871 Boss McManes's friends in the state assembly passed a bill that granted the city unlimited taxing power to construct new public buildings without being subject to any outside audit. The city promptly broke ground on a mammoth new City Hall—the world's largest building in terms of square footage—that would become a haven for crooked contractors until its completion thirty years later. The subsequent orgy of taxation to pay for that building so infuriated the city's most prominent businessmen that in 1880 a group including Tony Drexel, the dry goods magnates John Wanamaker and Justus Strawbridge, and the gadfly businessman Rudolph Blankenburg formed what they called "The Committee of One Hundred" to fight the Gas Trust.

Their first efforts were impressive. Enlisting support from the city's clergy and newspapers, in 1881 these reformers elected an honest Democrat as mayor and an equally honest Republican to the more important post of receiver of taxes. In 1885 the reformer John Bullitt—Tony Drexel's friend and lawyer—drafted a new city charter that restrained the Gas Trust and most other independent agencies—all of them havens for graft—by rendering them subservient to a strong mayor responsible (at least in theory) for all city government conduct.

Mistakenly believing they had achieved their goal, the businessmen dissolved the Committee of One Hundred and went back to their banks, factories and emporiums. But late in 1886 Boss McManes and his cronies from the Gas Trust resurfaced as the backers of the "South Mountain Water Company," a scheme to lease and operate Philadelphia's waterworks on their own terms, in much the same way that they had previously drained the city's gas works. The proposed company's borrowing requirements—$16 million over the following three years—attracted interest from, of all people, Junius Morgan in London, who cabled Tony for advice about the venture.

Tony cabled back: "The scheme is entirely on paper. No work done as yet or projected. . . . Scheme can be carried through only by corrupt means."

But Junius refused to drop the issue. "If ordinance passed honestly do you consider the proposed business desirable?" he cabled in reply.

Tony cabled back the next day: "Would not entertain proposition myself and take no stock in the parties here who are very unreliable in their statements." In a longer, gentler letter to Junius two days later in which he characterized himself as "your loving friend," Tony explained that McManes "is the devil of Philadelphia." The South Mountain Water Company's supporters, he added, "may get their bills through [the City Councils], but as far as we are concerned we can have nothing to do with such swindlers however compelling they may appear as to profit." Apparently it was not only Pierpont Morgan but Pierpont's father as well who required occasional reminders from Tony to do the right thing.

Before long Philadelphia's Gas Trust was succeeded by a new political machine, this one led by the even more corrupt and notorious Matthew Quay. But if Tony Drexel could not lead by civic exhortation, he could lead effectively by example.

In 1885, with the end of City Hall's construction nowhere in sight, Tony erected a new banking house for Drexel & Co. at the southeast corner of Fifth and Chestnut, just across from the Old State House (later called Independence Hall). It was a magnificent white marble structure, widely considered the handsomest private bank in the world, but it represented merely the beginning of Tony's vision. Just as he had assembled the land at the corner of Broad and Wall Streets in New York for Drexel, Morgan's headquarters in 1872, now Tony proceeded to buy up the rest of the block on which his new Philadelphia headquarters stood. He already owned the Law Building and the former Philadelphia Library structure to the south on Fifth Street. In December 1886, for $413,000, Tony bought the old post office to the east on Chestnut Street. His purpose was to build, above and around his new bank, Philadelphia's first large office building, an eleven-story structure—the city's tallest—complete with such modern amenities as wide corridors and an abundant supply of elevators, an invention then just in its infancy.

Two obstacles stood in his way. The Independence National Bank, which occupied the space on Chestnut Street between Drexel & Co. and the former post office, refused to sell, and in any case Tony's firm would need to do business in the banking house while construction proceeded around it. The challenge only seems to have enhanced Tony's passion for the project. The Drexel Building he commenced in 1887 was designed in the shape of an "H" so as to avoid the Independence Bank's property. For such a tall building, this design required reinforcing the foundations with huge pilasters of masonry, a difficult task in construction at that time.

Nevertheless, the building was completed in 1888 and quickly became one of the city's leading attractions—"a monument to finance and business," as one brochure of the 1890s described it. No expense had been spared. Halls connecting the building's 398 rooms were fashioned of hollow terra-cotta blocks; the corridor floors were finished with artificial stone. The building's elevators operated even on Sundays, an unheard-of service at the time. Visitors who flocked to the building's rooftop viewing pavilion, towering over Independence Square and the Old State House and the endless panorama of offices and factories, inevitably found themselves thinking more expansively about their quaint old city and its possibilities.

Within two years of the Drexel Building's opening, the Philadelphia Stock Exchange abandoned its Third Street location for a new hall in the Drexel Building which Tony had specially arranged. Virtually overnight, the term "Third Street" as a synonym for Philadelphia's financial district lost its meaning and vanished from local speech.

The Drexel Building of 1888 was eventually eclipsed when the taller City Hall opened thirteen years later, in 1901. Both buildings transformed the city visually and psychologically. Yet Philadelphians couldn't help noticing the drastic contrast between the two structures. City Hall had required thirty years from groundbreaking to completion; the Drexel Building had needed one year. City Hall had cost taxpayers more than $24 million (as opposed to its original $10 million estimate); the Drexel Building had cost taxpayers nothing. And the Drexel Building was hardly the last of Tony's civic improvements. His grandest gesture was still to come.

Two Social Revolutionaries

BY THE MID-1880s the huge capital pools mobilized by financiers like Pierpont Morgan and Anthony Drexel had altered the rhythms of American life. Railroads connected cities; streetcars connected neighborhoods within cities; and telegraphs and telephones connected people at great distances without their moving at all. A community's waking hours, once restricted by the rising and setting of the sun, were now extended as Thomas Edison's powerful electric lights lit up homes, businesses, and streets. Factories expanded their capacities and extended their hours. Migrants—from the countryside and Europe alike— poured into cities like Philadelphia to work. The smoke from these plants made living nearby repulsive and unhealthy, but the speed and comfort of rail-based streetcars meant workers didn't have to.

Warm bodies and strong backs no longer sufficed to serve the new economy's growing businesses and industries. Now these businesses needed workers trained in commerce, finance, and technology. Women previously confined to their homes began to be accepted in skilled occupations. Workers forming labor unions to protect themselves from exploitation began to perceive a more useful key to a better life: their access to education with which to acquire skills that were suddenly in great demand.

Philadelphia in the 1880s was already well known for its rich variety of traditional educational offerings. Its liberal arts colleges, like the University of Pennsylvania, Haverford College, and Swarthmore College, were famous. It had effective public and Catholic school systems. Its venerable network of Quaker secondary schools, like William Penn Charter and Germantown Friends, was nearly two centuries old. But like most cities, Philadelphia lacked facilities for practical, intensive, relatively rapid training in the new business and industrial specialties springing up: secretarial and office work, mechanics, commerce, home economics, crafts. "Industrial education"—so called because it served the needs of industry and industrial workers alike—became one of the great progressive causes of the day.

Central High School, the city's elite academic high school, added courses in engineering and other industrial skills. Peirce College, one of the first business schools, trained prospective secretaries and bookkeepers. The Spring Garden Institute, later Spring Garden College, offered technical and mechanical courses. The merchant prince John Wanamaker set up a school within his department store that provided high school classes (and even some college) for his clerks. But these small-scale ventures were merely stopgap responses to a broad social phenomenon.

Anthony Drexel was no educator; his own formal education had ended when he was thirteen. But his brother Frank's death renewed Tony's connection to his niece Katharine Drexel, and their relationship subsequently generated two remarkable educational innovations of the nineteenth century.

When Frank Drexel died in February 1885, he left one of the largest estates then recorded in the United States. Of its $15.5 million value, Frank bequeathed one-tenth to charities; the remaining $14 million was left in trust, providing an annual income for his three daughters. The will's tight "spendthrift clause" protected Elizabeth, Kate, and Louise from golddiggers by forbidding any husband from involvement with his wife's property. By assuring the daughters a regular income, and by stipulating that if they died childless the trust principal would go to charity, the will effectively discouraged suitors and encouraged the daughters' charitable instincts.

That Elizabeth and Louise eventually married anyway was a tribute to the devotion of their husbands. But Kate, who was twenty-six when her father died, was a harder case, high-spirited but also painfully serious, and possessed of the shrewdest business head among her generation of Drexels. Far more than Tony's three sons—then enduring perfunctory apprenticeships at Drexel & Co. —Kate seemed eager to learn from her Uncle Anthony about the relative value of investments and the creditworthiness of specific bonds. Tony for his part was grateful to find someone in the next generation who responded enthusiastically to his mentoring instincts. But of course Victorian society offered no place in banking for a woman. Some suitable activity would have to be found for her.

Since the mid-1870s Kate's father had generously supported Catholic institutions in Philadelphia. His second wife, Emma, extended these charitable instincts to benefit the poor, regardless of race or creed. But it was their daughters who focused on Indians and blacks in particular. Shortly after the Custer massacre in Montana in 1876, the family's priest and good friend, a vigorous Irishman named James O'Connor, had been appointed vicar of Nebraska, a diocesan district that then included Nebraska, the Dakotas, Wyoming, and Montana. O'Connor's letters reporting the harassment and embitterment of Indian tribes upset the three young sisters and motivated the family's first donations. Within five years, a chain of simple Catholic mission schools built for the Indians by Frank Drexel's family extended from the Great Lakes to the Columbia River and down to the Mexican border.

This was a radical notion at a time when many white Americans believed that education of blacks should be limited to reading the Bible and no one thought of educating Native Americans at all. Under a "peace policy" inaugurated by President Grant, the U.S. government agreed to pay $100 a year for each Indian child attending the Catholic mission schools. But these buildings, which were rudimentary to begin with, lacked priests and nuns to staff them. Kate and her sisters toured some of these agencies in the Pacific Northwest with their father in 1884; following that trip, Kate sent $100 of her own money to a small rectory in Tacoma, Washington to pay for a statue. In the summer of 1884 Kate also accompanied her father to the installation of Archbishop Patrick Ryan of Philadelphia, who subsequently became her close friend.

Kate's Uncle Anthony was an equally charitable Episcopalian; the internationally known stained glass windows at the Church (now Cathedral Church) of the Saviour were largely his gift. Yet to Tony—whom Frank had appointed co-executor of his will, along with George Childs and Tony's brother-in-law John D. Lankenau—now fell the primary responsibility for his devoutly Catholic niece's future.

The religious differences seem not to have fazed him. If anything, Tony encouraged his nieces' Catholic philanthropies. Following an earthquake in Charleston, South Carolina in 1886, he wrote to his nieces in Europe, "I think you all ought to contribute towards the suffering there and I will send Archbishop Ryan $500 for your account and have him send it to Charleston for the relief of Catholics there. I think you will approve of this." A few weeks later he elaborated:

> I knew there was a great deal of suffering among the Catholics in Charleston and I thought it right to direct your money should thus go to their relief. I know you are not sectarian where the interests of humans are concerned, but are always willing to take the *christian* [sic] view of it and distribute your alms irrespective of creed. That is what I have always done, and I am glad to have you do the same.

The three nieces were still traveling in Europe that fall when the cornerstone was laid for their first major philanthropic undertaking, the St. Francis de Sales Industrial School for poor orphan boys in Eddington, near their summer home. In their absence, Tony took charge of arranging what was essentially a Catholic ceremony. The zeal with which he pursued the details of the event is suggested in a letter to his nieces:

> The Archbishop has sent me a list of all the Catholic clergy of the city and sur-roundings and also of other gentlemen he wishes invited and I am now hav-ing the invitations directed. I have directed Wilson to have a platform 20 x 20 erected and also a covering for the guests in case of rain and also to place planks in all the muddy places between the station and the platform. Miss Cassidy will get some carriages and an omnibus at Holmesburg for the trans-portation of old and delicate people. A priest told me the other day he had been thinking over the refreshment question and had decided that milk was the best thing to be given your guests but I told him as it was not customary to serve refreshments on such occasions we would not milk the party.

Tony's unofficial guardian relationship with his nieces seems to have rein-forced his own unconventional philanthropic instincts. Like other business leaders of his day, he had always given generously to traditional charities and in-stitutions—the Church of the Saviour, the University of Pennsylvania, hospi-tals, the Society for the Prevention of Cruelty to Animals, the George C. Meade Post of the Grand Army of the Republic, the Fairmount Park Association, and the Spring Garden Institute. But virtually alone among businessmen in his po-sition, even at the peak of his wealth and influence Tony seems to have identi-fied most comfortably with underdogs.

This, after all, was the man who had once kept President Grant and the Cab-inet waiting in his parlor while he offered career advice to a struggling young physician. Tony almost always made his donations anonymously; when one re-cipient, Philadelphia's German Hospital, proposed to change its name in Tony's honor, he vehemently declined, and eventually the hospital was named for Tony's brother-in-law John Lankenau. "I consider that wealth comes to a man by accident," Tony was once overheard to remark. "I do not see why a man who has become wealthy should be different from the poor man who hoes corn or drives a streetcar. Why should one be unnatural? Why should he try to be other than he is—to consider himself above others because he has a large bank ac-count?"

Thus, even before the vogue for industrial education, Tony began to ponder ways of providing the poor not merely with handouts but with empowerment.

By the late 1870s his brother Joseph in New York was supporting revolutionary social experiments in home ownership for workers, better prison conditions, hospital sanitation, and other improvements in the quality of urban life. But many of Joe's well-intentioned schemes were too utopian to succeed. Dismayed by the depressing New York soup kitchens he supported, Joseph Drexel spent $15,000 to open several cheerful free coffeehouses, only to find that few people would patronize them. To protect the poor from freezing in the winter, Joe distributed free coal vouchers, which invariably wound up in the wrong hands. Tony—more cautious and pragmatic—was just as eager to promote social change but determined that his efforts would succeed.

The seeds of his thinking may have been planted as early as 1862, when he received a letter from the upstate New York brewer Matthew Vassar, seeking Tony's help in funding America's first college for women, in Vassar's home town of Poughkeepsie. His goal, Vassar wrote, was to educate "the mothers of coming generations" in a college "which shall be to them what Yale and Harvard are to young men."

Vassar—writing at the suggestion of that peripatetic intermediary George Childs—appealed to Tony's civic chauvinism by citing the example of another Philadelphia banker, the late Stephen Girard, whose will had established a first-class boarding school for white orphan boys in 1839. But unlike Girard, Vassar planned to proceed while he was still alive: "I prefer to be my own executor and see my money faithfully and judiciously expended under [my] own eye," he wrote.

Tony declined Vassar's request, apparently because he preferred to shape his own vision rather than support someone else's. But in the following years the cause of women's education seems to have germinated in his mind. He took a keen interest in October 1881 when his friend, the Philadelphia feminist teacher and reformer Eliza Sproat Turner, began conducting evening classes for working girls and women. These classes—possibly the first of their kind in the United States—evolved the following year into the New Century Guild, a kind of settlement house for working women. With funding from Anthony Drexel and George Childs, Mrs. Turner set up trade classes at the Guild in 1886, including courses in typesetting, glass cutting, leaded glass designing, and fabricating rope for frieze. By that time the Guild's student body had grown from a handful to 791 women in just five years.

That enthusiastic response, as well as the fact that most of the new industrial schools were intended for boys only, caused Tony to think seriously about endowing a women's college. Around 1886 he purchased a large estate in the distant Main Line suburb of Wayne for the purpose of creating an industrial college for girls, "somewhat similar to Girard College." Such a school, he explained, could instruct and train girls "in such way as to *help them* to employments and occupations in which they could earn *a liberal living.*" As Tony envisioned it, his school would board and train about two hundred girls, plus about four or five hundred more "who could get to the school during the day, get their luncheon there, and get back to their own homes in the evening."

In March 1888 Tony went public with his intention through a story in the *Ledger.* The proposed institution, the story announced, would be the first to bear Tony's name. Clearly, he saw the school as his life's crowning achievement.

Before proceeding, Tony dispatched Addison Burk, an editor of the *Public Ledger* and also president of the Spring Garden Institute, on a factfinding tour to New York, Boston, and other cities to investigate schools that might serve as suitable models. The schools in Burk's report that most impressed Tony were the Pratt Institute in Brooklyn, Cooper Union in New York, and Philadelphia's School of Industrial Art. But these were urban schools, and their successes forced Tony to rethink his vision yet again.

The isolated Wayne location, he now reflected, suffered from several drawbacks, "the chief of which was the withdrawal of the girls from home influence." The school's usefulness, he came to realize, would be strengthened by building his institute within the city limits. His change of heart may also have been influenced by the opening in 1885 of Bryn Mawr College, a women's school not far from Wayne, which effectively rendered Tony's vision redundant.

Tony shared his ruminations in these preliminary stages with just five close advisers: his wife, his friend George Childs, and his brother Frank's three daughters. In this group he found a circle of kindred spirits. Childs, perhaps because of his own impoverished childhood, was always ready with a hundred-dollar donation for almost any cause that approached him (he gave so often to synagogues, for example, that he was rumored to be Jewish). Frank Drexel's daughters, led by the oldest sister, Elizabeth, were opening their industrial school for Catholic working-class boys in Eddington, and Elizabeth and Louise were also thinking about converting an antebellum Virginia plantation into an industrial and agricultural institute for young black men.

These hopeful visions seem to have invigorated Tony as nothing had since he negotiated his bank's alliance with the Morgan family. In his excitement he failed to notice that his middle niece, Kate Drexel, was moving toward a separate idealistic vision of her own—a vision so far beyond Tony's comprehension that it never occurred to him.

Through her correspondence with Bishop O'Connor in Omaha as well as the writings of the author Helen Hunt Jackson, Kate had become sensitized to the injustices suffered by Native Americans. During her travels through the Pacific Northwest with her father and sisters in 1884, Kate had been dismayed by the primitive facilities the church schools provided for Indians and blacks, as well as by the lack of priests to staff them. From the sheltered perspective of her youth and wealth it did not occur to Kate that the Church's financial balance sheet might in fact be inferior to that of her own family.

In January 1887, while Kate and her sisters toured Europe, they attended a mass celebrated by Pope Leo XIII. At its conclusion Kate asked for a few minutes in private with the pope, during which she earnestly tried to explain the need for more missionary priests to work among the Indians. It was an audacious request for a twenty-eight-year-old woman, and the pope, lacking the resources to satisfy her complaint, replied in kind: "Why not, my child, yourself become a missionary?"

Kate could only stammer in reply that the missions already had enough nuns, but no priests. Still, the pope's offhand response had planted an idea in her mind. That fall, as Kate and her sisters again toured the Indian country, the concept gained force. She would take the veil herself and, utilizing her fortune as well as the financial acumen she had absorbed from her uncle, create her own order for the benefit of Indians and blacks.

In the context of her time, the idea was not illogical. Victorian women enjoyed more freedom and control over their lives in convents than they did in the outside world. The Church was one of the few institutions where an ambitious entrepreneurial woman like Kate Drexel could find an outlet for her talents. On the other hand, life in a nineteenth-century convent was rigorous and spartan. For a woman of material wealth and social prominence, such a step was akin to a millionaire's enlisting in the army as a private, and at first Kate kept her intentions from her Uncle Anthony. Instead, her confidant was Bishop O'Connor of Omaha, who accompanied the sisters on their Western trip. But even the bishop tried to discourage her.

"The question you will bear in mind," O'Connor wrote to Kate, "is, not which of the two states—the religious or the secular—is the better . . . but in which you can give more glory to God, be of more service to your neighbor, and acquire more merit for yourself."

O'Connor's reluctance to encourage Katharine's plan stemmed in part from the standard pastoral practice of discouraging a religious vocation as a means of testing the depth of intent. But at a subconscious level, O'Connor may well have opposed Katharine's becoming a nun for a different reason. Katharine was the primary support of Catholic Indian missions in the West—a cause dear to O'Connor's heart—and should she enter a convent she would have to leave all her money behind or donate it directly to her congregation. For whatever reason, O'Connor clearly favored maintaining Kate's status quo.

O'Connor's reluctance paled beside Tony's distress when Kate revealed her plans to him and George Childs on March 25, 1889. Both Tony and Childs sincerely loved Kate. But Tony felt about religion as he felt about arts and culture: It was vital and necessary, but it acquired meaning only when applied to life's central trilogy: one's family, business, and community. For a woman with Kate's advantages to willingly shut herself off from all three elements and live on forty-one cents a day struck him as not merely foolish but genuinely tragic.

Childs—presumably acting on Tony's behalf—went so far as to visit Archbishop Ryan to ask him to use his influence to dissuade Kate. The archbishop replied that the decision was Kate's to make. He tactfully added that if she became unhappy with it, she would have a long period before taking her vows, during which she could change her mind.

But Kate was not to be deterred. In the best rational tradition of her Uncle Anthony, she drew up a list of the pros and cons of entering religious life before making her decision. "On the Annunciation I told Uncle Anthony and Mr. Childs of my intentions and future plans," Kate wrote to Bishop O'Connor two weeks later.

> Uncle Anthony dropped four or five tears; but he said he would not oppose anything which would contribute to my happiness. He thinks, however, that I am making the mistake of my life if I become a religious; yet he consents and so does Mr. Childs. I told them both of my plans relative to my establishing an Order for Indians and Colored. They think I can do much more good by helping the Orders already established. I have told your plans to no one except Uncle A. and Mr. Childs.

After spending the spring and summer of 1889 as a visitor at St. Mary's Convent in Pittsburgh, Katharine was formally accepted as a novice in November. A carload of assorted family members and friends—including Tony Drexel and George Childs—traveled to Pittsburgh by train for the ceremony. "Miss Drexel," the *Philadelphia Times* announced to its stunned readers, "so well-known as the most attractive of the sisters of her branch of the family and one of the greatest heiresses in America, will henceforth be 'dead to the world'."

Yet in fact Kate Drexel never suffered such a separation. Despite her professed desire to be treated as an ordinary postulant, the Church needed her wealth and organizational skills too sorely to keep her buried in a convent. In anticipation of the new order she hoped to form, she was allowed more time to study religious rules and peruse spiritual books than her fellow novices. She was also given time to handle the mission correspondence and funding appeals that continued to flow in to her, just as they had before she took the veil. Early during her novitiate in Pittsburgh, Sister Katharine was permitted to travel to Philadelphia to confer with architects for her proposed new convent in Cornwells Heights and to consult with her Uncle Anthony on business matters.

How much Tony's radical vision of his institute and Katharine's radical vision of her order influenced each other is hard to say. But both ideas moved forward at the same time—between 1889 and 1891—and during this period uncle and niece remained in constant touch with each other.

By late 1889 Tony had abandoned both the concept of an all-girls' school and a suburban location. Now, perhaps inspired by the dedication of his Catholic niece, he became convinced that neither creed nor gender should bar any qualified applicant from attending his proposed institute. In a letter to Kate at the convent in August he discussed family gossip, provided summaries of her finances, and then added, "I also enclose a newspaper slip which will show you and explain why I changed my plans in reference to my proposed Industrial School. It will now be nonsectarian."

The slip was a long article in George Childs's *Ledger*, published with Tony's authority, to "correct erroneous impressions about the Drexel Industrial Institute" and provide "a review of the circumstances which have modified and enlarged that purpose."

> It is now the purpose of Mr. Drexel to provide funds to purchase and construct buildings and for the maintenance of a full corps of instructors for an Industrial Institute for young women and young men that will accommodate, for their instruction and training, as many as a thousand girls in the day time and a thousand boys at night.
>
> The facilities and instructions to be provided for this school are to be free of any and all cost to its students forever—that is, so far as the provision of ample funds and business foresight can assure.

Tony was proposing a revolutionary notion for his day: an institute that placed no restrictions on religion, race, gender, or social class. Instead of studying Latin, Greek, philosophy, and music, students would take courses in business, chemistry, cooking, dressmaking, art, and library science. The Drexel

Institute of Art, Science and Industry would offer such unprecedented features as low tuition, abundant full scholarships, night classes, and lectures and concerts open to the public. Instead of a cloistered suburban environment, Tony's institute would be located at 32nd and Chestnut Streets in West Philadelphia, near the confluence of two railroad lines and several trolley lines, so as to be accessible to students from anywhere in Philadelphia or its suburbs.

Lacking a formal education himself, Tony now cast his net wide for advice, in effect calling in his moral chits from a lifetime of connections. Eliza Turner agreed to share her faculty from the New Century Guild for classes in millinery, dressmaking, glass cutting, and typesetting at Tony's institute. Tony's social friends were prevailed upon to bequeath art and rare manuscripts with which to create the Institute's art gallery and museum.

Tony also turned to Henry Codman Potter, who had begun his career as an office boy at Drexel & Co. in the 1850s. Now Potter was the Episcopal bishop of New York and preparing to launch an ambitious vision of his own: the enormous gothic Cathedral of St. John the Divine on Manhattan's Morningside Heights.

"He brooded over this large plan," Bishop Potter wrote of Tony at this stage. "He considered each separate class of those whose higher education he had in mind and strove to understand both them and their best wants." To design the institute, Tony hired the noted Philadelphia architect Joseph M. Wilson, who had created the main building for Philadelphia's Centennial Exposition of 1876 as well as Tony's bank building downtown. Wilson himself was an ardent advocate of industrial education, and Tony sent him to Europe to study foreign institutions before embarking on the Institute's design phase.

Once construction began, Tony visited the site every day on his morning walk to his office. He had originally anticipated spending $1.5 million to build and endow the Institute, but by the time of its dedication in December 1891 he had committed twice that amount: $1 million for construction, furnishing, and equipment; $2 million for endowment and operating expenses.

All this activity took place while Ellen Drexel, long plagued by rheumatism, gradually withered away. The Drexel Institute had been her idea as much as Tony's, but as 1891 wore on she became an invalid, confined to Runnemede, their summer home at Lansdowne. The last great gathering she threw was a party for their friends and colleagues who had helped them create the Institute.

Although Tony had agreed to put his name on the Institute, he remained unwilling to impose his ideas on the school. "I know that the world is going to change," he wrote, "and, therefore, the Institute must change with it, and I do not want to tie it up." But the public anticipation of the Institute made it harder than ever for Tony to escape attention. At a dinner given by Mayor Edwin Fitler in 1891 for an array of national bankers and World's Fair Commissioners to discuss the coming Fair, Tony found himself the unwilling object of after-dinner toasts. For perhaps the only time in his life, he arose and spoke in public. His remarks amounted to three sentences: "Gentleman, I make no pretensions to oratory. On the contrary, I much prefer to be quiet. All that I wish to say is that whenever anything is wanted, call on me." After which he promptly sat down.

More than 2,000 people attended the Drexel Institute's official opening ceremonies on December 17, 1891. To the *Philadelphia Evening Bulletin*, the gathering was "in some respects the most remarkable ever brought together by a similar or any other occasion," attended by guests "whose names are household words the civilized world over." The list included Andrew Carnegie and Thomas Edison (both Drexel and Morgan clients), Pierpont Morgan, U.S. Vice President Levi P. Morton (whose New York investment bank had joined hands with Tony and Pierpont Morgan to defeat Jay Cooke in 1873), three members of President Benjamin Harrison's cabinet, the chief justice of the Pennsylvania Supreme Court, and U.S. Senator Chauncey M. Depew of New York, who was the principal speaker.

But the Institute's founder and chairman was not present to be embarrassed by their effusions. ("No single dollar that Mr. Drexel gives away today," declared one speaker, "represents any method of acquiring wealth except by open and straightforward methods.") Anthony Drexel declined to attend on the ground that he was in mourning for his wife Ellen, who had died just three weeks earlier, on November 27. In her death his self-effacing wife had performed her husband one final service: She had spared him once again from his greatest phobia, public attention.

One other critical figure was also conspicuous by her absence. Having taken her vows the previous February, the newly named Mother Mary Katharine Drexel had moved in with thirteen novices to the temporary headquarters of her new order—the Sisters of the Blessed Sacrament for Indians and Colored People—in her father's former summer home near Andalusia. Torn between her obligations to her church and her love for her family, Katharine wrote after Ellen's death to "My very dear Uncle,"

> If I cannot come to you now, it is not because I forget your love to us in our affliction—a love which made us your children. With the affection of a child for its father, my heart beats sympathy. Had I not loved my Aunt I should not have gone all the way to see her last week. You were so wise not to permit me

to see her. I did not know how very ill she was until I called. I had heard she was better. It will be best for me to convert all my love for her & you to the prayers which I owe you by the sweet title of being your affectionate child. . . . It is a grief for me to feel I cannot do anything for you. If there is, please let me have the pleasure and consolation of doing it.

Among the hundreds of condolence notes Tony received from the great and the unknown, one in particular addressed to "Dear Anthony" may have given him pause. It came from his oldest and bitterest rival.

This is indeed a great loss, the greatest that can happen to any man, especially to one of so affectionate a nature as yourself. I have gone through the same sad experience and to this day I can scarcely be reconciled to the change. Let us be faithful as Christians during the short period remaining and then we will be glad to go also and meet the beloved ones who have gone before us. With great sympathy,
Yr. old fr'd
Jay Cooke

More than any other note, Cooke's conciliatory message captured the tragic essence of Tony's situation. Despite Tony's success and relative youth—he was still only sixty-five—he had outlived his wife, both his brothers, and four of his nine children. His niece Elizabeth Drexel Smith, Kate's older sister, had died in premature childbirth the year before. Junius Morgan, whom Tony had continued to visit each spring in retirement in the south of France, was gone, too, the victim of a freak accident in his horsedrawn Victoria in April 1890. Nor had Tony witnessed his last tragedy. In the spring of 1892 his oldest surviving child, forty-year-old Frances Drexel ("Nanny") Paul, came down with an unidentified illness. Tony, taking his annual cure at Carlsbad, urged her to join him there, and on May 24 Nanny arrived with her husband—Tony's partner Jim Paul— and their three young children.

"Nanny has commenced taking the waters," Tony wrote hopefully to his niece Louise the next day. The doctor, he said, "thinks she will be benefited by them." But three weeks later, as Nanny lay in her room next to his at the Hotel Bristol, Tony wrote Louise:

She is desperately ill and it is about an even chance life or death. The doctors are not oversanguine but bid us hope for the best. We have three doctors, two natives and one English. It is three weeks today since she went to bed, where she lays patiently and uncomplaining. She has dwindled down to a shadow of herself and is deplorably weak. The crisis must be soon at hand and whether favorable or otherwise you will hear by my cable to the office before this reaches you. I know my dear child I have your sympathy in this new ordeal. I am resigned to whatever God shall send, feeling assured it will be for the best. I have full faith and confidence in His mercy.

Nanny died the following day. And now, as Jay Cooke had unwittingly foreseen, Tony's turn was coming. Like his father before him, Anthony Drexel had a rendezvous with the Reading Railroad.

The Burden of Conscience

WHEN THE READING RAILROAD emerged from its second bankruptcy in 1888, it seemed solvent at last. The reckless empire builder Franklin Gowen had been removed from the presidency and replaced with the handpicked choice of Tony and Pierpont Morgan, the more cautious and sober banker Austin Corbin. Corbin in turn answered to a voting trust created by Morgan. That same year, Tony had demonstrated his good faith in the arrangement by negotiating a new $24 million loan for the Reading. Three years later, together with Brown Brothers, he negotiated another $8.5 million loan for construction of the Reading Terminal in Philadelphia, the largest single-span train shed in the world.

But Tony raised these funds without great enthusiasm. Because he had not trusted the Reading to begin with, he and Morgan had restructured the railroad on their own terms. As a result, now Tony's credibility was tied up in the Reading. Thousands of small investors in Philadelphia had bought Reading stock and bonds through Drexel & Co. He would have to make the best of the situation; he was in for a penny and in for a pound.

As in all his financings, Tony had sought to anticipate every conceivable uncertainty in the Reading situation. In this case he failed to anticipate that the specter of Franklin Gowen, once removed from the Reading's presidency and even from life itself, would not simply disappear.

Gowen had been president of the Reading for virtually all of a seventeen-year period from 1869 to 1886. He was a civic fixture in Philadelphia, and his pretentious visions appealed to local civic boosters who dreamed of restoring the national economic leadership that New York had snatched from Philadelphia half a century before. Like Jay Cooke before him, Gowen appealed to investors' dreams rather than to their intellects. Frustrated and bitter after resigning from the Reading, he returned to the practice of law and, in 1889, shot himself in a hotel in Washington. But his death merely magnified his mystique, fostering the notion that Morgan and Drexel had somehow driven him to suicide.

Around the time of Gowen's death the Philadelphia merchant prince John Wanamaker and the railroad car builder George Pullman organized several other Philadelphia businessmen—all former Gowen supporters—into a rival syndicate of Reading investors. Unlike Tony Drexel and Pierpont Morgan, who believed the Reading must coexist with its competing Eastern railroads, these armchair warriors shared Gowen's militant belief that the Reading could flourish only by dominating or destroying its rivals. Marshaling the voting power of their stock, they forced Corbin's resignation in June 1889 and installed Corbin's second-in-command, Archibald A. McLeod, a railroad romantic who shared Franklin Gowen's preference for action over reflection.

McLeod was a native of Canada who had drifted into railroading in the West in the 1860s and come East in the early 1870s to operate small railroads owned by Austin Corbin. When Corbin became president of the Reading in 1888 he summoned McLeod to Philadelphia. As a railroad man answering to a banker, McLeod was an effective manager. But once in absolute charge of the Reading at the age of forty-one, McLeod became a whirling dervish.

He launched the Reading into an expansion program the likes of which even Gowen had not dared to conceive, acquiring the Jersey Central Railroad and the Lehigh Valley road. He also began work on the Reading's enormous new station on Market Street in downtown Philadelphia. Most ambitious of all, he tried to extend the Reading's coal operations into New England, acquiring controlling interest in several companies, including the New York & New England Railroad and the Boston & Maine Railroad. This rash invasion of the historic turf of the New Haven and the New York Central railroads flouted Pierpont Morgan's basic principle—that great railroads should protect their investors by cooperating rather than competing with each other.

To stop McLeod, Morgan and Drexel severed their financial relations with the Reading. But McLeod proceeded anyway, financing his New England acquisitions by using the Reading's mortgage bonds as collateral, or by pledging the stocks of other companies that the Reading had acquired on thin margin.

The result was a repeat of the Reading's disasters under Franklin Gowen. In January 1890 the Reading notified Drexel & Co. that it lacked the funds to meet its next interest payment. To Tony fell the burden of passing the grim news on to London, where much of the Reading's bonds had been marketed through J. S. Morgan & Co.

"We are thunderstruck," wired back Walter Burns, Pierpont Morgan's brother-in-law and now head of the London house. Burns had good reason to be shocked: Barely a month earlier the Reading had assured Burns that the railroad would "without doubt" earn $10 million above its fixed charges for the fiscal year then ending. On the strength of that forecast, Burns said, "we have assured everyone" in London that the Reading's bonds would be paid, "if not in full at least a large proportion." Yet now, with the Reading reporting only $200,000 in earnings, "Our position is most humiliating independent of heavy loss."

Burns's cable urged the Reading to pay "whatever earned, even if only small fraction." Not to pay any of the Reading's debt, he warned, would probably lead to "legal proceedings" and strong efforts to have the company's managers removed.

Burns's warning proved prescient. English bondholders representing firms and individuals holding some $7 million of the Reading's securities joined to protest the missed payment and demanded an independent audit of the Reading's books. The only reason J. S. Morgan & Co. did not sign the protest, the firm cabled Drexel, was to save the Philadelphia house from "any complication," even though Burns said his house felt "as much aggrieved as anyone."

Tony Drexel in Philadelphia and Pierpont Morgan in New York scrambled to save the Reading from failure with short-term loans and new debt issues, but this time J. S. Morgan would not join them. "Feeling" in London against the Reading was "extremely bitter," Burns wrote, and his firm would be "violently attacked" if it issued any more of the Reading's securities. Although money was growing scarce and demand for capital was greater than at any other time since the Panic of 1873, both Drexel and Morgan pumped new funds into the Reading without demanding even the customary charges that large lenders usually exacted. Three issues in 1890 and 1891 raised $14.5 million for the Reading; three term loans provided an additional $2 million; and in February 1892 Drexel's Philadelphia and New York houses sold yet another $2 million of Reading bonds. But none of these infusions prevented the Reading's failure. On February 25, 1893, the Reading declared bankruptcy, with debts of more than $125 million, a staggering sum for the time.

Although McLeod was the primary cause of the Reading's troubles, the bankruptcy court appointed him as one of the Reading's three receivers. Tony Drexel and Pierpont Morgan, who had repeatedly rescued the Reading over the past decade, now refused to render any further assistance as long as McLeod was involved. Other banks expressed interest in replacing the Drexel-Morgan combination as the Reading's financier, but none actually did. Cut off from further funding, McLeod finally resigned in April, blaming his downfall not on Morgan but on Tony Drexel. McLeod disingenuously claimed to reporters that Tony had turned against him because McLeod had threatened to seek refinancing from

Speyer & Co., the rival New York bank that since the mid-1880s had successfully weaned the Pennsylvania Railroad away from its exclusive relationship with the Drexels and Morgans.

As McLeod told it, the loss of a client like the Reading would have further damaged Drexel & Co.'s prestige. Tony "was enraged beyond expression," McLeod claimed to a reporter. "He foamed at the mouth, jumped from his seat and raising his hand exclaimed, 'That will be very bad for Speyers and for the Reading'." McLeod added:

> I knew perfectly well then, as I know now, that the Drexels have absolute con-
> trol of the money market of Philadelphia. It was Drexel and Childs of the
> *Philadelphia Ledger* that downed Jay Cooke in 1873, and they both boasted of
> it. . . . I knew that if I did not resign from the Reading as Drexel requested that
> I should have Drexel as my enemy, and Drexel is ten times worse as a fighter
> than Morgan.

McLeod's self-serving assessment contained just enough truth to infuriate Tony even more. At the very same time that Tony was wrestling with the Reading in the spring of 1893, his longtime client the Pennsylvania Railroad inexplicably awarded a 1.5-million-pound bond offering to Speyer's London house, despite a prompt and liberal competing offer from J. S. Morgan & Co. The Pennsylvania Railroad's president, George B. Roberts, was "evidently more anxious [to] secure participation for Speyer Bros . . . than to foster relations with us," the Morgans' London house complained to Tony in a cable of April 5.

But Tony had a better reason to feel exasperated by McLeod. Drexel and Morgan had already severed their financial ties with McLeod when he invaded the New England rail market. Their concern now, as the Reading's largest creditors, was to curb McLeod's reckless behavior—which further funding from Speyer would encourage.

Notwithstanding his desperate efforts to save the Reading over the previous three years, Tony now found himself reviled in Philadelphia as a vulture intent on plucking the bankrupt railroad's carcass. The disgrace suffered by his city, as well as the knowledge that his friends and neighbors would suffer the greatest losses from the Reading's defaults, seemed more than he could bear. The U.S. Treasury's reserve was shrinking dangerously and uncertainty about the nation's finances was growing; now the Reading's collapse undermined what little confidence remained in the nation's economy. The Panic of 1893 was underway, and Tony suffered the humiliation of knowing that his client, the Reading, was the primary catalyst.

Early in May, after the failure of the National Cordage Company, one of the country's best-known industrial concerns, the economy slid into one of the longest and severest depressions in U.S. history. Nearly one-third of the nation's railroad mileage would pass into receivership before the Panic ended.

Twenty years earlier, when Jay Cooke's failure had triggered the panic of 1873, Tony Drexel had bolstered public assurance by strolling confidently through Philadelphia's financial district. But now he was unable to conceal his own lost confidence. In a photograph taken in 1886, one newspaper noted, Tony appeared "bright-eyed, alert and destitute of deep care"; by contrast, "in his latest photograph all the lines of trouble are there—the brow is drawn, the lips are strongly set, as if struggling to suppress the cry of a heart which had felt many ills."

While Tony was embroiled in his struggle to remove McLeod from the Reading, the French artist Benjamin Constant arrived in Philadelphia to paint Tony's portrait. The painting had been commissioned by the Drexel Institute's board of managers the previous spring, while Tony was taking the waters in Carlsbad and was therefore unable to object. Tony predictably refused to sit for it. After several requests from his good friend Childs, Tony finally consented, but only on the condition that the $5,000 fee should not be paid for from the Institute's funds or the painting displayed there until after his death.

When Constant began his work in the Drexel Institute's art studio in March 1893, Tony asked Childs to be present for the first sitting. After Constant finished sketching Tony's face, Tony stood and motioned to Childs to take his place. "You have insisted upon my sitting," he said. "Now you must do as I have done; for as we have been together in life, you shall go down to posterity with me through Monsieur Constant's genius." Coming from someone who had never before expressed concern for posterity, such a melodramatic gesture suggested a man who was worn down and perhaps sensed that his own time was growing short.

With McLeod removed from the Reading—succeeded by Tony's choice, Joseph Harris, a fiscal conservative and a well-trained civil engineer with extensive experience in coal mining and transportation—Drexel & Co. assembled a rehabilitation plan for the railroad. The Drexel plan, made public late in May 1893, was largely the work of the Philadelphia banker J. Lowber Welsh, who was Tony's friend but not a Drexel & Co. partner. The plan concluded that some $30 million would be required to end the receivership and save the road from foreclosure and a formal reorganization.

But the plan was hastily prepared and relied on figures supplied by Reading officers. Pierpont Morgan himself had little enthusiasm for it. Experience had taught him not to depend on figures provided by a company's own officials un-less they were verified by independent accountants or, better still, by Morgan's expert partner Charles Coster. To his brother-in-law Walter Burns in London, Morgan characterized the Reading plan's figures as "disappointing & mislead-ing." But to Tony himself Morgan said nothing. Even at the height of his power and prominence Pierpont was unwilling to dispute his patron.

Despite Morgan's doubts, the financial press generally received the plan fa-vorably, and applications to subscribe to the new loan were so large that in late April, almost a month before the proposal was made public, Drexel & Co. ca-bled J. S. Morgan & Co. in London that most of the planned offering had already been taken. Believing that he had done all he could for the Reading, and des-perate for a change of scene, in late May Tony authorized the last expenditure to complete the Drexel Institute and boarded the steamship *City of New York*, bound for his offices in London and Paris and ultimately a long rest at Carlsbad.

He was unaccompanied by relatives or friends—his four surviving children, all married now, were at their summer homes or at Bar Harbor in Maine—but upon his arrival at Carlsbad on May 30 Tony found, as he had expected, "quite a number of nice people here, Philadelphians & New Yorkers." His two-room suite on the second floor of the Hotel Bristol offered a soothing view of the val-ley and distant mountains.

Cheerfully he fell into his familiar Carlsbad regimen. He arose each morning at 6 A.M., drank his Sprudel water, and then took a long walk to a jaegerhaus or an open-air restaurant, buying his rolls for breakfast on the way, in keeping with the Carlsbad custom. He dined simply at midday and took a light meal about 7:30 in the evening. "I get into a certain rut and find the time passes more rapidly," he wrote to his niece Louise.

At the end of the second week, after a hard walk through the woods on a very hot day, his physician found Tony in his room, writing at a table. He was gently perspiring from his walk and had seated himself between the open door and windows to benefit from the draft. The doctor, one A. Grunberger, warned him that he might catch a cold. "Oh, I stand all these things very well," Tony replied.

The next morning Tony sent Dr. Grunberger a note saying he had a severe chill and didn't feel at all well. The following morning—exactly one year after Tony's daughter Frances had died in the adjoining suite—Dr. Grunberger diag-nosed his ailment as pleurisy, an inflammation of the lungs that rendered deep breathing restricted and painful (the same ailment that had killed Tony's brother Frank). Grunberger called in a Dr. Neubauer, one of the best physicians in Carls-bad, who confirmed the diagnosis. But under the two doctors' treatment over the next ten days Tony seemed to recover: His pains ceased, his fever disappeared entirely, he regained his sleep and appetite and resumed his regular meals.

In any case, he would not permit his family to be advised of his illness. On June 20 Tony wrote a cheerful letter informing his niece Louise that he would soon be leaving Carlsbad: "Next week I will go to Paris via Frankfurt & Cologne at each of which places I will stop overnight." He expressed the hope of visiting Louise's sister's new convent: "How is Kate getting along with her enterprise? I take a look at it every time I pass going to N.Y. I want to go out and see it with you some time."

But on June 26 he received jarring news. The Reading Railroad's security holders in Philadelphia had declined Tony's reorganization plan. The bond holders objected to the arrangement to fund their coupons; the stockholders refused to assign their shares to a voting trust dominated by company officials who had been associated with McLeod's discredited administration; and all the railroad's security holders were unhappy with the plan's loan requirements. Now the whole plan would have to be scrapped, and Tony, or some competing banker, would have to devise a new one.

With this news, Tony suffered a relapse. The doctors seemed uncertain whether it was a recurrence of his gout, or pleurisy, or both. Restricted to his room with the barest minimum of visitors, on June 29 Tony weakly scribbled a note to Burns in London:

Altho I have passed the critical point I am [not] entirely out of the woods. I fear it will be some days before I get out again.

The pleurisy is disappearing but one of my legs is very much swollen & I can't put it to the ground.

In consequence of the pleurisy causing short breathing and a feeling of suffocation I could not go to bed but have had to pass the night in a chair . . . I am "hors du combat" but hope I will be all right again shortly.

I have postponed my day of sailing to the 29th [of July] by [the] "New York."

I would advise going very slowly about any RR reorganization plans. In my judgment you can't improve on the plan just withdrawn.

That would have gone through had it not been for the opposition of the "Income & General Management Comm.," a party of speculators and lawyers who want the reorganization job. Let them all flounder around & expose their hands. When the bell is rung for sale under foreclosure, then we can step in if we wish to do so. As the case stands now I can't see either honor or profit in doing anything.

I hope to see you in London before I sail & we can talk matters over.

In a faint, pathetic postscript, he added: "I don't know whether you will be able to read this but it is the best I can do."

That night Tony's two doctors examined him together and declared him safe. Tony asked when he might leave Carlsbad; in eight or ten days, they replied.

Dr. Grunberger visited him again the following morning as usual at 6:30 and found Tony in the best of spirits. He said he had slept seven hours and felt stronger than he had for a long time. He ate a hearty breakfast of tea, eggs, and rolls. At 9 A.M. he had a visit from H. C. Haskins of New York and his wife, who found him looking unusually well and cheerful. Mrs. Haskins, the daughter of the U.S. Minister to Austria and a favorite of Tony's, propped a bouquet of yellow roses on his table. Tony joked that it was good to be ill if it meant being taken care of by such a charming nurse.

Later that morning James Stebbins of Philadelphia stopped in for a visit. He too found Tony cheerful and seemingly on the road to recovery. When he left, the two men shook hands.

"Cheer up, old friend, and have pluck," Stebbins said.

"I have plenty of that," Tony replied.

Alone now, Tony turned to his newspapers and his mail. A letter from Walter Burns in London had just arrived, crossing with Tony's letter of the previous day, and Tony picked up his pencil to respond to it.

> I wrote you yesterday and today I have yours [of the] 28th. I have had a good night. The swelling and fever & pleurisy much better. My leg is still swollen & I can't stand on it, so I have to sit in one position day & night.
>
> I have a most careful nurse and lots of sympathy [from] my friends who are very kind, but the doctors prohibit my having company as I ought not to talk.
>
> I thank you very much for your kind sympathy.

His letter now turned to business questions and to the burning political issue of the day: the populists' demand to increase the money supply through the free coinage of silver, which Tony opposed as an inflationary gimmick. Tony had long admired President Grover Cleveland's personal integrity; he had supported Cleveland when he first ran in 1884 and then reluctantly opposed him in 1888 and 1892 over Cleveland's opposition to tariffs. Now, in the last thoughts he would express on any subject, Tony shared with Burns his feelings about Cleveland, a Democrat, and about James D. Cameron, the U.S. Senator from Pennsylvania.

Cameron always has been a silver man & in that respect disgraces the state he represents. I think he must have silver interests. He has always been a demagogue & not a statesman.

Cleveland can be counted on to do his duty in the silver business. He is an honest man & a statesman.

At 1:45 a waiter brought Tony's previously ordered dinner. Finding the door to the sitting room locked, he started to go through the bedroom. There he discovered Tony lying on his back, his mouth and eyes open. He had been dead, apparently since about noon, of a heart attack. On the table by his side were the *Philadelphia Public Ledger* of June 18, the *Philadelphia Bulletin* of June 16, the *London Times* of June 28, Tony's watch chain, his pencil, the private telegraph code of Drexel & Co., and a copy of Bradshaw's railroad timetable guide. On the chair was a pile of New York and Philadelphia newspapers. He had spent the last day of his sixty-six years immersed in the same minute details that had occupied him since he was a boy of thirteen.

While Anthony Drexel lived, the press had respected his wish for privacy: His name appeared occasionally in articles about other people, but only once in fifty-three years was he the central subject of an article in any publication, and that merely a brief and distant sketch written without his cooperation. Because he frowned on coverage, journalists took the path of least resistance and wrote about other, less reticent figures. But now that Tony was no longer present to object, the press cast off all constraints. His sudden death was front page news throughout America and Europe. Newspapers from New York to San Francisco dissected his final hours, his career, his background, the whereabouts of his children, and the progress of his body as it made its way across Germany to Bremen and then across the Atlantic aboard the German steamer *Kaiser Wilhelm II.*

His friends and beneficiaries, similarly constrained from praising Tony while he lived, now unleashed their feelings. Childs wrote a eulogy in *Harper's Weekly.* The unsentimental scholar Henry Charles Lea, who in the 1870s had joined Tony and Childs in founding the Reform Club to fight local political corruption, wrote a private condolence note to Childs: "I suppose that after all no one man is indispensable to the world, but it is not easy at the moment to look around and determine who there is to take his place."

Tony's memorial service at the Drexel Institute attracted two thousand mourners, among them the nation's business, political and educational leaders but also dozens of recipients of Tony's generosity whom Tony had sworn to secrecy. "No one but God and those he helped will ever know how wide and constant was the reach of his secret benefactions," declared Tony's former office boy, Bishop Henry Potter of New York. Such a high-powered gathering had been seen only once before in America, at the dedication of the Drexel Institute itself two years earlier.

Pierpont Morgan wrote a friend that he was "completely stunned by the death of Mr. Drexel. He was very dear to me, and I am at a complete loss to know how I am going to get along without him." He conveyed much the same sense of helplessness in a cable he sent on July 19 to his brother-in-law Walter Burns, now the head of J. S. Morgan & Co. in London.

> Laid Mr. Drexel peacefully to rest Woodlands Cemetery. Still feel quite dazed and staggered in deciding what best for future. Recognize importance all interests public as well as private in wise decision. Would you be willing to spare three weeks come over if I find it necessary help me decide. Will cable you when known what provisions in will as regards business.

There could be no mistaking his implication: The world's most famous banker was in the dark about his own future because Tony Drexel had never told him the provisions of his will. It was left to Burns to assure his brother-in-law, in a reply cabled the same day: "You must not allow yourself feel discouraged. A. J. Drexel told me recently had provided in will continue business."

At the age of fifty-six Morgan was on his own, with neither a father nor a patron looking over his shoulder. The world may not have recognized the extent to which he had relied on these elders, but Morgan did. Two months after Tony's death his daughter, Sallie Fell, sent Morgan a photograph of Tony as a keepsake. "I shall value it," Morgan wrote back, "not only as your gift but on account also of my associations with him. For he was the best friend I have ever had in every way."

Epilogue:
The Death and Rebirth of the House of Drexel

It is often said that the shoemaker's children go barefoot, that the minister's son becomes the village drunk, and that children of psychiatrists are notably maladjusted. Anthony Drexel's children suffered from a similar parental lapse on the part of their father. As a banker describing his business to Junius Morgan in 1871, Tony had astutely perceived how Robert Winthrop's "very large expectations" of inheritance had impaired Winthrop's entrepreneurial drive. Yet as a father Tony seemed incapable of applying this same insight to his own sons and daughters.

His will bequeathed $1 million as well as many of his art works to the Drexel Institute, and he left every clerk at Drexel & Co. $100 for each year of service. But these gifts as well as Tony's other bequests barely scratched the surface of his estate, which was valued between $25 and $30 million, one of the largest ever recorded up to that time. The three family trusts created by his will generated sufficient income to eliminate his descendants' material concerns for the next three generations. But it also destroyed their initiative. Although the will provided funds for the continuity of Drexel & Co. and offered capital incentives to encourage his three sons to maintain the bank, Tony's death became the signal for his family's virtual withdrawal from business of any kind.

Within four months of Tony's death, only one family member—his son-in-law, James Paul, Jr.—remained at Drexel & Co., and when James died in 1908 the family presence there vanished altogether. The next three generations of Tony's descendants numbered notable philanthropists, diplomats, lawyers, polo players, fox hunters, horse breeders, golf and tennis champions, bon vivants and one of the world's ten best-dressed men (the World War II diplomat Anthony J. Drexel Biddle, Jr., who was said to buy his monogrammed shirts in lots of 200). But the group included no one who could be described as commercially ambitious.

Tony's heir apparent, Anthony, Jr., who was made a partner at Drexel & Co.

in 1890, resigned just four months after his father's death. In a remarkably candid announcement, the firm explained, "He does not care to assume the cares and responsibilities which are attached to the business. He is a young man who is fond of life in the society he adorns." (At that "young man's" age—twenty-nine—his father had already been working at Drexel & Co. for 16 years and was firmly in charge.) Anthony, Jr., by most accounts a man of intelligence and wit, moved to England and happily devoted himself to yachting (a hobby that cost him $250,000 a year), consuming fine food and wines, and collecting stamps and mistresses with royal chums like King Edward VII. He cut a dashing figure in his goatee, white ducks, and blue blazer with red handkerchief. But when he and his wife Margarita were divorced in London in 1917, his wife's lawyer described Anthony, Jr. as "a man whose character and temper had been completely destroyed by his great wealth."

Anthony, Jr.'s brother John Rozet Drexel spent most of his life being dragged about Paris by his socially ambitious wife Alice; he "seemed a man without hobbies or avocations," an obituary observed when he died in 1935. The youngest brother, George Childs Drexel, succeeded his namesake George Childs as proprietor of the *Public Ledger* in 1894 and subsequently moved into Wootton, Childs's estate in the suburb of Bryn Mawr. But the reader will not be surprised to learn that this well-meaning attempt by Tony Drexel to create a surrogate son for his friend Childs failed as well. In 1902, when George Childs Drexel was just thirty-four, he sold the *Ledger* and devoted the remaining forty-two years of his life to his favorite hobbies: yachts and motor cars. He became an expert mechanic, drove one of the first automobiles in Philadelphia, and was instrumental in shaping the city's early speed laws.

The strongest members of the Drexel generations immediately following Anthony J. were generally not the men but the women. Tony's buxom, regal, eclectic daughter Sarah ("Sallie") Drexel Fell Van Rensselaer skillfully presided over Philadelphia society for more than thirty years from her mansion on Rittenhouse Square and from her court at Camp Hill, her suburban castle in Fort Washington. Sallie and her second husband Alexander Van Rensselaer were among the founders of the Philadelphia Orchestra in 1900; he served as its first president for thirty years. When they traveled the world, the Van Rensselaers were guests of the Japanese imperial family, the Court of St. James, the Rajah of Singapore, and the Viceroy of India. George Childs Drexel's wife Mary was another dominating Philadelphia grande dame, holding forth from her box at the Academy of Music until her death in 1948. Yet these and later generations of Drexel women were primarily characterized not by snobbery or pomposity but by free-spirited eccentricity interlaced with empathy and gentle politeness.

"We were all brought up with a jillion servants," Sallie's granddaughter Frances Cheston Train once remarked. "But what I remember is the extreme courtesy. My parents never gave an order; it was always, 'Would you mind bringing a horse?' They were culturally secure because they didn't have to impress anyone."

The generation following Tony Drexel did produce one genuine entrepreneur. The Sisters of the Blessed Sacrament—the ambitious nationwide network of missions founded by Katharine Drexel in 1891 and supervised by her in every detail for more than forty years—was in many respects organized along the lines of Tony's transatlantic banking network. And it succeeded largely by virtue of Mother Katharine's hardnosed financial acumen (and also because she required her nuns to enroll in practical courses at the Drexel Institute). During the sixty-six years from the time she took the veil until her death in 1955 at the age of ninety-six, Mother Katharine funneled all her personal income from her father's trust—some $20 million—to her order. At its peak, the order operated sixty missions and schools for blacks and Native Americans, including Xavier University in New Orleans. Even beyond her own order Katharine became in effect a one-woman foundation for bishops and priests seeking money to build or staff schools for Indians or blacks.

But Katharine's wealth and shrewdness were matched by her extraordinary courage. When the order opened a school for blacks in Beaumont, Texas in 1922, a hooded delegation of Ku Klux Klansmen rode up on horses, threatening to burn the school down. Mother Katharine came outside and confronted them—"No, we will not leave"—and began to pray. The Klansmen backed off.

Mother Katharine was canonized by Pope John Paul II in 2000, becoming in the process only the second native-born American saint. But her place in history was assured long before then. "If she had never done anything else than set an example to a frivolous, self-seeking world," Dennis Cardinal Dougherty of Philadelphia observed at Katharine's golden jubilee in 1941, "she should be regarded as a benefactress of the human race."

Anthony Drexel's death came at the worst possible time for his partners. The Panic of 1893 was underway and money was scarce. Had his will failed to direct his estate to continue temporarily as a de facto partner, the sudden withdrawal of his huge capital stake at such a moment might have ruined his partners, including even Pierpont Morgan. Over the long term, of course, the firms' capital was a less important asset than Morgan's influence and reputation.

Eighteen months after Tony Drexel's death—at the end of 1894, after the depression had subsided—Morgan summoned the partners of the Philadelphia and New York houses to the Metropolitan Club in New York, in the process assembling all the Drexel and Morgan partners together in one room for the first time. After dinner was finished and the waiters had left, Morgan unveiled his restructuring plan. The two houses would be combined under his leadership; their capital would be pooled and placed in the New York office, which would be renamed J. P. Morgan & Co. The Paris firm's name would be changed to Morgan, Harjes & Co. Only the Philadelphia house would continue under its original name, Drexel & Co., although no one named Drexel remained among its partners.

Over the next eighteen years until his death in 1913, Morgan supervised the streamlining of the chaotic American economy at a time when railroads, steam engines, electric power, and telephones were transforming life for practically all Americans. He bound America's railroads into a continuous system that ran from coast to coast. He organized the first modern corporations: U.S. Steel, General Electric, and International Harvester. He bailed out the U.S. government during a panic in 1895 and rescued the New York Stock Exchange during the Panic of 1907. Thanks to the awesome prestige of his stewardship, the firm of J. P. Morgan & Co. flourished through the entire twentieth century until it was subsumed into a merger with Chase Manhattan Bank in 2000.

Archibald A. McLeod survived his forced departure from the Reading Railroad, shortly afterward becoming president of the New York & New England Railroad, which the Reading had controlled. He continued to believe that Tony Drexel had forced him out of the Reading for some ulterior reason. Drexel "seemed to have something in his mind for the future," McLeod told an interviewer in the fall of 1893, "and I think that had Drexel lived I should have gone back into Reading after he had perfected some plans that he had in his mind." McLeod died in 1902 at the age of fifty-four.

Following Tony Drexel's death Pierpont Morgan at first refused to have anything more to do with the Reading Railroad. But after the Reading's security holders rejected a second reorganization plan offered in January 1894 and a third plan offered in October 1894, Morgan was approached in 1895 and asked to devise his own plan to reorganize the Reading. He did, and the Reading functioned until 1971, when it went bankrupt for the fourth and final time. Its world-famous train shed, built in 1893 with funds provided by Drexel & Co., survived as the roof for the Pennsylvania Convention Center's ballroom when the center opened in 1993.

Shortly after Morgan died in 1913, Woodrow Wilson signed into law the Federal Reserve Act, thereby creating America's first central bank since 1836, the year before Morgan was born. During that seventy-seven-year period the United States had experienced the most extraordinary long-term economic growth of any nation in world history, but it had also suffered through four devastating depressions. Conventional wisdom has held ever since that a central bank is necessary to smooth out such short-term jolts along the highway to prosperity. Yet the cyclical nature of the U.S. economy has persisted, and the greatest of all U.S. depressions—the one that began in 1930—was caused in large part by the Federal Reserve Board's paralysis in the face of falling stock prices. With the luxury of hindsight, and as the Internet decentralizes transactions between buyers and sellers of all types, economists of the future may well question whether central banks operated by political appointees do a better job of stabilizing markets than the cumulative private decisions of hundreds of financiers whose own fortunes are at stake, as Morgan's and Drexel's were.

George Childs, celebrated as an almost legendary figure who talked with kings yet retained the common touch, died in February 1894. Tony Drexel's death seven months earlier, suggested the *New York Press*, "may be said to have caused Mr. Childs' death, just as the bankruptcy of the Reading Railroad hastened Mr. Drexel's death. . . . From the hour of [Drexel's] death . . . his old buoyancy of spirit was gone. He missed Drexel every day of his life after that."

Although George Childs Drexel sold the *Ledger* just eight years later, the newspaper continued to distinguish itself under two subsequent owners, first Adolph Ochs of the *New York Times* and then Cyrus H. K. Curtis of the *Saturday Evening Post*. It was finally merged into the *Philadelphia Inquirer* when Curtis died in 1933. The *Evening Public Ledger*, an offshoot founded by Curtis in 1914, survived until 1942.

Jay Cooke never returned to banking after his failure in 1873. But he recouped his fortune through mining investments in Utah and discharged all of his debts by 1880. He lived until 1905, long enough to write his memoirs and persuade at least some financial historians that his downfall had been caused by the Drexels' unwarranted jealousy. After his shouting match with Childs at the *Ledger* in 1869 he never spoke to Childs again—until, a month before Childs's death in 1894, the two old antagonists met by chance one day in the street and Childs invited the aging financier into the *Ledger* building to talk and peruse his pictures and memorabilia.

John Harjes, the childhood friend whom Tony Drexel chose to open his Paris branch in 1868, remained at the renamed Morgan, Harjes & Co. for more than forty years until he retired at the end of 1908. He died in 1914 at the age of eighty-three. His son Henry succeeded him as resident senior partner in Paris until his death in a polo accident in 1926. The Paris house was subsequently renamed for its New York-based parent, J. P. Morgan & Co. But visitors to its office on the Place Vendôme will still find, in an interior office, a bust of the firm's founder, Anthony Drexel.

Edward Biddle went unmentioned in Anthony Drexel's will, but that will provided trusts of $1 million for each of the three sons Edward fathered with Emilie Drexel. A few years later those sons each contributed assets to establish a trust for their father. (Edward had three more sons with his second wife.) True to his original intentions, after leaving Drexel & Co. Edward became an art critic and historian. His published essays and his coauthored biographies of Thomas Sully and Jean Antoine Houdon demonstrated that he was no mere dilettante. But Edward never wrote anything about his own life or his relationship with Anthony Drexel. He remained a dashing, athletic figure in 1931 when, as the oldest living member of the Biddle clan, he presided over the family's celebration of the 250th anniversary of its arrival in America. Edward died two years later at the age of eighty-two, having outlived his first wife, Emilie Drexel, by half a century.

The prestige associated with the Drexel name at the time of A. J. Drexel's death produced marriages with so many wealthy and prominent families that Tony's blood descendants came to constitute a virtual financial-cultural-political clearing house for the Western world. At one time or another Drexels were related to Vanderbilts, Dukes, Roosevelts (both the Theodore and FDR branches), Bouviers, Biddles, Whartons, Wyeths, Whitneys, Mellons, Astors, Ingersolls, Cassatts, Cadwaladers, and Goulds, as well as the British nobility. By the end of the twentieth century only five American universities—Drexel, Vanderbilt, Duke, Brown, and Rutgers—were still linked to their founding families; all five families were related to the Drexels.

Indeed, "high society" in the twentieth century was virtually defined by

Drexel relatives. Harry Lehr, court jester to New York society in the 1890s, was the husband of Joseph Drexel's daughter Elizabeth. Maury H. B. Paul, society editor of the *New York Journal-American* until his death in 1942 and the first columnist to use the pseudonym "Cholly Knickerbocker," was related by marriage to the Drexels; so was the twentieth century's preeminent academic observer of the Protestant establishment, the University of Pennsylvania sociologist E. Digby Baltzell. And in 1961 a descendant of Frank Drexel's in-laws, the Bouviers, was installed in the White House in the person of the First Lady, Jacqueline Bouvier Kennedy.

Yet precisely because the Drexels were so prominently married and so geographically diffuse, many of them lost all cognizance of their family. By the end of the twentieth century the more than 300 descendants of Francis M. Drexel had been scattered as far as England, France, and Australia, but barely a dozen of them bore the surname Drexel and many were only dimly aware of their Drexel connections. Thus it was possible, one Saturday afternoon in the Cotswolds in 1991, for the three children of an English couple named Sue and Caspar Tiarks to watch the Walt Disney movie *The Happiest Millionaire* on television without any awareness that the film's protagonist—Tony Drexel's eccentric grandson, A. J. Drexel Biddle—was in fact their own first cousin three times removed. The diplomat Angier Biddle Duke and his philanthropist brother Anthony Drexel Duke once told this writer that they were vaguely related to the Drexel family, unaware that, like Caspar Tiarks, they too were direct descendants of Anthony Drexel—specifically, Tony's great-great-grandsons. Throughout his life Tony Drexel had persistently sought obscurity; in death, it seems, he achieved it even within his own family.

It took two world wars to reawaken the Drexel family's sense of purpose. In these global crises Tony Drexel's socialite descendants responded eagerly, as if grateful to have found at last a useful activity on a scale suitable to their background and wealth. In World War I Tony's son George Childs Drexel donated his yacht, the *Alcedo*, to the U.S. government; it subsequently became the first U.S. armed vessel sunk by a German torpedo. George's playboy brother Anthony Drexel, Jr. served as a stretcher-bearer with the British ambulance corps in France. His son J. Armstrong Drexel became the first American aviator to serve under France's commander, General Joseph Joffre.

With the outbreak of World War II in 1939, the Countess of Winchilsea—Armstrong Drexel's sister—became a leader of Britain's Women's Land Army, which trained 25,000 young women to replace British farmers summoned to military service. During the evacuation at Dunkirk in 1940, her son Christopher Maidstone jumped into his boat and helped ferry British and French soldiers across the English Channel. His sister Henrietta Finch-Hatton Tiarks, then twenty-four, became a motorcycle dispatch rider.

The rambunctious Colonel Anthony J. Drexel Biddle—protagonist of the Disney film *The Happiest Millionaire*—taught hand-to-hand combat to U.S. Marines in both world wars. As the German army advanced on Paris in the spring of 1940, his son, the well-dressed U.S. diplomat Tony Biddle, Jr., made a show of meeting frequently and conspicuously with French Premier Paul Reynaud in a valiant but futile effort (reminiscent of his great-grandfather's walk through Third Street in 1873) to bolster confidence among the French that American help was on the way. When German troops occupied Paris, another of Anthony Drexel's granddaughters, Mary Paul Munn Allez—then director of the American Aid Society in Paris—transformed herself into "Pauline," an underground informant who funneled information to the French Resistance gleaned from her contacts among Prussian officers who detested the Nazis (and who on at least one occasion protected her from arrest by the Nazis). Eva Drexel Dahlgren, granddaughter of Tony's brother Joseph Drexel, opened a Paris hospital during World War I, reactivated it during World War II, and was subsequently decorated for her service by the French government.

Such public service instincts have persisted among Tony Drexel's descendants ever since. The novelist Livingston Biddle, Jr. co-drafted the legislation creating the National Endowment for the Arts and headed that agency from 1977 to 1981. Ambassador Angier Biddle Duke was White House chief of protocol under Presidents Kennedy and Johnson. His brother Anthony Drexel Duke founded the Harbor for Boys and Girls in New York, which has provided summer camps and year-round programs for almost 3,000 poor children annually since 1937.

Josephine Brown was a founder in the 1960s of the radical Students for a Democratic Society. Pamela Drexel Walker helped found the Spoleto Festival in Italy. Christopher Finch-Hatton, 16th earl of Winchilsea, became a Liberal peer in the British House of Lords who assumed the mantle of unofficial champion for London's constables and taxi drivers, sometimes spending whole nights accompanying street cops on their beats. He was also the prime mover behind a continuing program of relief convoys to aid some 200,000 refugees in the desert of southwestern Algeria.

C. Howard Drexel, of Southern Pines, North Carolina, became a major force in the highly regarded restoration of Savannah, Georgia. His cousin Noreen

Drexel O'Farrell worked for Save the Children and Amnesty International, spent a year in India teaching Tibetan refugees, worked in a leper colony and helped overhaul the high school curriculum in Providence, Rhode Island. "Something," her older brother, John R. Drexel IV, has observed, "drives her to address inequities."

Although Drexel & Co. was effectively reduced to a branch office of J. P. Morgan & Co. after 1895, it retained its muscular prestige and power within Philadelphia. The house financed the expansion and integration of some of the country's great utilities systems—Philadelphia Electric Company, the United Gas Improvement Company, and Public Service Electric and Gas Company of New Jersey—as well as the construction and expansion in the 1920s of the University of Pennsylvania's famous sports arenas, the Palestra and Franklin Field. When the debts from these projects threatened to consume the university, Drexel & Co. came to the rescue by installing its own senior partner, Thomas S. Gates, as Penn's president in 1930.

The so-called "dual partnership" between the New York and Philadelphia houses was severed in 1940 when J. P. Morgan & Co., in order to handle trust business, became a corporation rather than a private bank. Nevertheless, one Drexel & Co. partner continued to serve on the J. P. Morgan board, and ties between the two houses persisted. Between 1961 and 1971 Thomas S. Gates, Jr., a second-generation Drexel partner, served as president and then chairman of J. P. Morgan & Co.

Drexel & Co., still private, became an investment banking and brokerage house, important in Philadelphia but nowhere else. The last of the Drexel family's investment was withdrawn from the firm in 1959. As hard times hit the brokerage industry in the late 1960s and early 1970s, Drexel & Co. underwent three mergers. But the Drexel name, by virtue of its prominence, survived each new combination, so that Drexel & Co. became successively Drexel Harriman Ripley, then Drexel Firestone, and finally, in 1973, Drexel Burnham Lambert. By the time Burnham & Co. effected this acquisition it was widely believed that the old Drexel & Co.'s sole remaining asset was the Drexel name. But in fact the transaction also brought Burnham a bright young Drexel Firestone trader named Michael Milken.

Like the Morgans and Drexels before him, Milken subsequently created and maintained a market for a new financial vehicle—the high-risk bonds of small entrepreneurial companies that had previously been despised by most investors. But Milken's market, unlike those of the Drexels and Morgans, functioned somewhat like a chain letter: Milken pressured some beneficiaries of his so-called "junk bonds" to invest in the junk bonds of other corporations, thus falsely creating the illusion that the market for junk bonds was sounder and more liquid than it really was. This deceptive (and consequently illegal) activity became both the source of Drexel Burnham's spectacular success in the 1980s and the cause of its equally spectacular collapse in February of 1990. Whatever the merits of his other exploits, in the process Michael Milken achieved something that no other financier had accomplished over the previous 150 years: the permanent devaluation of the Drexel name on Wall Street.

As required by Pennsylvania law, the three family trusts created in Anthony Drexel's will expired in 1985, twenty-one years after the death of his last surviving grandchild. At that time, some $48 million remaining in his estate was distributed among his living descendants—a pleasant surprise for the seventy-one beneficiary households, but hardly great wealth in the era of Ronald Reagan and the *Forbes* 400. No longer bound by money or by common ownership of a corporation, the descendants now found themselves connected through their loyalty to Tony Drexel's college and to Mother Katharine Drexel's religious order.

Mother Drexel's canonization by Pope John Paul in October 2000 was the occasion for some 200 Drexel family members—Catholics, Protestants, and nonbelievers alike—to fly to Rome for the ceremony. The Drexel Institute, renamed Drexel University in 1969, remained faithful to Tony Drexel's working class vision and to its gritty West Philadelphia location even as it evolved into an innovative university with 12,000 students. In 1983 it became the first American university to require access to personal computers for all students. At the dawn of the twenty-first century its engineering curriculum had been designated a national model by the National Science Foundation; its co-op program, one of the nation's first and largest such programs, enabled students to alternate full-time study with periods of professional employment. Only two of the founder's descendants have attended Drexel University, but several family members have always sat on the university's board of trustees. In retrospect, the Drexel family's philanthropic network outlasted its business empire.

After Tony Drexel died, his sons John and Anthony, Jr. moved from the family compound in West Philadelphia to the more fashionable vicinity of Rittenhouse Square downtown. Anthony Drexel's house itself was sold in 1906 to Samuel Fels, the developer of Fels-Naphtha Soap, who demolished the Drexel home to make way for his own new mansion. The rest of that 3800 block of Walnut Street, including the Fels mansion, has been subsumed into the University of Pennsylvania campus. Two of the Drexel children's homes—those of Anthony, Jr. and Frances Drexel Paul—survive today as the fraternity houses of Alpha Tau Omega and Sigma Chi respectively.

The Drexel Building at 23 Wall Street in New York, the six-story tower that Tony had erected for J. P. Morgan in 1873, was sold by the Drexel family to the House of Morgan in 1912 and torn down the following year to make way for the marble palace that stands there today. The eleven-story Drexel Building that Tony built at Fifth and Chestnut Streets in Philadelphia in 1888 was demolished by the U.S. government in 1956 to make way for the expansion of Independence National Park. A historical garden now occupies that site. The roll-top desks where Tony and his colleagues worked are still in use at 1838 Investment Advisors, a money management concern in the Philadelphia suburb of Radnor. That firm, which takes its name from the year Francis Drexel opened his Philadelphia office, is the last surviving vestige of Drexel Burnham Lambert.

One section of Philadelphia's old financial district—Third Street, between Chestnut and Market—still appears very much as it did when Francis Drexel and his sons worked there before the Civil War. As a result, it is possible—say, on a quiet summer Sunday morning, when no automobiles are cruising past—for visitors to stroll this block and imagine themselves back in the age of Andrew Jackson and Nicholas Biddle, in a street filled with horse carriages, stock runners, and brokers in top hats. The sole gap in the setting is a vacant lot at 34 South Third Street, where the elegant four-story Drexel Building of 1854 once stood. It was razed in 1976 for a parking lot, much to the outrage of preservationists, among them nuns from Katharine Drexel's Sisters of the Blessed Sacrament who picketed the site in protest.

Because this 1854 Drexel Building bore the same address as Francis Drexel's original 1838 office, historians assumed at the time that the first building had been replaced in 1854 and that therefore both buildings were now lost to posterity. They were mistaken. Shortly before completing this book the author discovered that Philadelphia's street numbering system had been changed a few years after the Drexels moved into their second building in 1854, so it was simply a coincidence that the Drexels' first and second offices bore the same address. The original fourteen-foot-wide home of Drexel & Co., renumbered in 1857 as 48 South Third Street, had survived unnoticed all along at the same spot —four doors north of Chestnut Street—where Francis Drexel opened his currency brokerage in 1838.

Today this three-story building houses a shoe repair shop on the ground floor and two small apartments upstairs. Its exterior and interior have been gutted and renovated at least twice, first in the 1870s and again in the 1970s. A curved dormer on the roof is the sole remaining recognizable link to Francis Drexel's day. The space where Tony Drexel worked behind the counter as a thirteen-year-old boy is now occupied by a Korean-born shoemaker, who in turn rents his shop from an Italian-born contractor. Like immigrants since the dawn of time, this tenant and his landlord crossed oceans and continents in the hope of improving their lives. And like this building's previous occupants, each day they persist at seemingly obscure and trivial tasks, uncertain where their efforts will lead but impelled by an innate sense that their work might, in some imperceptible manner, leave the world a better place than they found it.

Appendix I: Simplifed Genealogy

CHILDREN OF FRANCIS JOSEPH DREXEL (1762–1836)
AND MAGDALENA WILHELM DREXEL

- I. Susanna (1789– ?)
- II. Francis Martin (1792–1863)
- III. Anton (1796–1858 or later)

CHILDREN OF FRANCIS MARTIN DREXEL (1792–1863)
AND CATHERINE HOOKEY DREXEL (1795–1870)

- I. Mary Johanna (1822–1873) m. John Lankenau
- II. Francis Anthony (1824–1885) m. (1) Hannah J. Langstroth
  m. (2) Emma Mary Bouvier
- III. Anthony Joseph (1826–1893) m. Ellen Bicking Rosét
- IV. Joseph Wilhelm (1831–1888) m. Lucy Wharton
- V. Heloise (1837–1895) m. James Charles Smith
- VI. Caroline (1838–1911) m. John Goddard Watmough

CHILDREN OF ANTHONY J. DREXEL (1826–1893)
AND ELLEN R. DREXEL (1832?–1891)

- I. Emilie Taylor (1851–1883) m. Edward Biddle.
- II. Frances Katherine (1852–1892) m. James W. Paul, Jr.
- III. Marie Rozet (1854–1855)
- IV. Mae E. (1857–1886) m. Charles T. Stewart
- V. Sarah Rozet (1860–1929) m. (1) John R. Fell
  m. (2) Alexander Van Rensselaer
- VI. Francis Anthony (1861–1869)
- VII. John Rozet (1863–1935) m. Alice Gordon Troth
- VIII. Anthony J., Jr. (1864–1934) m. Margarita Armstrong
- IX. George W. Childs (1868–1944) m. Mary S. Irick

Appendix II: Principal Characters

Biddle, A. J. Drexel (1874–1948). Grandson of AJD (son of Edward and Emilie D. Biddle). B. October 1, 1874, d. May 27, 1948.

Biddle, Edward (1851–1933). Son-in-law of AJD. M. (1872) Emilie Drexel (d. 1883). Had six grown children from two marriages.

Biddle, Emilie Taylor Drexel (1851–83). AJD's eldest daughter. B. Philadelphia, September 15, 1851. M. Edward Biddle, March 7, 1872. D. January 21, 1883, age 31.

Bowdoin, George S. Drexel Morgan & Co. partner in New York from January 1, 1884. Retired December 31, 1899.

Burns, Walter H. (1838?–97). Son-in-law of JSM; became partner of J. S. Morgan & Co., London, January 1879; he and Junius were the only partners for the next five years. D. November 22, 1897.

Childs, George William (1829–94) (GWC). AJD's best friend. B. Baltimore, May 12, 1829. Married Emma Bouvier Peterson (1842–1928), daughter of his partner, publisher Robert E. Peterson. Her mother was Hannah Mary Bouvier Peterson, daughter of Judge John Bouvier, associate justice of the Court of Criminal Sessions and author of *Bouvier's Law Dictionary*, but unrelated to Philadelphia's Michel Bouvier family. D. Philadelphia, February 3, 1894.

Cooke, Jay (1821–1905). Senior, Jay Cooke & Co., 1861–73. B. Sandusky, Ohio, August 10, 1821; d. Ogontz, Pennsylvania, February 18, 1905.

Coster, Charles H. (1852–1900). Drexel Morgan & Co. partner in New York from January 1, 1884. D. March 13, 1900.

Dabney, Charles H. (1807– ?). Nominal senior partner to JPM at Dabney, Morgan & Co., New York, 1864–71.

Drexel, Anthony Joseph (1826–93) (AJD). B. Philadelphia, September 13, 1826. With Drexel & Co., 1839–93; partner from 1847. M. Ellen Bicking Rosét, Philadelphia, August 13, 1850. D. Carlsbad, Bohemia, June 30, 1893.

Drexel, Anthony J., Jr. (1864–1934) (AJD, Jr.) Partner, Drexel & Co., Philadelphia, January 1, 1890–October 21, 1893. M. Margarita Armstrong; divorced 1917. D. December 14, 1934.

Drexel, Anton (1796–1858 or later). Brother of FMD. Married Josefa Marllotte.

Drexel, Catherine Hookey (1795–1870). Mrs. FMD. B. Philadelphia, April 16, 1795. M. FMD, Philadelphia, April 23, 1821. D. Philadelphia, September 21, 1870.

Drexel, Ellen Bicking Rosét (1832?–91). Mrs. AJD. Daughter of John Rosét or Rozét, Philadelphia merchant of French descent. M. AJD, Philadelphia, August 13, 1850. D. Runnymede, Lansdowne, Pennsylvania, November 27, 1891.

Drexel, Emma Mary Bouvier (1833–83). FAD's second wife. M. FAD April 10, 1860. D. Philadelphia, January 29, 1883.

Drexel, Francis A. (1824–85) (FAD). AJD's brother; father of Saint Katharine Drexel. B. Philadelphia, January 20, 1824. M. Hannah Langstroth, September 28, 1854 (d. 1858). M. Emma Bouvier, April 10, 1860 (d.1883). D. Philadelphia, February 15, 1885.

Drexel, Francis Anthony (1861–69). AJD's sixth child and first son. D. April 25, 1869.

Drexel, Francis (or Franz) Joseph (1762–1836). FMD's father. D. Austria, January 23, 1836.

Drexel, Francis Martin (1792–1863) (FMD). AJD's father. B. Dornbirn, Austria, April 7, 1792. To U.S., 1817. M. Catherine Hookey, Philadelphia, April 23, 1821. D. Philadelphia, June 5, 1863. Buried at Church of the Holy Trinity, Philadelphia.

Drexel, George W. Childs (1868–1944). AJD's ninth and last child. B. Long Branch, New Jersey, July 24, 1868. M. Mary S. Irick, November 18, 1891. Succeeded G. W. Childs as editor and publisher of *Public Ledger*, 1894; sold paper and retired, 1902. D. September 9, 1944. No children. His widow died December 16, 1948, age 84.

Drexel, Hannah J. Langstroth (1826–58). First wife of FAD; mother of Saint Katharine Drexel. B. Philadelphia, January 14, 1826. M. FAD September 28, 1854. D. following childbirth, Philadelphia, December 30, 1858.

Drexel, John Rozet (1863–1935). AJD's seventh child. B. March 3, 1863. M. 1886 to Alice Gordon Troth (1866–1947). D. May 18, 1935.

Drexel, Joseph Wilhelm (1831–88). AJD's younger brother. B. Philadelphia, January 24, 1831. Married April 18, 1865 to Lucy Wharton (1841–1912). D. New York, March 25, 1888.

Drexel, Katharine (1858–1955). AJD's niece; daughter of FAD. B. Philadelphia, November 26, 1858. Founded Sisters of the Blessed Sacrament, February 12, 1891. D. March 3, 1955. Canonized by Roman Catholic Church October 1, 2000.

Drexel, Marie Rozet. (1854–55). Third child of AJD. D. Media, Pennsylvania, August 8, 1855.

Fabbri, Egisto P. (1839?–94). Drexel Morgan & Co. partner, New York, January 1, 1876–December 31, 1885.

Godfrey, Charles H. Longtime Drexel & Co. employee who was made a partner in January 1875, remained through January 1, 1884. Spent his last year at Drexel Morgan & Co. in New York.

Goodwin, James Junius (1835–1915). JPM's first cousin and partner in early 1860s.

Harjes, John H. (1830–1914). Philadelphia friend of AJD from about 1849. B. Bremen, Prussia; to U.S. 1849. Joined family banking house of Harjes Brothers, Philadelphia, 1853; became resident head partner of Drexel, Harjes & Co., Paris, 1868. Retired from Morgan, Harjes & Co. December 31, 1908. D. February 15, 1914.

Hookey, Anthony (1755–1833). FMD's father-in-law. B. Philadelphia, April 1755. Had six children; fourth was Catherine H. Drexel (b. 1795). Grocer and a founder of Holy Trinity Church. D. December 12, 1833.

Lankenau, John D. (1817–1901). AJD's brother-in-law. B. Germany, came to U.S. 1836, became a banker. M. Mary Johanna Drexel, October 9, 1848. D. August 30, 1901.

Lankenau, Mary Johanna Drexel (1822–73). FMD's oldest daughter; AJD's oldest sister. M. John D. Lankenau, Philadelphia, October 9, 1848. D. May 27, 1873.

Ludlow, John, D.D. (1793–1857). Father of John Livingston Ludlow. Pastor of First Reformed Dutch Church, New Brunswick, New Jersey, 1818–23; First Reformed Dutch Church, Albany, New York, 1823–34; provost, University of Pennsylvania, 1834–53. Officiated at AJD's wedding, 1850.

Ludlow, John Livingston (1819–88). Physician; brother-in-law of AJD's wife Ellen R. Drexel. B. New Brunswick, New Jersey, May 14, 1819, son of the Rev. John Ludlow, D.D. M. Mary Ann Rozet. D. Philadelphia, June 21, 1888.

McCulloch, Hugh (1808–95). Friend and partner of Jay Cooke. U.S. controller of the currency, 1863–65; Secretary of the Treasury, 1865–69, 1884–85. Partner, Jay Cooke, McCulloch & Co., London, 1870–73.

McKean, William V. Chief of staff of *Public Ledger* under George Childs, 1864–?. Veteran journalist previously at *Philadelphia Inquirer*.

McLeod, Archibald A. (1848–1902). President of Reading Railroad, 1889–92, later of Boston & Maine. Forced out of Reading by AJD and JPM April 1893. Became receiver of the Reading. President of New York & New England Railroad, 1893.

Morgan, J. Pierpont, Sr. (1837–1913) (JPM). AJD's partner. B. April 17, 1837. Partner, Drexel Morgan & Co., 1871–94. D. Rome, March 31, 1913.

Morgan, Junius S. (1813–90) (JSM). Father of JPM. Partner, Peabody & Co., London, 1853–64; senior partner, J. S. Morgan & Co., 1864–90. D. Monte Carlo, April 8, 1890.

Morrell, Louise B. Drexel (1863–1945). AJD's niece; younger half-sister of Saint Katharine Drexel. B. Philadelphia, October 2, 1863. M. Edward Morrell, January 17, 1889. D. November 5, 1945.

Morton, Levi P. (1824–1920). New York banker and politician. U.S. Representative, 1879–81; Vice President of U.S., 1889–93; Governor of New York, 1895–97.

Paul, Frances Katherine Drexel (1852–92). AJD's second child, known as "Fanny" and "Nanny." M. James W. Paul Jr., of Philadelphia, December 6, 1877. D. Carlsbad, Bohemia June 16, 1892.

Paul, James W., Jr. (1851–1908). AJD's son-in-law. Son of distinguished Philadelphia lawyer. Drexel & Co. partner from January 1, 1883 until his death, September 25, 1908.

Robinson, John Norris (1831–?). B. Wilmington, Delaware, January 8, 1831. Began banking career at father's firm, R. R. Robinson & Co. Left 1856 to become a partner at Drexel & Co. Moved to Drexel, Winthrop & Co., New York, 1868. Drexel Morgan & Co. partner in New York July 1, 1871–January 1, 1875. Retired due to poor health.

Rogers, Jacob C. (?–1900). Husband of one of George Peabody's sisters. Head of Boston brokerage firm R. G. Dun & Co. Accepted partnership in J. S. Morgan & Co., London, October 1873. Retired from J. S. Morgan & Co. December 31, 1878, but became head of its Boston agency. D. January 2, 1900.

Rosét, Jacques Marie (1765–1851). Grandfather of Ellen Bicking Rosét Drexel. B. Lyon, France; to Austria 1777. Arrived U.S. December 10, 1792. M. Elizabeth Stubert (1775–1843) and had eight children, four of whom reached maturity. Moved to Germantown 1821. Educated a Catholic, attended Dutch Reformed Church in Philadelphia, joined Lutheran Church in Germantown in his eightieth year.

Rosét (or Rozét), John. Father-in-law of AJD; eldest son of Jacques Marie Rosét;

father of Ellen Rosét Drexel. M. Mary Laning of Wilkes-Barre, Pennsylvania, a granddaughter of Judge Matthias Hollenback of Wilkes-Barre. Had four daughters and one son. Son George Hollenback Rozet, b. February 21, 1829, was still living in Chicago in 1893. Daughters: Mary Ann, m. Dr. John Livingston Ludlow; Antoinette (or Elizabeth), m. John Brodhead or Broadhead (d. before 1882); Ellen, m. AJD; Sarah, m. Charles M. Smith of Chicago.

Smith, Elizabeth L. Drexel (1855–90). AJD's niece; oldest sister of Saint Katharine Drexel. B. Philadelphia, August 27, 1855. M. Walter G. Smith, January 7, 1890. D. in childbirth, September 26, 1890.

Smith, Heloise Drexel (1837–95). FMD's fifth child; AJD's younger sister. B. August 6, 1837. M. James Charles Smith, November 7, 1867. D. Oct. 15, 1895. Husband (1827–93), a University of Pennsylvania graduate (Class of 1847) and a merchant, d. December 13, 1893.

Stewart, Mae E. Drexel (1857–86). AJD's fourth child. M. Charles T. Stewart (1857–1901). D. January 4, 1886, age 28.

Stotesbury, Edward T. (1849–1938) B. Philadelphia, February 26, 1849. Son of Thomas Stotesbury, member of firm of Harris & Stotesbury, leading Philadelphia sugar refiners. Joined Drexel & Co. as office boy October 22, 1866; partner from January 1, 1883 until death; senior partner 1904–38. D. May 16, 1938.

Swain, William M. (1809–68). Founder of *Public Ledger*, 1836. B. Manlius, New York, May 12, 1809. D. Philadelphia, February 16, 1868. Wife Sarah Swain d. June 24, 1891, age 81.

Thomas, George C. (1839–1909). AJD's successor at Drexel & Co. B. Philadelphia, October 28, 1839. Joined Jay Cooke & Co. bank, 1863; partner 1868–73. Became Drexel & Co. partner 1883. Succeeded AJD as Philadelphia resident senior partner 1893. Retired December 31, 1904. D. April 21, 1909.

Van Rensselaer, Alexander (1850–1933). AJD's son-in-law; second husband of Sarah Drexel Fell. B. October 1, 1850. A founder of Philadelphia Orchestra (1900) and long its president. D. July 18, 1933.

Van Rensselaer, Sarah Drexel Fell (1860–1929). AJD's fifth child. B. August 28, 1860. M (1) John R. Fell (1858–95); m (2) Alexander Van Rensselaer, January 27, 1898 at Camp Hill, Fort Washington, Pennsylvania. D. February 3, 1929.

Watmough, Caroline Drexel (1838–1911). AJD's youngest sister. Married John Goddard Watmough (1837–1913), a stock broker, October 10, 1861.

Welsh, John Lowber (1842–1904). AJD friend. Philadelphia banker and financier. Negotiated loan for Reading Railroad in Europe, 1870. Appointed its receiver, 1886. President, Buffalo, Bradford & Pittsburgh Railroad, 1893, and of People's Traction Co. of Philadelphia, 1895. Elected director of reorganized Reading company, 1893. D. Philadelphia, August 23, 1904.

Winthrop, Eugene (?–1893). Brother of Robert Winthrop. Partner, Drexel, Harjes & Co., Paris, 1868–93. D. January 27, 1893.

Winthrop, Robert. Brother of Eugene Winthrop. Resident senior partner in Drexel, Winthrop & Co., New York, throughout firm's existence, 1863–71. Retired 1871. Son-in-law of Moses Taylor, president of National City Bank.

Wright, J. Hood (1846–94). Drexel & Co. partner. Started there as clerk 1861. Made junior partner 1865. With FAD and AJD, one of only three Drexel & Co. partners through December 1874. Became Drexel Morgan & Co. partner in New York 1875. M. Mary Robinson, widow of Drexel Morgan & Co. partner John M. Robinson. D. November 12, 1894.

Abbreviations

AJD: Anthony J. Drexel

BBP/London: Baring Bros. & Co. papers, Baring Bros. Archives, London

DFN/HL: Drexel family notes, Hagerty Library, Drexel University, Philadelphia

DFS/DUM: Drexel family scrapbooks, Drexel University Museum

DUM: Drexel University Museum files, storage room, main building, Philadelphia

EIA: 1838 Investment Advisors, Radnor, Pennsylvania

FAD: Francis A. Drexel

FMD: Francis Martin Drexel

FMD/DUM: Francis Martin Drexel folder, Drexel University Museum

GWC: George W. Childs

GWC/HL: George W. Childs notes, Hagerty Library

HL: Hagerty Library, Room L-20, Drexel University

HSP: Historical Society of Pennsylvania, Philadelphia

JPM: J. Pierpont Morgan

JPM, Jr.: J. Pierpont Morgan, Jr.

JPM/NY: J. P. Morgan & Co., New York

JPM/Paris: J. P. Morgan & Co., Paris

JSM: Junius S. Morgan

JSMP/GL: Junius S. Morgan papers, Guildhall Library, London

MFP: Morgan family papers

PML: Pierpont Morgan Library, New York

RGDCL: R. G. Dun & Co. Ledgers

SBS: Sisters of the Blessed Sacrament archives, Cornwells Heights, Pennsylvania

Notes

The date March 8, 1871 is deduced from a letter from AJD to Junius Morgan, March 10, 1871: "your son came to see me the night before last & we talked over matters fully" (J. S. Morgan & Co. archives, Guildhall Library, London, Ms 21,760, HC 1.9).

"... 'or a parlor car, as his taste or inclination may require.'" Sipes, *The Pennsylvania Railroad*, 79.

"... a few blocks from Manhattan's financial district." Morgan's office address is taken from W. H. Wilson's New York City Directory for 1869. The successor firm of Drexel, Morgan & Co. continued at this address.

"... twelve tracks headed for points north, south, and west." Sipes, *The Pennsylvania Railroad*, 43–45. Also see Burgess and Kennedy, *Centennial History of the Pennsylvania Railroad*, 237–40.

"... this same journey between America's two largest cities had required . . ." Weigley, *Philadelphia: A 300-Year-History*, 398–99, describes transport of Civil War troops from New England to Philadelphia, citing Taylor, *Philadelphia in the Civil War*, 207–15.

"... and proceeded from there by horse-drawn rail car." Sipes, *The Pennsylvania Railroad*, 20.

"... could still remember when the trip required twenty-two hours . . ." *Poulson's Daily Advertiser*, October 23, 1821, 1, has an ad for the Union Line between Philadelphia and New York. It left Philadelphia at noon by steamboat to Trenton, went by stagecoach 25 miles to New Brunswick with an overnight stay in New Brunswick, went by steam ferry the next morning, and arrived in New York at 10 a.m.

"... barely three and a half hours after boarding the ferry from lower Manhattan." For discussions of rail travel between New York and Philadelphia, see Sipes, *The Pennsylvania Railroad*, 19–20, 43–45, 54; and Burgess and Kennedy, *Centennial History of the Pennsylvania Railroad Co., 1846–1946*, 237–41, 256, 266, 268. I am also indebted to Bill Brady of Philadelphia, a third-generation Pennsylvania Railroad employee, who helped me through the logistics of the connection as of 1871.

"'I will be on hand to meet you.'" AJD to JPM, March 4, 1871 (PML).

"... 'he has no doubt written to you about it.'" AJD to JPM, March 2, 1871 (PML).

"'I have had a visit from Mr. A. J. Drexel . . .'" Letter cited in JPM, Jr., "Reminiscences." Also see Carosso, *The Morgans*, 136.

PAGE 3

". . . 'his peculiar brusqueness of manner has made him & his house unpopular . . .'" Strouse, *Morgan: American Financier*, 137.

". . . everything from his lapses of character to his irregular bowel movements." Strouse, *Morgan: American Financier*, 82.

". . . at a time when 80 percent of American families earned less than $500 . . ." Redlich, *Molding of American Banking*, vol. 2: 382. Strouse, "The Brilliant Bailout," 64, discusses Americans' earnings in the 1880s.

PAGE 4

". . . the geniality of Robin Hood's merry friar." Description from a profile in the *Press* (probably the *New York Press*), October 30, 1873 (Childs scrapbook, GWC/HL).

CHAPTER 1

PAGE 9

"Dornbirn, his birthplace . . ." Dornbirn today is part of Vorarlberg province, created in 1815 out of the western Tyrol. When Francis M. Drexel grew up there, the region was an integral part of the Tyrol.

". . . was the first Drexel to leave the land . . ." One possible exception: An undated, unidentified news clip in the SBS archives—apparently from a New York newspaper prior to 1929—mentions a collateral ancestor of Francis M. Drexel named Rev. Jeremias Drexel, born in 1581, a Jesuit priest, master of rhetoric, court preacher at Munich, adviser to the Elector Maximilian I, and author of the *Helioropium*, a Latin work translated into other languages even into the twentieth century. I have not verified this relative or found him mentioned elsewhere. The article's author, one "Bill Benedick," describes himself as distantly related by marriage to the Drexels, but his article contains enough errors to cast doubt on its reliability. I mention it here for those who wish to pursue it further.

". . . developed the family's first connections across the nearby national borders . . ." FMD, *Peregrinations of an Artist*, 4, refers to people he encountered across the Rhine in Switzerland who knew his father.

". . . the elder son among his three children." Francis had an older sister, Susanna, born in 1789, and a younger brother, Anton, born in 1796. See Historical Society Note, FMD/DUM; also Geber G. Gearhart Collection, Genealogical Society of Pennsylvania, cited in Fisher, "The Anthony Joseph Drexel House."

PAGE 10

"The elder Francis Drexel appears to have been an officer . . ." FMD, *Peregrinations of an Artist*, 7, mentions in passing a man who "was an officer among the insurgents, as well as my father."

". . . both of which suggest his devotion to the Tyrolese cause." Boies Penrose, "Early Life of F. M. Drexel," 332.

PAGE 12

"His father had given him letters of introduction . . ." FMD, *Peregrinations of an Artist*, 4, notes, "I had letters of recommendation from my father to some gentleman in Altstatten, but did not present them," without further explanation.

"'Nothing, I am sure, calls forth the faculties . . .'" Wollstonecraft, *Thoughts on the Education of Daughters*, 1787.

PAGE 16

". . . calling Francis, 'a friend of hers from some miles off.'" FMD, *Peregrinations of an Artist*, 15.

". . . 'for which my sister got rather wrongfully suspected . . .'" FMD, *Peregrinations of an Artist*, 15.

PAGE 18

"When he next returned, more than forty years later . . ." A scribbled note on a Drexel family tree (DFN/DL) mentions that Francis visited Dornbirn in 1858 or 1859—the only reference I have found to such a visit.

CHAPTER 2

PAGE 20

". . . 'the Athens of America'. . . " Weigley, *Philadelphia: A 300-Year History*, 257.

PAGE 21

". . . an innkeeper on Bread Street . . ." Penrose, "Early Life of F. M. Drexel," mistakenly refers to this street as "Broad Street." Bread Street (or Moravian Alley, its alternate name) runs north and south between Second and Third Streets, below Race. "Grundlock" is listed in the 1817 Philadelphia City Directory as an innkeeper at the Columbian Hotel, 29 Bread, and in 1819 as a tavernkeeper at Bread and Fetter Lane.

"In 1820 he was elected to the Musical Fund Society . . ." Mactier, *The Musical Fund Society of Philadelphia*, 33.

". . . later founded the brokerage house of W. H. Newbold's Son." Sargent and Sargent, *Epes Sargent of Gloucester and His Descendants*, 85, gives details of the family of William and Mary (Smith) Newbold, married in 1794. Their son William H. Newbold, born 1807, founded W. H. Newbold's Son.

". . . listed in newspaper advertisements as one of five references . . ." Ad for Mrs. Matthews's school, *Poulson's Daily Advertiser*, July 1, 1822, 1, col. 5.

". . . elected to membership in the German Society of Philadelphia." Seidensticker, *Erter Teil der Geschichte der Deutschen Gesellschaft von Pennsylvanien*, 601.

"He augmented his portrait commissions by teaching art at a girls' seminary . . ." FMD, *Peregrinations of an Artist*, 30.

PAGE 22

"'. . . but after that sad catastrophe Mrs. Fisher did me the honor to detract from my conduct . . .'" FMD, *Peregrinations of an Artist*, 29.

". . . Francis married twenty-six-year-old Catherine Hookey . . ." From the *Philadelphia*

Freeman's Journal, April 24, 1821: "Married, last evening, 23rd inst., by the Right Rev. Dr. Conceal, Mr. Francis M. Drexel, Limner, to Miss Catherine, daughter of Anthony Hookey, Esq." (PHS). The name was also spelled Hooke.

"The Hookeys seem to have sprung largely from English Quaker stock . . ." Penrose, "Early Life of F. M. Drexel," 344.

"Francis and Catherine settled into a house at 40 South Sixth Street . . ." The Philadelphia directory for 1821 shows "Mr. & Mrs." Francis M. Drexel at 40 South Sixth St. His studio remained at 171 Chestnut until 1823, when it too was listed at 40 S. Sixth.

PAGE 23

"Bolivar . . . had reached the height of his popularity . . ." Some accounts of Francis's life suggest that he met or even became friendly with Bolivar, but this is almost certainly false; the two men never came closer than a few miles from each other. See Penrose, "Early Life of F. M. Drexel," 346. In any case, Francis's journal of his travels contains no mention of his having met Bolivar.

PAGE 25

". . . the birth of their fourth child, Joseph Wilhelm, on January 24, 1831 . . ." Most biographies of Joseph, published during his life as well as after his death, record his birth date as January 24, 1833. However, his baptismal record indisputably shows him baptized at Holy Trinity Roman Catholic Church on April 24, 1831, having been born on January 24, 1831. See Philadelphia records at Philadelphia Archdiocesan Historical Research Center, St. Charles Borromeo Seminary, Wynnewood, Pennsylvania. Why Joseph consistently subtracted two years from his age is a mystery.

". . . attempted a career as a brewer in partnership with a man named Partenheimer . . ." Penrose, "Early Life of F. M. Drexel," 357. The ledger book of Drexel & Partenheimer is stored in HL.

"The estate records of Stephen Girard record a payment of $119.24 . . ." *Retrospective of Holy Trinity Parish, 1794–1914*, 88, cited in Baldwin, *A Call to Sanctity.*

". . . spent some time painting portraits in Princeton, New Jersey." An item about Francis in the Princeton (New Jersey) *Whig*, August 19, 1836, 3, refers to "his short stay here two years since" (Princeton University Archives).

PAGE 26

"'. . . has made me anxious to leave this to my children.'" FMD, *Peregrinations of an Artist*, 1. A cover note to this manuscript written by FMD's granddaughter, Katherine Drexel Penrose, in December 1901 remarks that "This account was written probably after Mr. Drexel returned from Chile, about 1830, and before he went to Mexico, in 1835."

"Madame Buchey, who operated the school until 1853, appears to have been a progressive educator." A paid notice in the *Philadelphia National Gazette*, August 24, 1833, 1, announced the opening of the school on September 1. Also see recollection of Francis J. Dallett, a great-great-grandson of Madame Buchey, in a letter to William Borsock, August 27, 1982. Dallett was then archivist of the University of Pennsylvania. Madame Buchey's school operated at her house until 1853, according to Dallett.

"In 1835 Francis was off on his wanderings again, this time to Mexico . . ." Penrose, "Early Life of F. M. Drexel," 357. Penrose notes that a Mexican official "kindly but vainly looked through the public archives in Mexico for further material."

"'the ladies and gentlemen of Princeton and vicinity.'" Princeton (N.J.) *Whig*, August 19, 1836, 3 (Princeton University Archives). Also, Francis's fifth and sixth children, Caroline and Heloise, are believed to have been born in 1837 and 1838 respectively, which seems to suggest that Francis was back in Philadelphia no later than 1836.

PAGE 27

"So banks were rarely called upon to lend or invest large quantities of capital." Weigley, *Philadelphia: A 300-Year History*, 255.

PAGE 28

"In 1832 Jackson vetoed the renewal of the Second Bank's national charter . . ." This timing was especially unfortunate because in 1835 the Bank of England restricted its lending. This action led to a financial panic in England, which was a leading source of capital for the United States. The English panic in turn created financial problems for U.S. banks at precisely the moment that the Bank of the United States was losing its charter. See Temin, *The Jacksonian Economy*.

". . . thousands of banks and businesses from New Orleans to Boston had closed their doors . . ." Guadella, *The Hundred Years* (1936), excerpted in *Harper's*, May 1998, 50, describes the panic of 1837.

PAGE 29

". . . probably the longest economic contraction in America's history." Carosso, "The House of Drexel," 7.

". . . in partnership with a broker there named James M. Franciscus." FMD's obituary from the *Public Ledger*, June 6, 1863, mentions J. M. Franciscus as his Louisville partner. The Louisville City Directory for 1838–39 by Gabriel Collins lists a James M. Franciscus with F. A. Massol & Co., lottery & exchange brokers, at 56 Wall Street. This presumably was FMD's partner in his original 1837 brokerage. I could find no Louisville directory for 1837, and the 1836 directory carries no listing for either Drexel or Franciscus.

"Francis Drexel chose Louisville . . ." AJD obituary, *Philadelphia Press*, July 1, 1893, and other newspapers, many of which carried virtually identical reports.

". . . Mexican gold and silver could be shipped by steamboat to or from a port city like New Orleans in just five days." Groner, *American Heritage History of American Business & Industry*, 88.

". . . expected to capitalize on his foreign contacts and his linguistic fluency . . ." Hopkinson, *Drexel & Co.*, 14–15. Also Staub, "Francis Martin Drexel: An Artist Turned Banker."

CHAPTER 3

PAGE 33

". . . his Philadelphia-born wife Catherine insisted that he return to her home . . ." AJD obituary in unidentified newspaper, July 1, 1893, says of his father: "although successful there, his wife desired to return to her old home in Philadelphia." On the other hand, the *Philadelphia Press*, same date, attributes the relocation solely to Francis: "Desiring to return to his old home in this city, he changed his plans" (DFS, vol. 1, DUM).

". . . in a narrow fourteen-foot-wide building at 34 South Third Street . . ." The building's address today is 48 South Third St., Philadelphia's street numbering system having been changed in 1857.

". . . all of them still packed into two square miles between the Delaware and Schuylkill Rivers." Davis, *The Bouviers*, 44.

"'. . . is no where brought so broadly out as it is in the city of Philadelphia.'" Alexander Mackay, *Western World, or, Travels in the United States in 1846–47*, quoted in Weigley, *Philadelphia: A 300-Year History*, 330.

"'. . . did not show the taint of his origins.'" Davis, *The Bouviers*, 96.

PAGE 34

"'. . . it would exclude grace, wit and worth.'" Davis, *The Bouviers*, 97–98.

"One such refugee was Michel Bouvier . . ." Davis, *The Bouviers*, 111. To note one other common thread, both Francis M. Drexel and Michel Bouvier are buried at Old St. Mary's Church in Philadelphia.

"Another such immigrant was Jacques Marie Rosét . . ." For background on Jacques (later Jacob) Rosét, see Ward, "The Germantown Road," 7–9.

"His son John Rosét married into wealth through the Laning and Hollenback families . . ." For the family background, see Ward, "The Germantown Road," 9; also portrait description—John Jacob Rosét and Mary Ann Laning Rosét (wife)—by John F. Sheldon, May 1, 1980 (FMD/DUM).

PAGE 35

". . . boasted of importing window glasses for prominent customers . . ." John Rosét's glass imports are mentioned in Garvan, *Federal Philadelphia: The Athens of the Western World*, 56.

". . . preferring a plain black suit and black tie." Condolence note on Ellen Drexel's death, to AJD from D. M. Godwin, Baugh & Sons Co., Philadelphia, November 28, 1891, recalls "the happy hours when we were children together, and we enjoyed our childhood sports in her father's house on Pine Street above Fifth. She was a lovely girl, and we were all much attached to her." See Drexel family Box 2, DFN/HL. Philadelphia city directories beginning 1830 list John Rosét, merchant, at 221 High St. (now 523 Market). Beginning in 1845 his home is listed at 130 Pine St. (now 504 Pine St.). AJD obituary, *Philadelphia Press*, July 1, 1893, 12–13 (DFS, vol. 1, DUM).

". . . well informed about art and music . . ." Carosso, "The House of Drexel," manuscript, April 24, 1980, 13; also AJD obituary, *Philadelphia Press*, 13.

". . . his attentiveness as a listener." AJD obituary, *Philadelphia Press*, 12.

"Rosét's third daughter . . ." Ellen was probably born in 1831 or 1832. The family tree in

The Drexel Heritage (1975) lists her birth year as 1832. The census of September 13, 1850 (just after her marriage) lists her age as 19. The census of June 9, 1860 lists her age as 32 (born in 1828), which seems unlikely: her presumably older brother George H. Rozet was born February 21, 1829.

". . . who as the future Mrs. George H. Boker and Mrs. Oliver Hopkinson . . ." See biography of George H. Boker in Jackson, *Encyclopedia of Philadelphia*, vol. 2. On Elisa (or Eliza) Swaim Hopkinson, see Jordan, *Colonial and Revolutionary Families*, vol. 12, 285; also vol. 18, 133; also Montgomery, *Encyclopedia of Pennsylvania Biography*, vol. 25 (1945), 449.

". . . they had left that faith far behind them." In Rosét family papers on file at HSP, 1800–1841, the family name is interchangeably spelled "Rosét" and "Rozet," both in French and in English.

". . . upon moving to Germantown in his eightieth year . . ." Ward, "The Germantown Road," 9.

PAGE 36

". . . waited on Third Street to buy and sell this uncurrent money . . ." Drexel & Co., *A New Home for an Old House*, 19. Also see "Personal Recollections of Francis M. Drexel," by "B.S.R.," *Public Ledger*, apparently 1893. The original of this undated clipping, signed only with the author's initials, was found by the author among the Drexel family materials in DFN/HL. The date 1893 is surmised from the article's reference to "the recent death of Anthony J. Drexel," which occurred on June 30, 1893. Also see Stevenson, "Looking Back 50 Years on Financial Philadelphia."

"'I would be given a package of money . . . and finally sell to the one whose bid was highest.'" "Personal recollections of Francis M. Drexel."

PAGE 37

"'kept a barrel of soda crackers under the office counter . . .'" In "Girard's Talk of the Day," the pseudonymous columnist published this recollection from the deceased Philadelphia banker John Sailer.

PAGE 38

"'that Mr. Drexell [sic] had used Mr. Brooks as a means of collecting a debt . . .'" "Commotion Among the Brokers, or the Shavers Shaving," 2, col. 3.

"'They had a banknote clerk . . . without stopping work, call out, 'Counterfeit!'" Stevenson, "Looking Back 50 Years on Financial Philadelphia."

". . . Anthony and his brothers were expected to come early and stay late . . ." AJD obituary, *Philadelphia Press*, 1.

". . . and one or the other sometimes served as night watchman . . ." Duffy, *Katharine Drexel*, 21.

"But their father was also liberal about bestowing responsibility to his sons . . ." Witt Bowden in *Dictionary of American Biography*, 455.

PAGE 39

". . . to claim the gold and silver of interior banks . . ." Hopkinson, *Drexel & Co.*, 14–15.

Curiously, an unlabeled newspaper obituary for AJD from July 1, 1893 uses the same sentence as Hopkinson but says "imperial banks" instead of "interior banks." The latter term seems more appropriate; Hopkinson in 1952 probably corrected the original. Also see *Biographical Dictionary of Pennsylvania*, 1874, 24–25.

"'he never knew what it was to be idle.'" AJD obituary, *Philadelphia Press*, 1.

"'I know Danl Webster was notorious for not paying his debts . . .'" AJD to Caleb Cope, September 1887, from Earl Moore Autographs, Wynnewood, Pennsylvania, Catalogue #3 (1979).

PAGE 40

"Yet by 1840 America's railroads operated some 2,300 miles of track . . ." For growth of railroads, see Carosso, "The House of Drexel," 2ff.

"'I felt sorry for Drexel's . . . in that line since.'" Stevenson, "Looking Back 50 Years on Financial Philadelphia."

"Banks chartered by states. . . . First Bank of the United States." Chartered banks increased and flourished after 1811, when they rushed in to fill the void created by the failure of the First Bank of the United States.

PAGE 41

"'mercantile banking is concentrating in the hands of private houses . . .'" Larson, *Jay Cooke: Private Banker*, 52.

". . . private bankers who functioned as the cutting-edge entrepreneurs . . ." For further discussion, see Redlich, *Molding of American Banking*, vol. 2: 72; also Wainwright, *The Philadelphia National Bank*, 118.

". . . was the first Treasury loan subscribed for in specie . . ." Hopkinson, *Drexel & Co.*, 15.

". . . that same year Francis Drexel bought the building at 34 South Third Street . . ." The title chain for the building (now 48 S. Third St.) is on file at the Philadelphia Historical Commission. It describes the sale price as "2,500, subject to $5,000 mortgage" and the date of sale as December 20, 1847.

". . . on Chestnut Street near what is now 17th Street." Philadelphia city directories for 1841 through 1854 list Francis M. Drexel at 506 Chestnut, near Schuylkill Sixth, the old term for what is now 17th Street.

". . . requiring the rightful owner to pay Francis $1,786 in rents and profits lost . . ." The case of *Drexel v. Man* is discussed in *Public Ledger*, March 10, 1846, 2, 4.

PAGE 42

"This agitation culminated in the so-called 'Awful Riots' of 1844 . . ." Weigley, *Philadelphia: A 300-Year History*, 356–57. Contrary to widespread belief, most of the fatalities suffered in these riots were Protestant attackers rather than Catholics. In the May 1844 riots, four Protestants and one Catholic died. In a second riot in July 1844, 14 Protestant rioters and two federal soldiers died. See articles by Lou Baldwin in the *Catholic Standard & Times*, Philadelphia, May 26, June 2, June 9, 1994.

"... either to embrace or repudiate the unruly Irish Catholic immigrant workers ..." Light, *Rome and the New Republic*, 291.

"... among other things, Hogan refused to board with his fellow priests ..." Light, *Rome and the New Republic*, 90–92.

PAGE 43

"'Catholics so zealous that they had been and were then rearing Protestant families.'" Mahony, *Historical Sketches: St. Mary's Church*, 40.

"... values and beliefs of the 'inherited religion of the West.'" Light, *Rome and the New Republic*, 104–5.

"... ended in a riot at which the railing and part of the church wall were torn away." The best description of the riot can be found in Light, *Rome and the New Republic*, 144–47.

"... a similar revolt by St. Mary's trustees was suppressed again ..." Light, *Rome and the New Republic*, 263ff.; Tourscher, *The Hogan Schism and Trustees Troubles in St. Mary's Church, Philadelphia, 1820–29*, 18, cited in Baldwin, *A Call to Sanctity*, 10. See also Mahony, *Historical Sketches: St. Mary's Church*, 40–41.

"... whose seminary employed the senior Francis Drexel as an art teacher ..." Connelly, *The History of the Archdiocese of Philadelphia*, 110, cited in Baldwin, *A Call to Sanctity*, 10.

"... and Francis himself served briefly as a trustee ..." *Retrospective of Holy Trinity Parish, 125th Anniversary, 1794–1914*, cited in Baldwin, *A Call to Sanctity*, 10.

"... these Philadelphia Catholic families like the Drexels, Bories, and Bullitts ..." Lukacs, *Philadelphia: Patricians and Philistines*, 25, cites these three families as examples of converts.

PAGE 44

"... more than half a billion dollars in gold would be taken out of California over the next five years ..." Groner, *American Heritage Dictionary of History of American Business & Industry*, 125.

"... more gold would be mined in the world than in the previous 350 years." *Encyclopedia Britannica* (1964), vol. 10: 535.

CHAPTER 4

PAGE 45

"... the 1850 census found them living near Seventh and Mulberry ..." Schedule I, South Mulberry Ward, Dwelling #1073, Philadelphia, U.S. Census, September 13, 1850. South Mulberry Ward encompassed the area from Race to Mulberry (now Arch) Streets west of Seventh Street to the Schuylkill River.

PAGE 46

"... not by its eldest member, Francis Drexel, but by his second son Anthony." Carosso, "The House of Drexel," 11–12.

"... he was also the father-in-law of Ellen Drexel's oldest sister, Mary Ann Rosét Ludlow."

John F. Sheldon paper, May 1, 1980 (FMD/DUM), says Ellen Rosét's oldest sister Marianne married Dr. John Livingston Ludlow, son of John Ludlow, provost of Rutgers College. Meyerson and Winegrad, *Gladly Learn and Gladly Teach*, 238, says Rev. John Ludlow was provost at Penn from 1834 to 1853. F. J. Dallett, interviewed March 10, 1999, says that AJD's and Ellen Rosét's wedding was performed by the Rev. Dr. John Ludlow, a Dutch Reformed clergyman who had been provost at Penn (1834–53). Ward, "The Germantown Road," 9, says one Rosét daughter married Dr. John L. Ludlow.

"When Anthony's and Ellen's first child, Emilie, was born . . ." Emilie Taylor Drexel, first child of AJD, born Sept. 15, 1851, baptized June 29, 1852.

". . . Hannah Mayer Rothschild had been ostracized by her famous Jewish banking family for marrying outside the faith." See, among others, Niall Ferguson, *The House of Rothschild: Money's Prophets*, 319–21.

". . . found themselves searching in vain for a son or nephew willing to travel to America . . ." Ferguson, *The House of Rothschild*, 370–71.

"He resolved to set up a branch house in San Francisco." Larson, *Jay Cooke: Private Banker*, 77.

". . . . by May had set up the banking house of Drexel, Sather & Church on Montgomery Street." The firm had been formed as Sather & Church in August 1850 by Edward W. Church of San Francisco and Peder Sather of New York (his home as of 1852) and San Francisco (his home as of 1854). The firm of Sather & Church, bankers, apparently also operated in New York, according to San Francisco city directories. Drexel, Sather & Church also had an office at Third and J. Streets, Sacramento, as of January 1, 1856. FMD apparently withdrew from the firm in 1857. He may never have lived in San Francisco. Colville's San Francisco Directory of 1856–57 says Sather & Church was founded August 1850 and became Drexel, Sather & Church in May 1851. FMD obituary in June 1863 says he left for California 12 years earlier—1851. How Francis Drexel traveled to California is my conjecture, based on (a) a later reference to the gold he shipped home via the isthmus of Panama; (b) the relative speed with which he went to California and returned (the trip via the isthmus normally took two months, compared to six months across the continent or around Cape Horn); and (c) his familiarity with jungle terrain from his journey through Bolivia in the late 1820s.

"Like the Drexel house in Philadelphia, the San Francisco house also provided local merchants with the credits they needed . . ." Carosso, "The House of Drexel," 8–9.

PAGE 47

". . . but he maintained his San Francisco partnership until 1857." In *First-Class Business Houses in San Francisco*, October 1852, 16, an ad for Drexel, Sather & Church, bankers, lists Francis M. Drexel as domiciled in Philadelphia. Several Drexel histories and biographies say Francis remained in San Francisco until 1857—that is, until his partnership dissolved--but this seems impossible: Francis is known to have been in Philadelphia at least at some point in 1853 (he was involved in designing the bank's new building there, which opened in 1854) and in London in 1854 (George Peabody, writing from London to Junius S. Morgan, August 25, 1854: "Francis M. Drexel . . . called on me," JSMP/GL). San Francisco city directories (as well as New York and Philadelphia directories) indicate that Francis was a Philadelphia resident throughout this period. FMD and Drexel, Sather & Church are listed in the San Francisco directory for 1856–57, but in 1858 only Sather & Church is listed. This seems consistent with Drexel biographies which say he dissolved his San Francisco partnership shortly before the Panic of 1857, which broke in September of that year.

"... when a steamer bearing $300,000 in gold from California was lost at sea." AJD obituary, *Chicago Herald*, July 1, 1893 (DFS, vol. 1: 10). It is impossible to say whether this ship was the *Central America*, which sank off the Carolina coast in 1857 with 21 tons ($1.6 million 1857 dollars' worth) of California gold and was later immortalized in Gary Kinder's book, *Ship of Gold in the Deep Blue Sea*.

"... America's railroads added some 22,000 miles of track, at a cost of more than $838 million." Carosso, *The Morgans*, 55.

"... ultimately financed the completion of Philadelphia's first railroad to Lake Erie." Larson, "Jay Cooke's Early Work in Transportation," 365–66.

PAGE 48

"To extend their reach, large private banks ... were part owners or managers." Redlich, *Molding of American Banking*, vol. 2: 75.

"... Chicago ... was the Drexels' first such branch." At some point in the early 1840s, Francis apparently opened a Chicago office styled Drexel & Smith, although nothing indicates that he actually lived there. At the time, Chicago was a struggling frontier town whose viability as a commercial crossroads depended on its ability to dig a canal connecting Lake Michigan to the Illinois River. To finance this canal, the Michigan Canal Commission sold portions of its land, including a large tract south of the city limits in what is now Hyde Park, to a Dr. William Egan, who financed his purchase with a $50,000 loan from Drexel. When Egan defaulted on the loan a few years later, his land became Drexel property. It was laid out as the "Drexel & Smith Subdivision," but Francis Drexel donated a wide center strip to the city for a boulevard, apparently in the hope of stimulating development. Nearly forty years later this beautiful street was named Drexel Boulevard, and in gratitude Francis Drexel's sons presented Chicago with the Drexel Fountain, installed in 1882. This episode suggests that the Drexels played a role in Chicago's early development; it also may have been their first philanthropic venture. How they got involved in Chicago or who were the named partners of Drexel & Smith remains a mystery. Tony Drexel's younger brother Joseph set up a branch office in Chicago in 1860, but he was too young to have been there in the 1840s—when the Illinois-Michigan Canal was completed in 1848, Joseph Drexel was only seventeen. Tony Drexel's wife Ellen Rosét had a younger sister named Sarah who married a Chicagoan named Charles M. Smith (see *Genealogies of Pennsylvania Families*, 668); it's possible that he was the Smith of the Drexels' Chicago partnership as well as their initial Windy City contact. But this is merely speculation. See memo at SBS from Sr. Roberta to Sr. Mary Hottenroth, July 17, 1981; also Knutson, "Statue Honors Drexel."

"... by acquiring an interest in an established Wall Street house, J. V. Van Vleck, Read &

Co . . ." Carosso, "The House of Drexel," 16. The earliest reference to the firm of Van Vleck, Read & Drexel, bankers, at 27 Wall St., appears in *Trow's N.Y.C. Directory 1855–56* (for year ending May 1, 1856).

". . . possibly Drexel & Co.'s first government financings since the Mexican War . . ." Redlich, *The Molding of American Banking,* vol. 2: 365.

". . . the U.S. was a debtor nation that relied heavily on foreign investment." Geisst, *Wall Street,* 30.

". . . estimated that foreign investment in U.S. railroads alone amounted to nearly $83 million." Strouse, *Morgan: American Financier,* 71.

". . . the legendary London bank that helped Thomas Jefferson finance the Louisiana Purchase in 1803." Geisst, *Wall Street,* 16.

". . . one of just three preeminent London banks specializing in Anglo-American trade." Carosso, "The House of Drexel," 9.

PAGE 49

". . . his opinion was based almost exclusively upon a letter her received that year from Abraham Barker. . . ." The letter is dated July 12, 1851. Barker is briefly described in Stevenson, "Looking Back 50 Years on Financial Philadelphia."

"Barker . . . added that the Drexel sons were considered more amiable." Hidy, *House of Baring in American Trade,* 398, 582–83. Barker's firm was Barker Bros. & Co. Carosso, *The Morgans,* 36, identifies Ward as Baring Brothers' U.S. agent from February 1853, although Ward seems to have filled this role informally at least as early as 1850.

". . . and their four remaining unmarried children settled there as well, on the south side of the Square at 19th Street." When the modern street numbering system was adopted in 1857, Francis Drexel's address became 1900 S. Rittenhouse Square. In Philadelphia city directories, from 1845 to 1853, FMD is listed as living at 506 Chestnut Street near "Schuylkill 6th" (now 17th Street), and in 1853 AJD is on "Rittenhouse Sq." In 1854 Francis M. Drexel and sons FAD and JWD are listed as living at "SW corner of 19th & S. Rittenhouse Sq." (called 1900 S. Rittenhouse beginning 1858); AJD was still on "S. Rittenhouse Sq." By 1855 Francis A. Drexel lived at 33 Race, renumbered 433 Race the following year. AJD was listed in 1854 at "S. Rittenhouse Sq.," in 1855 and '56 at "3 S. Rittenhouse Sq." In 1857 and 1858 he is listed at "William and Walnut," West Philadelphia—his new home between 38th and 39th Streets.

PAGE 50

". . . were routinely greeted by visitors as Frank, Tony, and Joe without their taking any offense." Description taken from Stevenson, "Looking Back 50 Years on Financial Philadelphia."

"'The first floor is appropriated to the operations of the firm . . . furnished with all the modern improvements, and are well-lighted and ventilated.'" *Public Ledger,* January 16, 1854. A copy is on file at Philadelphia Historical Commission in the folder for 34 S. Third St., as the building was renumbered three years after it opened.

PAGE 51

"Most of the nineteenth century's great 'merchant bankers' . . ." For a good discussion of the origins of merchant bankers, see Wechsberg, *The Merchant Bankers*, esp. 6–8.

". . . but he lacked an heir to assure his bank's continuity." Strouse, *Morgan*, 52.

"'We shall require an active, clever agent . . . His firm is Drexel & Co., Bankers, Phila.'" George Peabody to JSM, August 25, 1854 (JSMP/GLL).

PAGE 52

". . . Drexel & Co. was named Peabody's Philadelphia correspondent." Perkins, *Financing Anglo-American Trade*, 136. Also Carosso, *The Morgans*, 39–40.

"Now financing trade . . . became the bank's primary business." Carosso, "The House of Drexel," 10.

". . . Tony and other parishioners to pay $500 each to architect Samuel Sloan . . ." *The Church of the Saviour*, 100th anniversary pamphlet, November 1950. Also see Silver, "The Anthony J. Drexel Mansion," 8, and Baltzell, *Philadelphia Gentlemen*, 277.

". . . the church's huge onyx baptismal font, which is still in use." *Philadelphia Bulletin*, 1952 (DFS, vol. 10: 37).

"Its design seems to bear the imprint of Samuel Sloan . . ." Samuel Sloan (1815–84). The first vestry book for the Episcopal Church of the Saviour at 38th and Ludlow (then Mary and Oak Streets) contains pledges by AJD and others to pay $500 each to Sloan for his 1856 design of the church. See Silver, "The Anthony J. Drexel Mansion," 7–8.

". . . 'everything that wealth could purchase or taste could choose' . . ." AJD biographical sketch (SBS, 4).

PAGE 53

"Three afternoons a week she invited Philadelphia's needy . . . an astonishing sum for the time." Duffy, *Katharine Drexel*, 27.

PAGE 54

". . . where Childs learned to strike a bargain by calling for the 'balance' . . ." The best source on Childs is Stern, "George W. Childs: Poor Richard the Second," 3332ff. Also see Burt, *The Perennial Philadelphians*, 417–18.

". . . offering what he called 'amusements as well as instruction.'" G. W. Childs letter, 1858, cited in Stern, "George W. Childs: Poor Richard the Second," 3335–36.

"Childs's first introduction to Tony Drexel, perhaps about 1853 . . ." Childs's eulogy to AJD, *Harper's Weekly*, July 15, 1893, remarks, "For 40 years he was my friend and companion"—that is, presumably since 1853 or thereabouts.

". . . Peterson, who in the 1830s had practiced law on Sixth Street . . ." The Philadelphia directory for 1830 shows Francis M. Drexel at 40 S. Sixth and Peterson practicing law in the office of his father-in-law, John Bouvier, very close by at 56 S. Sixth. This John Bouvier (1787–1851), a jurist best known for his *Law Dictionary* (1839), was apparently unrelated to the family of Michel Bouvier, who was friendly with Francis Drexel and whose daughter Emma married Frank Drexel in 1860. George Childs married Peterson's daughter (Judge Bouvier's granddaughter), Emma Bouvier Peterson, in the late 1850s.

". . . 'such an example of the better things of life . . . who saw its long unbroken consistent beauty.'" GWC obituary by Talcott Williams, *Harper's Weekly*, February 10, 1894 (Box 4, GWC/HL).

PAGE 55

"Francis M. Drexel was one of only two brokers on that list." Philadelphia city directory, 1857; also Weigley, *Philadelphia: A 300-Year History*, 327–29.

"The confusion quickly spread to New York insurance companies . . . calling in loans to cover their own positions." Geisst, *Wall Street*, 47–48.

". . . returned to San Francisco to withdraw from his partnership there." Most Drexel & Co. histories and FMD biographies report without elaboration that he withdrew from the San Francisco house shortly before the panic of 1857, a judgment supported by the firm's disappearance from the San Francisco City Directory in 1858. The closest contemporary report, *Biographical Encyclopedia of Pennsylvania* (1874), 24–25, remarks that Francis "returned to San Francisco, found the business flourishing, and withdrew from it on his return to Philadelphia."

PAGE 56

"'A prudent people would make prudent banks . . . but some 600 to 1,000 are killed by them every year.'" Fisher, *The Diary of Sidney George Fisher, 1834–1871*, 279.

CHAPTER 5
PAGE 59

"'I felt a shock & thrill of terror . . . *we must* come well out of it.'" Katherine Brinley Wharton, diary, 14 April 1861 (HSP), cited in Gallman, *Mastering Wartime*, 4.

PAGE 60

". . . by 1861 the city's defenders of racial equality were in a distinct minority." See Gallman, *Mastering Wartime*, 2.

". . . and sent them away with a band and a blessing." This description is taken largely from MacKay, "Philadelphia During the Civil War."

". . . there was not even enough money in the Treasury to pay Congressional salaries." Gordon, *The Great Game*, 91ff.

"The stock market plunged to low points not seen even during the panic of 1857." Geisst, *Wall Street*, 51; also Gallman, *Mastering Wartime*, 266.

"The federal government's expenses . . . to $1 million a day by early summer 1861 and to $1.5 million by December." Gordon, *The Great Game*, 91ff.

PAGE 61

". . . but their bid was refused because of the Treasury's arbitrary cutoff at 94." Larson, *Jay Cooke: Private Banker*, 100–104.

"Drexel & Co. at this point possessed . . . that was spending that much every day." Geisst, *Wall Street*, 52, says Jay Cooke had $150,000 in capital in 1861 and Drexel & Co. had ten times that amount.

PAGE 62

"The second type, exemplified by Cooke, 'is lacking in realism . . . when its members will get into difficulty.'" Gras, Introduction to Larson, *Jay Cooke: Private Banker*, xi.

". . . arrived on the Mayflower in 1620 and built the third house in Plymouth, Massachusetts." *National Cyclopaedia of American Biography*, 253.

". . . 'from a family that had for generations . . . the narrowness of its culture.'" Larson, *Jay Cooke: Private Banker*, 42.

PAGE 63

". . . a brownstone building at 114 South Third Street, a block south of the Drexels." Larson, *Jay Cooke: Private Banker*, 98, gives Cooke's address.

". . . in the federal government's desperate financial situation, he saw his opportunity." Larson, "Jay Cooke's Early Work in Transportation."

". . . the group began dabbling in the stock market." Oberholtzer, *Jay Cooke*, vol. 1: 96.

". . . they entered a joint venture to purchase warrants for prairie lands . . ." Larson, *Jay Cooke: Private Banker*, 75.

". . . a stake that in 1860 led Cooke and Drexel to fight unsuccessfully to remove the railroad's corrupt management." Larson, *Jay Cooke: Private Banker*, 94–95.

"Cooke had supported himself during his freelance years by borrowing from Drexel & Co . . ." Larson, "Jay Cooke's Early Work in Transportation."

". . . Jay Cooke & Co. took $141,000 for four banks and one individual in Philadelphia." Larson, *Jay Cooke: Private Banker*, 100–104.

PAGE 64

"'Toney [sic] Drexel and Company and myself . . . succeeded in getting 300,000 bid for.'" Oberholtzer, *Jay Cooke*, vol. 1: 140–41.

"This action instantly solved Cooke's capital needs . . ." Larson, *Jay Cooke: Private Banker*, 105–6; also see Geisst, *Wall Street*, 52.

PAGE 65

". . . 'you had no cash capital and that I would run great risk if I did it.'" Moore to Jay Cooke and William Moorhead, March 1, 1871, cited in Larson, *Jay Cooke: Private Banker*, 107.

". . . 'respectfully appeal to the patriotism and State pride . . . a six per cent Loan free from any taxation.'" Larson, *Jay Cooke: Private Banker*, 105.

". . . 'yet we had the valuable aid of his counsel . . . the high character and standing of his house.'" Oberholtzer, *Jay Cooke*, vol. 1: 120.

"The loan was oversubscribed." Larson, *Jay Cooke: Private Banker*, 107.

"'We would refer to Drexel & Co. as the heaviest house in Philadelphia . . . and stands very high as a business man.'" Larson, *Jay Cooke: Private Banker*, 108

PAGE 66

". . . Cornelius Vanderbilt offered his fleet of 60 vessels for as much as $2,500 a day." Jackson, *J. P. Morgan*, 65.

PAGE 67

". . . sometimes raising as much as $2 million in a single day." Jackson, *J. P. Morgan*, 66.

"Bankers visiting Cooke's Third Street office gaped . . . 6 percent bonds at 100 percent of their par value." See Stevenson, "Looking Back 50 Years on Financial Philadelphia."

". . . Cooke's Washington banking house opened for business in February 1862 . . ." Oberholtzer, *Jay Cooke*, vol. 1: 184.

". . . but Francis found his brother Anton, four years his junior, still living in Dornbirn." F. J. Dallett notes, from genealogical material compiled by Frances Wright and Carolyn Cotton, both of whom scoured original sources (Drexel papers, DFN/HL).

PAGE 68

"Francis, who remained conscious, was informed that his injury was fatal . . . 4,000 miles from the Austrian village where it had begun." *Public Ledger*, June 6, 1863; *Philadelphia Bulletin*, June 6, 1863; Konkle, "Francis Martin Drexel"; letter from J. L. Ludlow, M.D., dated June 6, 1863, to unidentified newspaper (DFS, vol. 6, DUM).

". . . the first of its periodic credit reports . . ." 32 R. G. Dun & Co. credit reports for Drexel & Co., April 13, 1864 (Hagley Library, Wilmington, Delaware).

". . . had devastated Drexel & Co.'s business in commercial credits." Carosso, "The House of Drexel," 13–14.

PAGE 69

"On that same July 1, 1863 the Drexels dissolved . . . Robert Winthrop, the firm's resident partner in New York, one-third." Partnership agreements of July 1, 1863 (PML, Box B-2, Folder 2).

"His father-in-law . . . was president of the National City Bank." Carosso, *The Morgans*, 138.

PAGE 70

"'These are qualities more rarely found than genius . . . meaning so plainly that there could be no mistaking it.'" Grant, *Personal Memoirs*, 47.

". . . Grant was describing himself as much as Taylor." For a discussion of Grant's views on Taylor, see McPherson, "The Unheroic Hero."

". . . bringing the total raised to $511 million." MacKay, "Philadelphia During the Civil War."

"One of these Cooke was advised . . . 'he could obtain money at a lower rate.'" Oberholtzer, *Jay Cooke*, vol. 1: 544–47.

"... 'his gratuitous advice not to become agent for the loan.'" Jay Cooke to Henry Cooke, February 21, 1870, quoted in Oberholtzer, *Jay Cooke*, vol. 1: 546.

"... he was under severe pressure to cut costs." Carosso, *The Morgans*, 110.

"Jay Cooke did not make his fortune selling the government's war loans . . . 'We were whipped in the Treasury Department.'" Oberholtzer, *Jay Cooke*, vol. 1: 574.

"Cooke's relatively meager commissions . . . came from the exposure he gained." Geisst, *Wall Street*, 55–57.

"... selling it at once to Mr. Drexel . . ." Hopkinson, *Drexel & Co.*, 16–17.

"(Cooke's name did not appear on the list . . .)" Baltzell, *Philadelphia Gentlemen*, 130; also *Philadelphia Inquirer*, May 29, 1940 (DFS/HL, vol. 7).

CHAPTER 6

"(He owned it until 1872 . . . the bible of the book publishing trade.)" Stern, "George W. Childs," 3339.

"'I will yet be the owner of the *Public Ledger*' . . ." Childs obituary, *Public Ledger*, February 3, 1894, quoting Dr. R. Shelton Mackenzie, to whom the remark allegedly was made.

"Their *Ledger* sold for only one cent . . ." Calkin, "The *Public Ledger*: An Independent Newspaper," 43.

"... Joseph Sailer, who began writing his daily 'money article' in 1840 and continued it for more than forty years." Calkin, "The *Public Ledger*," 45.

"... by 1850 its circulation had risen to 40,000." Calkin, "The *Public Ledger*," 46.

"In 1846 the *Ledger* became the first newspaper to install . . . in a single high-speed press run." Emery and Smith, *The Press and America*, 224.

"... awarded by statute to the local paper with the largest circulation." Calkin, "The *Public Ledger*," 50.

"The *Ledger* alone remained nonpartisan." Calkin, "The *Public Ledger*," 54–55.

"... aided Jay Cooke in promoting the sale of government securities . . ." Calkin, "The *Public Ledger*," 53.

"Swain had been at the paper's helm . . . a third inactive partner was dead." James Parton, Childs biography in unidentified New York publication, August 27, 1870 (Childs scrapbook, GWC/HL).

"... but lacked the $150,000 purchase price." Childs, *Recollections*, 14–15. Also see undated clip (c. 1869) from unidentified paper (Childs scrapbook , Box 2, GWC/HL).

". . . he would received a one-third interest in the paper." In most accounts the Drexels owned two-thirds of the *Ledger* and Childs one-third. One exception is Townsend, *The Old "Main Line"* , 83–84, which says the Drexels had three-quarters and Childs one-quarter.

". . . would buy back Childs's interest at the prevailing market value upon Childs's death." See AJD's will, Article 23, which refers to a partnership agreement with Childs dated March 27, 1865 and amended November 27, 1869. Since Childs acquired the *Ledger* in December 1864, these dates suggest that AJD may have become involved a few months later. See *Philadelphia Bulletin*, December 7, 1949: "AJD became interested in the *Public Ledger* after George W. Childs took control of it in 1864" (DFS, vol. 9, DUM).

". . . 'always raise its voice . . . in support of the Government.'" Calkin, "The *Public Ledger*," 52.

"The paper had been losing . . . showed a profit of $2,000 a day for many years." Childs obituary, *New York Press*, February 4, 1894.

"'There are about 70,000 houses in Philadelphia . . . just one copy for each house.'" *New York Ledger*, March 4, 1865 (Childs scrapbook, Box 2, GWC/HL).

"'The rules which governed the newspaper . . . many respects identical.'" Childs obituary, *New York Press*, February 4, 1894.

"'The *Ledger* is in "fine" order . . . injure your health without doing any good to the paper.'" AJD to GWC, March 25, 1869 (Childs scrapbook, Box 2, GWC/HL).

"Cooke returned to the *Ledger* office to apologize." Oberholtzer, *Jay Cooke*, vol. 1: 546–47.

"He never lived in the Philadelphia house." *Philadelphia Bulletin*, December 3, 1924 (DFS, 113 col. 3, DUM). Grant's widow sold the house after his death in 1885, and the house was torn down in 1924.

CHAPTER 7

". . . the foundation for skyscrapers, railroads, and modern factories . . . " Fischer, *The Great Wave*, quoted in Easton, "Deflationary Winners," 262. Also see Holbrook, *The Age of the Moguls*, 19.

". . . J&W Seligman & Co. had already opened European branches . . ." Redlich, *The Molding of American Banking*, vol. 2: 75; also Birmingham, *Our Crowd*, 73–74.

"That left Drexel & Co. . . . . as the only leading investment banker with a relatively long and respected track record." Redlich, *The Molding of American Banking*, vol. 2: 361.

"On three occasions in 1867. . . and the North Missouri Railroad." Larson, *Jay Cooke, Private Banker*, 223–24, 245–46.

"By 1870 Cooke had a London branch as well . . ." Redlich, *The Molding of American Banking*, vol. 2: 75.

"... in alliance with the emerging New York German-Jewish firm of Kuhn, Loeb & Co." Jackson, *J. P. Morgan*, 95–96.

"... was largely a Cooke-Clark operation; Drexel & Co. was merely one of its 73 minor incorporators." Larson, *Jay Cooke: Private Banker*, 139.

"... Drexel & Co. was again merely a minor shareholder." Oberholtzer, *Jay Cooke*, vol. 1: 188.

"Before Drew died in 1867 ... than by adding value to it." Geisst, *Wall Street*, 71.

"When Fisk and Gould took over the Erie Railroad in 1869 ... diluted the holdings of their existing stockholders." Geisst, *Wall Street*, 59.

"... Lyman Trumbull sat in the Senate while on retainer from the Illinois Central." Strouse, *Morgan: American Financier*, 156. Trumbull represented Illinois in the U.S. Senate from 1855 to 1873.

"During the war Cooke had performed a patriotic service ..." See Larson, *Jay Cooke: Private Banker*, 245, 318, 375.

"In the heat of the Civil War, the press and the public had overlooked Cooke's practice ... just like any other influence seeker." Strouse, *Morgan: American Financier*, 156.

"'Indeed it may be said that no other measure is supported ... manipulation of the funds.'" *Public Ledger*, February 17, 1869.

"'not in any way control or interfere ... until it appeared in print.'" Oberholtzer, *Jay Cooke*, vol. 2: 134–35.

"'I have not much fear of these fellows ... snap my fingers at the whole crew.'" Larson, *Jay Cooke: Private Banker*, 222.

"Then, in late 1867 ... three most prominent American financial firms in the French capital." Kindleberger, "Origins of United States Direct Investment in France."

"Instead, Tony assigned two other resident general partners ... who effectively became the new Paris firm's 'senior.'" J. P. Morgan & Co., "Co-partnership Notices," I (2 vols.) (PML).

"Harjes was four years younger than Tony ..." "Memo for Mr. Stoddard from W. H. Wilson," August 15, 1927 (MFP, PML); "Memorandum," undated, Benjamin Strong Correspondence (File 1122.1, Benjamin Strong Papers, Federal Reserve Bank of New York). See also *Commercial & Financial Chronicle* 98 (February 21, 1914): 569; *New York Times*, February 16, 1914; and *National Cyclopaedia of American Biography*, 19: 262.

"Tony personally pledged to advance Harjes the funds ..." Partnership agreement, January 31, 1868 (Box B-1 (6), folder 1, MFP/PML). The Paris house was formed January 31, 1868 and opened for business on May 1, 1868.

". . . it developed a market in France for American securities . . ." Kindleberger, "Origins of United States Direct Investment in France," 387–88. Also J. P. Morgan & Co., "Co-partnership notices."

". . . and enhanced the bank's reputation for standing behind its guarantees at any cost." From biography of AJD in Scharf and Westcott, *History of Philadelphia*, 3: 2101–2.

". . . decorated him with the order of Chevalier of the Legion of Honor." Carosso, *The Morgans*, 135.

". . . patched up his differences with Junius Morgan and moved his account back to J. S. Morgan's bank in 1868." Carosso, *The Morgans*, 110.

PAGE 87

"Morgan was turning his London house into a major distributor . . . lacked both the necessary experience and character." See Carosso, *The Morgans*, 105–7, 119.

PAGE 88

"But at this moment that man was laboring . . . J. Pierpont." See Carosso, "The House of Drexel," 19–20; also *The Morgans*, 135.

CHAPTER 8

PAGE 91

"Until his death in 1847 . . . investigating and settling claims." Carosso, *The Morgans*, 15–16.

"In the Jacksonian era large merchants like Howe Mather . . . Junius remained there for the next fifteen years." Strouse, *Morgan: American Financier*, 17, 26.

". . . and in 1854 Junius accepted and moved to London." Strouse, *Morgan: American Financier*, 29, 33, 42.

"Pierpont's poor health . . . all his time with his parents and grandparents." Strouse, *Morgan: American Financier*, 27.

PAGE 92

". . . communicated through long and informative letters." Strouse, *Morgan: American Financier*, 60–61, 86.

"'You are altogether too rapid in disposing . . . with all attendants evils is sure to be upon you.'" JSM to JPM, March 15, 1859, quoted in Strouse, 82.

". . . with $300,000 in capital provided by his father." Strouse, *Morgan: American Financier*, 90–91. The capital figure is provided by JPM, Jr. in "Reminiscences" (JPM/NY), 2.

". . . operated out of a one-room office at 53 Exchange Place . . ." Strouse, *Morgan: American Financier*, 90–91.

PAGE 93

"(Pierpont's commission . . . a time of great risk and uncertainty.)" Strouse, *Morgan: American Financier*, 92ff.

". . . Junius gradually transferred the London firm's New York accounts to J. P. Morgan & Co." Strouse, *Morgan: American Financier*, 94–95.

"This move caught the markets by surprise . . . more than $60,000 for each of the two friends." Strouse, *Morgan: American Financier*, 110–11.

PAGE 94

". . . forging an additional $1.5 million in gold certificates, some of them in Pierpont's name." Strouse, *Morgan: American Financier*, 117.

"The newly rechristened Dabney, Morgan & Co. opened . . . at 53 Exchange Place." Carosso, *The Morgans*, 105.

". . . when in fact he was worth about $350,000." Strouse, *Morgan: American Financier*, 137. Pierpont Morgan's net worth of some $350,000 is taken from the closing balances in his personal accounts at Dabney, Morgan & Co. in 1871. See Carosso, *The Morgans*, 682.

"Although he was considered 'of excellent character'. . . 'brusqueness of manner.'" Strouse, *Morgan: American Financier*, 137.

PAGE 95

"Pierpont's own poor health. . . ." Carosso, *The Morgans*, 135.

". . . he paid a call on Junius Morgan in London." Precisely when this visit took place is unclear. Carosso, *The Morgans*, 135, says Tony visited Junius Morgan's office "early in January 1871." But several months' mail correspondence between Tony and Junius Morgan, beginning December 23, 1870, suggests that Tony was in Philadelphia during that time. See letters and cables in JSMP/GL.

". . . he and Tony had developed a trusting relationship." Carosso, *The Morgans*, 131.

"'My pressing business interests in this country . . . prevent my living abroad for any length of time'. . ." AJD to JSM, January 27, 1871 (JSMP/GL).

PAGE 96

". . . 'I have just returned home this week . . . to go to New York soon.'" AJD to JPM, March 4, 1871 (Box B-4, folder 1, MFP/PML).

"The sprawling three-story, forty-one-room mansion. . . . were more simply decorated than those below." Silver, "The Anthony J. Drexel Mansion." The number of rooms in the mansion is taken from Cooke and Cooke, "The Philadelphia Biddles," 396.

PAGE 97

". . . he was dissatisfied with his New York arrangement." JPM, Jr., "The New York Firms," memorandum dated July 29, 1942 (New York Firms folder, PML).

"'I want you to come into my firm as a partner.'" Allen, *The Great Pierpont Morgan*, 32.

". . . Pierpont would be entitled to 50 percent of the new firm's profits . . ." See Carosso, *The Morgans*, 138.

"On the back of an envelope . . . 'profits or loss to be divided half & [illegible] ratio.'" AJD's notes on envelope, March 8, 1871 (Box B-4, folder 1, MFP/PML).

". . . 'your son came to see me the night before last & we talked over matters fully.'" AJD to JSM, March 10, 1871 (JSMP/GL, Ms 21,760, HC 1.9 (b)).

"Perhaps most important, in Tony Drexel . . . smooth out his rough edges as no father could." See AJD to JSM, January 27, 1871 (JSMP/GL); also Carosso, "The House of Drexel," 23–24.

"Robert Winthrop was a proud, wealthy man . . ." AJD to JSM, January 27, 1871 (JSMP/GL).

"Within a week of their first meeting . . . at the National City Bank." Carosso, *The Morgans*, 138.

"'I received yesterday a very kind letter . . . we both felt alike on that subject.'" AJD to JPM, March 15, 1871 (MFP/PML).

"'I am very glad to hear your father . . . to see you there and we can have a full talk.'" AJD to JPM, March 17, 1871 (MFP/PML). The "Mr. Peabody" referred to in the letter is S. Endicott Peabody, a relative of George Peabody who joined J. S. Morgan & Co. as a partner early in 1871. George Peabody, a bachelor, had died in 1869.

". . . 'Would it not be a good plan to write Mr. Harjes . . . by next mail if you approve of it.'" AJD to JPM, April 7, 1871 (MFP/PML).

". . . 'I will try to see you next week . . . points occur to you that ought to be discussed.'" AJD to JPM, April 13, 1871 (MFP/PML).

". . . 'As the time is getting short . . . too crowded when we commence.'" AJD to JPM, May 17, 1871 (MFP/PML).

". . . . 'Your son wishes to leave . . . in case we carry out the arrangement.'" AJD to JSM, March 10, 1871 (JSMP/GL).

"'I think your son is just in that condition . . . to be proud of him in many ways.'" AJD to JSM, April 4, 1871 (JSMP/GL).

". . . J. Hood Wright, the other Philadelphia partner, put in $5000 . . ." J. Hood Wright (1846–94), who had started his banking career with Drexel & Co. in 1861 at age 15, was made a junior partner four years later, and quickly became one of its most active and respected members. Carosso, *The Morgans*, 138.

"Pierpont Morgan's capital contribution was just $15,000 . . . whichever was higher." DM & Co., "Private ledger" (MFP/PML).

"Tony had told Junius in January 1871 . . ." AJD to JSM, January 27, 1871 (JSMP/GL).

"Junius at the time was worth more than $5 million . . ." Carosso, *The Morgans*, 141.

". . . 'one of the most important changes in banking circles announced at this time.'"

Commercial & Financial Chronicle, July 1, 1871, 11, quoted in Carosso, *The Morgans*, 141.

"Of these banks . . . in the same class with Drexel, Morgan." Carosso, *The Morgans*, 140.

PAGE 102

". . . 'the first articles of partnership of Drexel, Morgan & Co.'" Quoted in Hopkinson, *Drexel & Co.*, 19. Also see Carosso, "The House of Drexel," 22; and Carosso, *The Morgans*, 136.

". . . 'among the few leading banking houses in the world.'" *Commercial & Financial Chronicle*, July 1, 1871, 11, quoted in Carosso, *The Morgans*, 141.

"He would not return until late September 1872 . . ." There is at least some evidence that Pierpont Morgan was already active in the affairs of the London and Paris houses before his return to New York that fall. A letter from J. S. Morgan & Co. of London to Drexel, Harjes & Co. of Paris, July 26, 1872, reports, "Your Mr. Morgan has explained to us the terms upon which the Banque de Paris has offered to receive your subscriptions to the new French loan" (Private Copy-Out Letter book, 1867–75, 720, JSMP/GL).

PAGE 103

". . . 'the biggest transaction which has ever occurred in New York' . . ." *New York Commercial Advertiser*, February 28, 1872 (GWC/HL).

". . . 'the highest price ever paid for land in the world . . .'" Hopkinson, *Drexel & Co.*, 19.

"The small building . . . was jointly owned by six siblings. . . . The deal ultimately fashioned . . . an annuity for all six heirs." JPM, Jr., "Reminiscences," 4, says the building was owned by seven siblings, each of whom received a $50,000 mortgage, totaling $350,000. But the deed itself lists six owners and a purchase price of $250,000. See Anastasia L. Burtsell et al. to AJD, April 20, 1872, New York City Register, N.Y. County, Liber 1208 of Conveyances, 366 (also at JPM/NY).

". . . 'if I could only use it easily and regularly.'" JPM, Jr., "Reminiscences," 4–5. AJD's remark was made to Jack Morgan, presumably years after the sale, which took place when Jack was only four years old.

PAGE 104

". . . 'Is it really possible that Drexel, Morgan & Co. have bought all that ground?'" *Journal of Commerce*, quoted in *Delaware Tribune*, February 15, 1872 (GWC/HL).

". . . 'throws New York enterprise into the shade, in this case at least.'" *National Republican*, Washington, D.C., February 12, 1872 (GWC/HL).

". . . 23 Wall Street—would be as famous as the name of its principal tenant." Carosso, *The Morgans*, 173.

"'No native banking house stands higher' . . ." R. G. Dun & Co., notes re Drexel & Co., November 18, 1872 (Hagley Library, Wilmington, Del.).

PAGE 105

"He yearned not for a banking career . . . the company of fashionable gentlemen." Cordelia Drexel Biddle, *My Philadelphia Father*, 23–24.

"Although Edward made little attempt to hide his contempt for business . . . a share in the bank's profits." Cooke and Cooke, "The Philadelphia Biddles," 393–98.

CHAPTER 9
PAGE 108

"The settlement brought the United States a $15.5 million award from Britain . . ." Carosso, *The Morgans*, 154; *Manchester Guardian*, May 9, 1872 (GWC/HL); *Anglo-American Times*, May 11, 1872 (GWC/HL).

". . . the Rothschilds had never established a significant presence in America . . ." The Rothschilds were unable to persuade any member of their family to move to America. Instead, they settled for the services of their New York agent, August Belmont, whose reputation was more negative than positive. See, among others, Ferguson, *The House of Rothschild: Money's Prophets*, 369–73.

PAGE 109

"The decision . . . 'entirely with Morton & Pierpont as they being on the ground . . .'" AJD to JSM, January 14, 1873 (JSMP/GL).

"But Cooke needed the money desperately and badly." Larson, *Jay Cooke*, 396.

"(The loan wasn't entirely placed until early 1876.)" Carosso, *The Morgans*, 179–80.

". . . 'remarkably well. . . never better' . . ." JPM to JSM, April 17/18, 1873 (MFP/PML), quoted in Strouse, *Morgan: American Financier*, 150.

PAGE 110

". . . 'but he is kept in check by the Drexels.'" R. G. Dun & Co., "Credit ledgers," 468 (300/NN, RGDCL/Baker Library, Harvard University).

". . . 'saved Morgan two or three times, for Morgan is a plunger.'" Barron, *More They Told Barron*, 125, interview with Alexander A. McLeod (Reading Railroad ex-president), September 8, 1893. McLeod was repeating what he had been told by George Childs— who, as Tony Drexel's best friend, was hardly an unbiased observer.

". . . 'the aspect of affairs at the moment . . . the other side of the Atlantic.'" JPM to JSM, April 1, 1873 (MFP/PML).

". . . 'Mr. Drexel and family have arrived safely . . . to have him here to consult and act with.'" JPM to JSM, June 7, 1873 (MFP/PML).

". . . 'Mr. Drexel is always in New York on that day . . . I go down for that purpose.'" JPM to JSM, July 24, 1873 (MFP/PML).

". . . 'I would not for a moment . . .'" JPM to JSM, March 28, 1873 (MFP/PML).

"On his way back to the office . . . calling in all Drexel, Morgan's loans." JPM, Jr., "Reminiscences," 1.

PAGE 111

"Joseph Wilhelm Drexel . . . was a colorful sight on Wall Street." Lehr, *King Lehr and the Gilded Age*, 16.

". . . prevented the band being torn to pieces by its infuriated victims." "Big Banker Drexel."

". . . that he often fell suddenly asleep at dinner . . ." Lehr, *King Lehr and the Gilded Age,* 16.

". . . Joe was neither a good banker nor an astute business man, and Pierpont rarely consulted him." JPM, Jr., "Reminiscences," calls Frank and Anthony Drexel "men of very considerable ability and high character," whereas Joseph was "a very uninspiring sort of person, and was treated, I think, rather roughly at times by the senior partner in New York"—that is, by Pierpont Morgan.

"'You will find him very different from his brother' . . ." JPM to JSM, June 7, 1873 (MFP/PML).

". . . 'a rough, uncouth fellow, continually quarreling with Drexel in the office.'" Carosso, *The Morgans,* 693n. Presumably the "other partner" quoted is J. Norris Robinson, the firm's only other partner at the time.

". . . Pierpont knocked it to the floor with his cane." Several of Joseph Drexel's descendants have related this "hat incident" to me. Precisely when it took place is unclear. According to Joseph's great-granddaughter Frances Penrose Haythe, Joseph went home following this incident and never returned. Later correspondence suggests that Joseph withdrew more gracefully and less dramatically.

PAGE 112

"*You do what I say* . . .'" JPM, Jr., "Reminiscences," 1–2. Jack Morgan's source for this anecdote appears to be either Pierpont Morgan himself or the Drexel, Morgan partner J. Hood Wright, or perhaps both men.

". . . America's most famous banker was bankrupt." Oberholtzer, *Jay Cooke,* 421–22.

". . . 'dread deemed to take possession of the multitude.'" Robert Sobel, *Panic on Wall Street,* 165.

PAGE 113

". . . 'as cheerful as if there was not a woe in the world . . . to that degree confidence was improved.'" AJD obituary, *Philadelphia Press,* July 1, 1893 (DFS, vol. 1: 13, DUM).

". . . 'Everything satisfactory with us with ample margin.'" JPM to JSM, September 19, 1873 (MFP/PML).

". . . 'a letter from Mr. Drexel to me on the subject . . . and we will talk the matter over.'" JPM to JSM, November 7, 1873 (MFP/PML).

"'I think you make a mistake in not appreciating the strength . . . to protect and promote your interests.'" JPM to JSM, February 13, 1874 (MFP/PML).

PAGE 114

"Frank had remained a devout but socially conscious Catholic . . . to church-related institution." See *Dictionary of American Biography,* Supp. S, 185.

PAGE 115

". . . he always made out in advance a map of his route . . . reach him by cable wherever he happened to be." AJD obituary, *Philadelphia Press*, July 1, 1893.

"'I always write under difficulties . . .'" AJD to Elizabeth, Katharine, and Louise Drexel, September 7, 1886 (SBS).

"'I don't know if you will be able to read this disconnected scrawl . . .'" AJD to Walter Smith, March 24, 1890 (SBS).

". . . 'Tell the gentleman my next free hour . . .'" "Men and Things," unidentified Philadelphia news clip, Nov. 8, 1927 (SBS).

"When Grant sought out business leaders . . . needed their support more than they needed his." See, for example, McFeely, *Grant: A Biography*, 393.

"'I regret very much that important business . . . when I will be able to do so.'" AJD to Representative Horace Maynard, Jan. 10, 1874 (DFN/HL).

PAGE 116

"Tony was 'simply a liberal, conscientious citizen . . .'" AJD obituary, *Philadelphia Times*, July 1, 1893 (DFS, vol. 1: 8, DUM).

"'Here was a subject he had considered . . . he changed his opinions and wrote the veto message.'" Childs, *Recollections*, 84. But certainly Grant consulted other advisers as well. See McFeely, *Grant*, 394.

PAGE 117

"He talked with the young doctor for ten minutes . . ." AJD obituary, *Philadelphia Press*, July 1, 1893. Years later, about 1891, the same physician found himself sitting next to Tony Drexel at a civic dinner. He recalled Tony's kindness to him when Tony had Grant and the cabinet at his house. Tony, according to the physician, smiled and answered, "I do not see why you should feel obligated to me for that."

"But I do," said the physician, "and I shall never stop praising you, for that is all that I can possibly hope to do to repay you."

"I am sure that I can ask for no greater honor than to be well thought of," Tony is said to have replied.

". . . Childs later recalled, 'I got a telegram from Mr. A. J. Drexel . . .'" Childs, *Recollections*, 106.

"The general was living and traveling on the income from the gifts . . ." McFeely, *Grant*, 453–54, 465.

"In December 1879 Tony and Ellen Drexel threw an enormous reception. . . ." Hopkinson, *Drexel & Co.*, 24.

"In 1881 Childs and Drexel successfully raised still another house fund for Grant . . ." McFeely, *Grant*, 488.

PAGE 118

"'Of course as long as Mr. J. W. D. continues business, any such arrangement . . . I don't feel good for much anyway.'" JPM to JSM, March 30, 1875 (MFP/PML).

"'Never mix business with friendship' . . ." AJD obituary, *San Francisco Chronicle*, July 1, 1893 (DFS, vol. 1, DUM).

"'Mr. Joseph Drexel told me, a day or two ago, that he had made up his mind . . . But I can write more fully after seeing Mr. Drexel.'" JPM to JSM, September 14, 1875 (MFP/PML).

PAGE 119

"'My grandfather, Joseph Drexel . . . a far from gentle manner.'" Letter from Boies Penrose, August 16 (no year) to Mrs. Jones (SBS).

CHAPTER 10

PAGE 120

". . . by February 1878 Drexel, Morgan had taken over the entire first floor." Carosso, *The Morgans*, 173.

"Even the mail . . . opened and read only by the partners." By the mid-1870s correspondence at the New York house had grown to about 175 letters a day, causing Pierpont, over his father's disapproval, to assign the job of opening mail to a trusted senior clerk. See Carosso, *The Morgans*, 172.

PAGE 121

"The task . . . 'must be done with the greatest caution in every way.'" AJD to JSM, January 27, 1871 (JSMP/GL).

"'When Mr. A. J. D. was here on Monday he suggested . . . and hope all for the best.'" JPM to JSM, September 17, 1875 (MFP/PML).

". . . Welsh declined the offer after all." In any event, Welsh subsequently worked closely with both Tony and Pierpont on several railroad reorganizations.

PAGE 122

"'When we were discussing Fabbri, AJD said . . . but Mr. D. would not listen to that so it was dropped.'" JPM to JSM, October 19 1875 (MFP/PML).

"Through the 1870s and 1880s the Drexel and Morgan partnerships added twelve new partners . . ." Carosso, *The Morgans*, 282.

"His philosophy held that no one at the firm could stand still." G. W. Childs obituary, *New York Press*, February 4, 1894. The article discusses Childs's attempts to apply AJD's philosophy to a newspaper operation.

PAGE 123

". . . 'for their services.'" Partnership agreement, July 1, 1871; amended agreement, January 1, 1875 (MFP/PML).

PAGE 124

"One day early in 1878 . . . Edward, who prided himself on his boxing skills, promptly knocked the clerk down . . ." Cordelia Biddle, in *My Philadelphia Father*, places this incident in 1879; Nicholas Biddle, in *Personal Memoirs*, says it occurred after Edward had been at the bank some ten years, that is, 1878. The best source is a letter from Pierpont Morgan to Edward Biddle, dated March 4, 1878 (letterpress books, MFP/PML), expressing regret at Edward's departure from the firm. This clearly suggests that the incident occurred some time before then.

"Tony further eased the transition by purchasing . . ." The "million-dollar punch" is discussed in two books by AJD's great-grandchildren: Cordelia Biddle, *My Philadelphia Father*, 31; and Nicholas Biddle, *Personal Memoirs*, 1–2. Both authors were amateurs whose accounts seem embellished and contain some factual errors, but they're the best we have.

"The year 1880 found him studying law at 32 South Third Street . . ." Philadelphia City Directory, 1880.

"In 1881 he was admitted to the Philadelphia bar." Cooke and Cooke, *The Philadelphia Biddles*, 399.

PAGE 125

"On a dare from friends . . . She died shortly afterward, at the age of 31." Cordelia Biddle, *My Philadelphia Father*, 31. Emilie Drexel Biddle died January 21, 1883.

"Tony promised to create three trusts of $1 million each . . ." Cordelia Biddle, *My Philadelphia Father*, 32.

"When Edward wanted to see them . . ." Cordelia Biddle, *My Philadelphia Father*, 33.

PAGE 126

"Tony was fond of Edward's oldest son . . ." Cordelia Biddle, *My Philadelphia Father*, 35.

". . . grew up considering themselves the Drexel family's poor relations." See numerous passages in Nicholas Biddle, *Personal Memoirs*.

". . . Runnemede, the Drexels' sprawling summer estate in Lansdowne . . ." The estate was said to have been built for (but never occupied by) Queen Isabella II of Spain following her abdication in 1868. She ultimately chose exile in Paris instead.

"'It was a Spartan regime' . . ." Cordelia Biddle, *My Philadelphia Father*, 34.

CHAPTER 11

PAGE 127

"In 1880 Drexel, Morgan led the syndicate formed in Paris for construction of the Panama Canal." Fisher, "The Anthony J. Drexel House," 10.

". . . grew from $2.5 billion in 1870 to $10 billion in 1890." Carosso, *The Morgans*, 219.

PAGE 128

"'We quite realize the trouble Mr. Anthony Drexel has . . . in which he has managed the affair.'" JSM & Co. to Drexel, Morgan & Co., Oct. 12, 1873 (Private Copy-Out Letter Books, 1867–75, 844, JSMP/GL).

". . . 'I felt disposed to do somewhat more . . . I have no doubt he was right.'" JPM to JSM, August 24, 1877 (MFP/PML).

"'both Mr. Drexel and myself felt as we feel . . . of the efforts made in his behalf.'" JPM to JSM, December 24, 1877 (MFP/PML).

PAGE 129

"When word of the sale reached the public. . . ." *Commercial & Financial Chronicle* 29 (November 29, 1879): 554. See also Carosso, *Investment Banking in America: A History*, 37.

". . . 'I thought I would wait and sound Mr. A. J. Drexel . . . to let the thing stand as at present.'" JPM to JSM, October 19, 1880 (MFP/PML).

"Gowen was the son of middle class Irish immigrants to Philadelphia . . ." Burt, *The Perennial Philadelphians*, 205–6.

PAGE 130

"'Directly or indirectly . . . all prices move with Reading pulsations.'" "Money Market Column," *Public Ledger*, February 17, 1886 (JSMP/GL).

". . . in what one historian called 'an orgy of borrowing.'" "History of the Reading System," Hagley Museum and Library Summary, xiv.

"Since more than 50 percent of the Reading's stock was then held by the McAlmont family . . ." "History of the Reading System," xiii–xiv.

"'We do not consider the proposed business desirable . . .'" AJD to JSM, September 29, 1882 (JSMP/GL).

"'F. B. Gowen has always understated his fixed charges . . . therefore proposed business cannot be made attractive to me.'" Private cables, JSM to AJD, September 29, 1882; AJD to JSM, September 30, 1882 (JSMP/GL).

PAGE 131

". . . Junius should make certain to keep complete control of the transaction." Carosso, *The Morgans*, 259ff.

"'Being unable to secure your cooperation . . .'" Private cables, JSM to AJD, October 2, 1882 (JSMP/GL).

". . . the New York house had added two partners—Charles Coster . . ." Hopkinson, *Drexel & Co.*, 20–21. See Keyes, *Bound Chronological Record of J. P. Morgan & Co., etc.*, 1939 (MFP/PML).

PAGE 132

". . . 'that the railroad should be worked in harmony with other coal-carrying roads.'" "History of the Reading System," xvi.

"In 1885 Pierpont negotiated the famous New York Central-Pennsylvania peace pact . . ." Carosso, *Investment Banking in America: A History*, 37–38.

PAGE 133

"Two other partners . . . had reserves exceeding $1 million." Drexel & Co. records (EIA).

"At a time when 80 percent of American families earned less than $500 . . ." Strouse, "The Brilliant Bailout," 64.

"'have been of the most friendly character . . . fair-minded person would say was our right in the matter.'" Drexel & Co. to J. S. Morgan & Co., March 31, 1885 (JSMP/GL).

". . . 'he did think an opportunity should have been offered us . . .'" Drexel & Co. to J. S. Morgan & Co., March 31, 1885 (JSMP/GL).

PAGE 135

". . . 'As I telegraphed Mr. Drexel, I saw but one thing to do . . . and uncertainty attending all such transactions.'" JPM to JSM, March 1, 1881 (MFP/PML).

"Pierpont's character had indeed undergone a radical change since his alliance with Tony Drexel." A contrary view of the methods of Tony Drexel and Pierpont Morgan was provided by the irresponsible Archibald McLeod, who was forced to resign as president of the Reading Railroad in 1893 after Drexel and Morgan refused to fund the railroad further unless McLeod departed. "Drexel," McLeod told a reporter later that year, "is ten times worse as a fighter than Morgan." See Barron, *More They Told Barron*, October 20, 1893, 126–28.

"The transcription of these messages bear dates—late December—but no year . . ." December 26, the date of the first exchange of telegrams, fell on Saturday in 1885 and Sunday in 1886, which leads me to believe that 1885 is the more likely year.

"A. J. Drexel to J. P. Morgan, Dec. 26: . . . 'perfectly agreeable.'" MFP/PML.

CHAPTER 12
PAGE 139

". . . leaving bequests totaling $19,000 to seven Philadelphia institutions . . ." *Public Ledger,* October 11, 1870. Catherine died Sept. 21, 1870.

PAGE 140

"By February 15 he was dead, at the age of sixty-one." Duffy, *Katharine Drexel*, 68-72.

"After Frank's death, his daughters Elizabeth, Kate, and Louise moved in at Tony and Ellen's summer estate . . ." Baldwin, *A Call to Sanctity*, 19.

"Miss Cassidy, as she was called, was a devout Catholic . . ." "Giving Up Millions to Live on 41 Cents a Day," *Philadelphia Inquirer*, April 25, 1937 (DFS, vol. 6, DUM).

PAGE 141

"Tony's greatest pleasure came from presiding at the family dinner table . . ." "Heritage," quoting reminiscence of J. Peterson Ryder, *Drexel University News*, Summer 1978, 8.

". . . .Tony built homes on or adjacent to his Walnut Street lot . . ." Fisher, "The Anthony J. Drexel House," 3-4 (DUM).

"'I have always felt towards you three girls as towards my own daughters' . . ." AJD to Katharine Drexel, January 24, 1891 (SBS).

". . . 'lots of love and kisses' . . ." AJD to Elizabeth, Kate, and Louise Drexel, October 1, 1886 (SBS).

". . . at the spa resort of Carlsbad, Bohemia . . ." AJD obituary, *Philadelphia Record*, July 3,

1893 (DFS, vol. 1: 21, DUM), quotes a Dr. A. Grunberger, who said AJD had been coming to Carlsbad annually for ten years for treatment of rheumatic gout.

". . . 'His companionship has been the seasoning of our pleasure here . . . has been more delightful than I can express.'" Elizabeth Drexel to Helen Smith, June 15, 1889, cited in Sister M. Dolores, *The Francis A. Drexel Family*, 366.

PAGE 142

". . . his daughters Emilie and Frances were said to rank among Philadelphia's finest amateur pianists . . ." AJD obituary, *Philadelphia Press*, July 1, 1893 (DFS, vol. 1: 13, DUM).

"'I went on Monday night and found it unsatisfactory . . .'" AJD to Louise Drexel Morrell, January 20, 1889 (SBS).

"'None of you go to it, you understand.'" Lehr, *King Lehr and the Gilded Age*, 21.

PAGE 143

"(When asked why they built this new development so far out . . . more time to read the *Ledger*.)" Baltzell, *Philadelphia Gentlemen*, 232; Childs obituary, *New York Press*, February 4, 1894; author's interview with F. J. Dallett, March 10, 1999; AJD obituary, *Chicago Herald*, July 1, 1893.

"'Loafing is, they say . . .'" AJD to Elizabeth, Kate, and Louise Drexel, March 8, 1887 (SBS).

"'She doesn't want to leave me . . .'" AJD to Elizabeth, Kate, and Louise Drexel, September 28, 1886 (SBS).

"'I am quite content to stay home and not go abroad . . .'" AJD to Elizabeth, Kate, and Louise Drexel, November 29, 1886 (SBS).

"'I don't go out any but go to bed early and enjoy myself that way.'" AJD to Elizabeth, Kate and Louise Drexel, December 15, 1886 (SBS).

"By the mid-nineteenth century it had become a gathering place for Europe's wealthy invalids . . ." Strouse, *Morgan: American Financier*, 124. Also *Encyclopedia Britannica* (1964), vol. 13: 282.

PAGE 144

"After dinner, she said, 'Uncle Anthony dozes off . . .'" Sister M. Dolores, *The Francis A. Drexel Family*, 365.

"'My dear children . . . to your loving uncle, A. J. Drexel'" AJD to Elizabeth, Kate, and Louise Drexel, July 29, 1886 (SBS).

PAGE 145

"'I have felt anxious all the time you have been in Spain . . .'" AJD to Elizabeth, Kate, and Louise Drexel, January 27, 1890 (SBS).

". . . their reception in December 1879 for General Grant at their West Philadelphia home . . ." The Grant reception is referenced, among other sources, in Hopkinson, *Drexel & Co.*, 24.

"'The wedding passed off nicely and I am glad it is over . . .'" AJD to Elizabeth, Kate, and Louise Drexel, September 15, 1886 (SBS).

"He served quietly as president of the Fairmount Park Art Commission . . ." Fisher, "The Anthony J. Drexel House," 6 (DUM).

PAGE 146

"'Would not entertain proposition myself . . . however compelling they may appear as to profit.'" Private cables, Drexel & Co. to J. S. Morgan & Co., December 6, 7, 1886; JSM to Drexel & Co., December 6, 1886; AJD to JSM, December 9, 1886 (JSMP/GL).

PAGE 147

". . . led by the even more corrupt and notorious Matthew Quay." Guinther: *Philadelphia: A Dream for the Keeping*, 118.

"The Drexel Building he commenced in 1887 . . ." Re the Drexel Building, see "Drexel Building," promotional brochure (DFN/HL; apparently printed after 1893—it refers to AJD's will); Oberholtzer, *History of Philadelphia*, vol. 2: 431; "Men and Things," unidentified Philadelphia news clip, November 8, 1927 (SBS); Drexel & Co.,"A New Home for an Old House," 21; McMichael, *Philadelphia and Popular Philadelphians* (DFN/HL).

CHAPTER 13

PAGE 150

"By assuring the daughters a regular income . . . encouraged the daughters' charitable instincts." Baldwin, *Saint Katharine Drexel*, 51–54.

"That Elizabeth and Louise eventually married . . ." Frank Drexel's will notwithstanding, his daughters' spouses did indeed participate in their wives' financial affairs. According to the final report filed with Philadelphia Orphans Court by the Francis Drexel Trust after Katharine Drexel died in 1955, Louise Drexel's husband Edward Morrell served longer than any other individual as one of the estate's three trustees.

". . . Kate seemed eager to learn from her Uncle Anthony about the relative value of investments . . ." See, for example, AJD's letter to Kate of September 16, 1889 (SBS).

"But it was their daughters who focused on Indians and blacks in particular." The Frank Drexel family's social consciousness and their interest in reaching out to non-Catholics were rare among Catholics of their day. Their attitude most likely was influenced by Frank's first wife Hannah Langstroth, who belonged to the Dunkards, a religious sect whose beliefs fell somewhere between those of Baptists and Quakers.

PAGE 151

"Within five years, a chain of simple Catholic mission schools built for the Indians . . ." *Philadelphia Record*, April 12, 1941 (DFS, vol. 7: 94, DUM).

". . . the U.S. government agreed to pay $100 a year for each Indian child attending the Catholic mission schools." Ibid.

". . . installation of Archbishop Patrick Ryan of Philadelphia, who subsequently became her close friend." Baldwin, *A Call to Sanctity*, 17.

"'I think you ought to contribute towards the suffering . . . I think you will approve of this.'" AJD to Elizabeth, Kate, and Louise Drexel, September 28, 1886 (SBS).

"'I knew there was a great deal of suffering . . . I am glad to have you do the same.'" AJD to Elizabeth, Kate, and Louise Drexel, October 25, 1886 (SBS).

PAGE 152

"'The Archbishop has sent me a list of all the Catholic clergy . . .we would not milk the party.'" AJD to Elizabeth, Kate and Louise Drexel, November 3, 1886 (SBS).

". . . the hospital was named for Tony's brother-in-law John Lankenau . . . " Butler and Strode, *Drexel U.*, 69.

PAGE 153

". . . his brother Joseph in New York was supporting revolutionary social experiments . . ." Concerning the philanthropic experiments of Joseph W. Drexel, see *Dictionary of American Biography*, 457; *National Cyclopedia*, 366; *Colonial Families of Philadelphia*, vol. 1, 536; "Division of Drexel Estate Is Asked," undated clip from *Public Ledger*, about 1912 (DFS, vol. 3, DUM).

"'I prefer to be my own executor. . .under [my] own eye.'" Matthew Vassar to AJD, March 25, 1862, in Vassar, *Autobiography and Letters of Matthew Vassar*.

"With funding from Anthony Drexel and George Childs, Mrs. Turner set up trade classes . . ." Toll and Gillam, *Invisible Philadelphia*, 350–52.

PAGE 154

". . . 'somewhat similar to Girard College.'" Fee, *Origin and Growth of Vocational Education in Philadelphia to 1917*, 95, quoted in Fisher, "The Anthony J. Drexel House," 12 (DUM).

". . . 'who could get to the school during the day . . .'" Undated *Public Ledger* clip, probably August 1889 (SBS). The article explains Tony's change of plans. He refers to it in letters to his nieces in August 1889 (SBS).

". . . would be the first to bear Tony's name." *Public Ledger*, March 11, 1888, 20.

". . . Tony dispatched Addison Burk . . . on a factfinding tour . . ." Fee, *Origin and Growth of Vocational Education*, 95, quoted in Fisher, "The Anthony J. Drexel House," 12 (DUM).

"The schools in Burk's report that most impressed Tony were . . ." Butler and Strode, *Drexel University*, 70.

". . . 'the chief of which was the widthdrawal of the girls from home influence.'" Undatred *Public Ledger* clip, probably August 1889 (SBS).

". . . it did not occur to Kate that the Church's financial balance sheet might in fact be inferior to that of her own family." Between 1885 and 1891 Katharine helped fund the building of 57 Indian missions in 15 states. One statistic suggests the extent of the Church's dependence upon Drexel wealth: In the dozen or so years after the U.S. government withdrew its aid to Catholic Indian schools, Katharine annually gave about $100,000 for the maintenance of Catholic Indian missionary schools, while her 12 million fellow U.S. Catholics combined gave about $75,000. See Fr. William Ketcham, of the Catholic Bureau of Indian Schools, in the *Indian Sentinel* (1904–5): 31, in SBS Annals (SBS).

"'The question you will bear in mind . . . and acquire more merit for yourself.'" Bishop O'Connor to Katharine Drexel, April 21, 1887 (SBS).

PAGE 156

". . . should she enter a convent she would have to leave all her money behind or donate it directly to her congregation." When it became apparent that Kate was intent on taking the veil, O'Connor ingeniously solved his funding problem by urging her to found her own congregation dedicated to working exclusively among Indians and blacks. In effect this arrangement would enable her to continue the philanthropy in which she was already engaged. Thus the idea to create the Sisters of the Blessed Sacrament may have been O'Connor's more than Katharine's.

". . . during which she could change her mind." Baldwin, *A Call to Sanctity*, 23.

"'Uncle Anthony dropped four or five tears . . . to no one except Uncle A. and Mr. Childs.'" Duffy, *Katharine Drexel*, 138

". . . traveled to Pittsburgh by train for the ceremony." Baldwin, *A Call to Sanctity*, 26.

PAGE 157

"She was also given time to handle the mission correspondence . . . before she took the veil." Duffy, *Katharine Drexel*, 145.

". . . and to consult with her Uncle Anthony on business matters." SBS Annals, 3–20.

"'I also enclose a newspaper slip . . . will now be nonsectarian.'" AJD to Katharine Drexel, August 22, 1889 (SBS).

"'It is now the purpose of Mr. Drexel . . . business foresight can assure.'" Undated clip from *Public Ledger*, probably August 1889 (SBS).

"Instead of studying Latin, Greek, philosophy . . ." Butler and Strode, *Drexel U.*, 75.

PAGE 158

"Tony's social friends were prevailed upon to bequeath art and rare manuscripts . . ." Fisher, "The Anthony J. Drexel House," 13.

"'He brooded over this large plan . . . to understand both them and their best wants.'" Butler and Strode, *Drexel U.*, 70.

"Wilson himself was an ardent advocate of industrial education . . ." Butler and Strode, *Drexel U.*, 70.

"The last great gathering she threw . . . who had helped them create the Institute." Ellen R. Drexel obituary, unidentified, undated (DFS, vol. 2, DUM).

"'I do not want to tie it up . . .'" "Heritage," *Drexel University News*, Summer 1978, 10 (excerpted from McDonald and Hinton, *Drexel Institute of Technology, A Memorial History*).

PAGE 159

"His remarks amounted to three sentences . . ." AJD obituary, *Philadelphia Press*, July 1, 1893 (DFS, vol. 1: 13, DUM). Mayor Fitler left office April 6, 1891, so the dinner presumably occurred prior to that date.

". . . 'whose names are household words the civilized world over.'" Silver, "The Anthony J. Drexel Mansion," Sec. 8, continuation sheet 1 (DUM).

"'If I cannot come to you now, it is not because I forget . . . let me have the pleasure and consolation of doing it.'" Condolence letter to AJD from Katharine Drexel, undated, but presumably late November or early December 1891 (DFN Box 2, DFN/HL).

PAGE 160

"'This is indeed a great loss . . . Jay Cooke'" Jay Cooke to AJD, Dec. 14, 1891 (DFN/HL).

". . . had died in premature childbirth the year before." Elizabeth died September 26, 1890.

"'Nanny has commenced taking the waters . . .'" AJD to Louise Drexel Morrell, May 25, 1892 (SBS).

"'She is desperately ill and it is about an even chance . . . I have full faith and confidence in His mercy.'" AJD to Louise Drexel Morrell, June 15, 1892 (SBS).

CHAPTER 14

PAGE 162

". . . he negotiated another $8.5 million loan for the construction of the Reading Terminal . . ." Fisher, "The Anthony J. Drexel House," 10 (DUM).

". . . in 1889, shot himself in a hotel in Washington." Burt, *The Perennial Philadelphians*, 206.

PAGE 163

"But once in absolute charge of the Reading at the age of forty-one . . ." Holton, *The Reading Railroad: History of a Coal Age*, 298, 300.

". . . by pledging the stocks of other companies that the Reading had acquired on thin margin." "History of the Reading System," xvii.

"To Tony fell the burden of passing the grim news on to London . . ." Private cables, AJD and JPM to J. S. Morgan & Co., January 7, 1890 (JSMP/GL).

PAGE 164

"Burns's cable urged the Reading to pay . . . efforts to have the company's managers removed." Private cables, J. S. Morgan & Co. to AJD, January 7 and 9, 1890, replying to earlier cable of January 7, 1890 from JPM and AJD (JSMP/GL).

". . . 'as much aggrieved as anyone.'" J. S. Morgan & Co. to Drexel & Co., January 22, 1890 ("Private telegrams," 6, JSMP/GL).

". . . pumped new funds into the Reading without demanding even the customary charges . . ." "Mr. Drexel's Friends and Foes."

"But none of these infusions prevented the Reading's failure." Carosso, *The Morgans*, 378ff.

". . . with debts of more than $125 million, a staggering sum for the time." Gordon, *The Great Game*, 163–64.

PAGE 165

"'I knew perfectly well then . . . Drexel is ten time worse as a fighter than Morgan.'" Interview with President A. A. McLeod of New York & New England Railroad, October 20, 1893, Barron, *More They Told Barron*, 126–28. The *New York Times*, February 9, 1893, also mentions Speyer & Co. as a potential banker for the Reading.

". . . 'evidently more anxious [to] secure participation . . . foster relations with us' . . ." J. S. Morgan & Co. to Drexel & Co., April 5, 1893 (JSMP/GL). See also Carosso, *The Morgans*, 359.

PAGE 166

"Nearly one-third of the nation's railroad mileage would pass into receivership . . ." Carosso, "The House of Drexel," 25–26.

"'bright-eyed, alert and destitute . . . a heart which had felt many ills.'" AJD obituary, *Philadelphia Press*, July 1, 1893 (DFS vol. 1: 13, DUM).

"'You have insisted upon my sitting . . . through Monsieur Constant's genius.'" George W. Childs eulogy to AJD, *Harper's Weekly*, July 15, 1893.

PAGE 167

". . . the Reading plan's figures as 'disappointing & misleading.'" Carosso, *The Morgans*, 380.

". . . Pierpont was unwilling to dispute his patron." Pierpont himself continued to acknowledge this reluctance as late as 1890. During a panic in London, Burns asked Pierpont whether J. S. Morgan & Co. should assist the Reading Railroad with a highly speculative bond issue. Morgan replied that the New York market was stronger and encouraged J. S. Morgan & Co. to do "whatever you think best" to assist the Reading's situation, but added: "In view of A. J. Drexel's reluctance doubt wisdom Drexel & Co., Drexel Morgan & Co. joining." See private cables, W. H. Burns to AJD, October 20 and 21, 1890; Drexel & Co. to J. S. Morgan & Co., October 21, 1890; JPM to W. H. Burns, October 22, 1890 (JSMP/GL).

". . . most of the planned offering had already been taken." Carosso, *The Morgans*, 380. Also Holton, *The Reading Railroad*, 325–26.

". . . boarded the steamship *City of New York* . . . a long rest at Carlsbad." The steamer is identified in *Philadelphia Item*, June 30, 1893 (DFS, vol. 1: 19, DUM). The reference to the Drexel Institute expenditure is from "Heritage," *Drexel University News*, Summer 1978, 10. A private cable from AJD, W. H. Burns, and JPM in London to Drexel & Co., May 29, 1893, notes, "AJD Paris tonight, Carlsbad Tuesday night"—that is, May 30 (JSMP/GL). AJD obituary, *Philadelphia Record*, July 3, 1893 (DFS, vol. 1: 21, DUM), says AJD arrived at Carlsbad June 1, but this date is probably mistaken.

"He was unaccompanied by relatives . . . 'quite a number of nice people . . .'" Whereabouts of his children taken from *Philadelphia Call*, July 1, 1893 (DFS, vol. 1: 75, DUM). Also see *Philadelphia Item*, June 30, 1893 (DFS, vol. 1: 19, DUM). Quotation is from AJD to Louise Drexel Morrell, June 20, 1893 (SBS).

"He dined simply . . ." AJD obituary, *Philadelphia Record*, July 3, 1893.

"'I get into a certain rut . . .'" AJD to Louise Drexel Morrell, June 20, 1893 (SBS).

PAGE 168

". . . he would not permit his family to be advised of his illness." Telegram from H. C. Haskins to George W. Childs, June 30, 1893, quoted in AJD obituary, *Philadelphia American*, July 1, 1893 (DFS, vol. 1, DUM).

"'How is Kate getting along with her enterprise? . . .'" AJD to Louise Drexel Morrell, June 20, 1893 (SBS).

"Now the whole plan would have to be scrapped . . ." Carosso, *The Morgans*, 380; also see Reading Railroad resolution of June 22, 1893 (JSMP/GL). The resolution was dated June 22; Drexel & Co. notified J. S. Morgan & Co. in London of the Reading plan's rejection on June 26; presumably AJD was notified in Carlsbad the same day.

"'Altho I have passed the critical point I am . . . we can talk matters over.'" AJD to Walter Burns, June 29, 1893 (DFN/HL).

PAGE 169

"'I wrote you yesterday and today I have yours . . . for your kind sympathy.'" AJD to Walter Burns, June 30, 1893 (DFN/DL).

PAGE 170

"He had spent the last day of his sixty-six years . . ." The best description of AJD's last hours appears in the *Philadelphia Record*, July 3. 1893.

"Newspapers from New York to San Francisco dissected his final hours . . ." *Philadelphia American*, July 19, 1893 (DFS, vol. 1: 37, DUM). AJD's body arrived in New York July 18.

"'I suppose that after all no one man is indispensable to the world . . .'" Bradley, *Henry Charles Lea*, 207–8.

PAGE 171

". . . 'completely stunned by the death of Mr. Drexel . . .'" JPM to Edward Coles, July 10, 1893 (MFP/PML, Letterpress book #3, 917).

"'Laid Mr. Drexel peacefully to rest . . . in will as regards business.'" JPM to W. H. Burns, July 19, 1893 (MFP/PML, Letterpress book #3, 933–34).

"'You must not allow yourself feel discouraged . . .'" W. H. Burns to JPM, July 19, 1893 (MFP/PML, Letterpress book #3, 933–34).

"'I shall value it . . .'" JPM to Sarah Drexel Fell, September 2, 1893 (MFP/PML, Letterpress book #3, 961).

EPILOGUE

PAGE 172

". . . 'He does not care to assume . . .'" *New York Times*, October 21, 1893.

PAGE 173

"... 'a man whose character and temper ...'" *Public Ledger*, 1917, undated (DFS, vol. 3, DUM).

".... 'seemed a man without hobbies ...'" AJD obituary, *Philadelphia Inquirer*, May 20, 1935 (DFS, vol. 5, DUM).

"He became an expert mechanic ..." GWC obituary, *Philadelphia Record*, September 10, 1944 (DFS, vol. 8, DUM).

PAGE 174

"... 'But what I remember is extreme courtesy ...'" Author's interview with Frances Train, 1991. See also Rottenberg, "The Drexel Century," 288.

"... 'No, we will not leave' ..." *Dallas Morning News*, April 26, 1991, G1.

"... 'she should be regarded as a benefactress ...'" Baldwin, *Saint Katharine Drexel*, 185.

PAGE 175

"... although no one named Drexel remained among its partners." Carosso, "The House of Drexel," 26. Also see JPM, Jr., "Reminiscences."

"Archibald A. McLeod survived his forced departure from the Reading ..." Barron, *More They Told Barron*, 126.

"... 'and I think that had Drexel lived I should have gone back ...'" Barron, *More They Told Barron*, 127.

"... Morgan was approached in 1895 and asked to devise his own plan to reorganize the Reading." Carosso, *The Morgans*, 380.

PAGE 176

"'... He missed Drexel every day of his life after that.'" Childs obituary, *New York Press*, February 4, 1894.

"Although George Childs Drexel sold the *Ledger* ... survived until 1942." Emery and Smith, *The Press and America*, 527–28.

PAGE 177

"... to talk and peruse his pictures and memorabilia." Oberholtzer, *Jay Cooke*, vol. 1: 544–47.

"He died in 1914 at the age of eighty-three." *New York Times*, February 16, 1914; *National Cyclopaedia of American Biography* 19: 262; Carosso, *The Morgans*, 442.

"... until his death in a polo accident in 1926." Keyes, *Bound Chronological Record of J. P. Morgan & Co., etc.*, 1939 (MFP/PML).

"His published essays ... he was no mere dilettante." Edward Biddle's writings included "Early American Portrait Painters Including Local Annals Connected with a Number of Them"; Biddle and Mantle Fielding, *Life and Works of Thomas Sully*; and Charles Henry Hart and Biddle, *Memoirs of the Life of Jean Antoine Houdon, the Sculptor of Voltaire and of Washington*.

". . . having outlived his first wife, Emilie Drexel, by half a century." Cooke and Cooke, *The Philadelphia Biddles*, 401; also see *New York Times*, February 25, 1933.

PAGE 179

". . . to bolster confidence among the French that American help was on the way." Liebling, *Liebling Abroad*, 85.

". . . 'drives her to address inequities.'" Author's interview with John R. Drexel IV, 1991.

PAGE 180

"The house financed the expansion and integration of some of the country's great utilities systems . . . sports arenas, Franklin Field and the Palestra." Hopkinson, *Drexel & Co.*, 25.

PAGE 181

". . . demolished the Drexel home to make way for his own new mansion." Fisher, "The Anthony Joseph Drexel House," 4; also Silver, "The Anthony J. Drexel Mansion," 3.

PAGE 182

". . . survive today as the fraternity houses of Alpha Tau Omega and Sigma Chi respectively." Author's interview with architectural historian George E. Thomas, March 15, 2000.

Bibliography

*indicates works that were especially useful

PRIMARY COLLECTIONS

"There is no significant collection of Drexel records," the late Vincent P. Carosso remarked in the notes to his 1987 classic, *The Morgans*. After 23 years of searching, I am happy to report the existence of, if not significant Drexel records, then at least far more abundant records than Professor Carosso and other scholars might have imagined. These are scattered in many locations, public and private, but are principally concentrated in six venues—four in the Philadelphia area and one each in New York and London.

⁕ The Pierpont Morgan Library, New York (PML) holds several ledgers and boxes dealing with the business of Drexel, Morgan & Co. and its successor, J. P. Morgan & Co., from 1871 to 1914. These include Anthony J. Drexel's original 1871 proposal to J. P. Morgan (scribbled on an envelope), AJD's letters to Morgan that spring, and three volumes of Morgan's 1873–93 correspondence, which include a few letters to and from AJD and many more letters referring to AJD.

⁕ The Guildhall Library, London (GL) is the current repository for the nineteenth-century papers of George Peabody & Co. and its successor firms J. S. Morgan & Co., Morgan, Grenfell & Co., and Deutsche Morgan Grenfell. Its holdings include four letters from AJD to Junius Morgan in 1871 proposing the alliance with Morgan's son and voluminous copies of J. S. Morgan's correspondence and cables, many of them to, from, and about Anthony Drexel or Drexel & Co.

⁕ The archives of the Sisters of the Blessed Sacrament, Cornwells Heights, Pennsylvania (SBS) contain Drexel family news clippings and memorabilia, including more than fifty letters from AJD to his nieces from 1885 on—virtually the only personal AJD correspondence I have found.

⁕ The archives of Hagerty Library, Drexel University, Philadelphia (HL) hold four boxes of unsorted Drexel family papers, correspondence, and memorabilia, including two letters written by AJD on the last two days of his life; also four boxes of George W. Childs papers and scrapbooks, many of them related to the Drexel family or Drexel & Co.

⁕ At the Drexel University Museum, Philadelphia (DUM) the storage room houses eleven Drexel family scrapbooks maintained by the Drexel Family Office from AJD's death in 1893 to the late twentieth century; these contain virtually every published reference to any Drexel matter throughout that period. One drawer of a file cabinet holds other Drexel family materials, including descriptions of Francis M. Drexel's paintings and two student term papers dealing with AJD's mansion.

⤙ The money management firm 1838 Investment Advisors, Radnor, Pennsylvania (named for the year Francis Drexel opened his Philadelphia currency exchange) is the last surviving vestige of Drexel Burnham Lambert. It has a small but valuable cache of old Drexel & Co. papers and news clips, as well as pictures, paintings, and furniture (including AJD's roll-top desk, still in use).

Other helpful archival sources:

Berks County Historical Society, Reading, Pennsylvania. Has research done on F. M. Drexel & family.

Chicago Historical Society, Chicago. Some records and clips concerning F. M. Drexel's early Chicago dealings and the origins of Drexel Boulevard there.

Firestone Library, Princeton University, Princeton, New Jersey. Special collections division has G. W. Childs materials, including letters referring to AJD.

Genealogical Society of Pennsylvania, Philadelphia, Geber G. Gearhart Collection.

German Society Library, Philadelphia.

Hagley Library, Wilmington, Delaware. Large collection of papers of Pennsylvania Railroad, Reading Railroad; also early Dun & Co. credit reports on microfilm. (The originals of the Dun & Co. reports are at Harvard University.)

Historical Society of Pennsylvania, Philadelphia (HSP). Biddle and Rosét family papers, as well as a very few AJD items.

Luddington Library, Bryn Mawr, Pennsylvania. Detailed files on Main Line mansions.

J. P. Morgan & Co., New York (JPM/NY). Some papers and pictures relating to the Drexels, including unpublished typescript reminiscences of J. P. Morgan, Jr.

J. P. Morgan & Co., Paris (JPM/Paris). Some records and memorabilia of the early Drexel Morgan & Co.

Philadelphia Archdiocesan Historical Research Center, St. Charles Borromeo Seminary, Wynnewood, Pennsylvania. Holdings include baptismal records.

Philadelphia Club Library, Philadelphia.

Philadelphia Historical Commission, Philadelphia. Its files contain deeds, correspondence, records, and photos of the original Drexel & Co. office (now 48 South Third St.) and the second office at 34 South Third St.

Railroad Museum of Pennsylvania, Strasburg, Pennsylvania.

Union League Library, Philadelphia.

DREXELS AND MORGANS

Allen, Frederick Lewis. *The Great Pierpont Morgan*. New York: Harper, 1949.

"Anthony J. Drexel: Services in Memory of the Great Philanthropist." *Public Ledger*, January 22, 1894, 1.

Baldwin, Lou. *A Call to Sanctity*. Philadelphia: Catholic Standard & Times, 1988. Originally published as supplement to *Catholic Standard & Times*, February 19, 1987.

*Baldwin, Lou. *Saint Katharine Drexel: Apostle to the Oppressed*. Philadelphia: Catholic Standard & Times, 2000.

Biddle, Cordelia. *Beneath the Wind*. New York: Simon and Schuster, 1993.

Biddle, Cordelia Drexel (later Robertson). *My Philadelphia Father*. New York: Doubleday, 1955.

Biddle, Edward. "Early American Portrait Painters Including Local Annals Connected with a Number of Them." *Philadelphia Numismatic and Antiquarian Society Proceedings* 28 (1893): 69–87.

Biddle, Edward and Mantle Fielding. *Life and Works of Thomas Sully (1783–1872)*. Philadelphia: n.p., 1921.

Biddle, George. *An American Artist's Story*. Boston: Little Brown, 1939.

Biddle, Nicholas. *Personal Memoirs*. Philadelphia: Privately printed, 1975.

Burk, Kathleen. *Morgan Grenfell, 1838–1988: The Biography of a Merchant Bank*. New York: Oxford University Press, 1989.

Burton, Katherine. *The Golden Door*. New York: P.J. Kenedy, 1957.

Carosso, Vincent P. "The House of Drexel." Address to Philadelphia Cultural Consortium, April 1980. Manuscript at EIA.

*Carosso, Vincent P. *The Morgans: Private International Bankers, 1854–1913*. Cambridge, Mass.: Harvard University Press, 1987.

Chernow, Ron. *The House of Morgan*. New York: Atlantic Monthly Press, 1990.

Childs, George W. "Tribute to Anthony J. Drexel." *Harper's Weekly*, July 15, 1893.

Dolores, Sister M. (Marie Elizabeth Letterhouse). *The Francis A. Drexel Family*. Cornwells Heights, Pa.: Sisters of the Blessed Sacrament, 1939.

*Drexel, Francis M. *Journal from Guayaquil*. Philadelphia: Privately printed, 1914.

*Drexel, Francis M. *The Peregrinations of An Artist*. Introduction by David A. Drexel. Southern Pines, N.C.: Privately printed, 1976.

Drexel & Co. *A New Home for an Old House*. Philadelphia: Privately printed, 1927.

Duffy, Sister Consuela. *Katharine Drexel: A Biography*. Cornwells Heights, Pa.: Sisters of the Blessed Sacrament, 1966.

Fisher, Nicole. "The Anthony Joseph Drexel House." Graduate thesis, December 10, 1991. DUM.

"Girard's Talk of the Day." *Philadelphia Inquirer*, February 17, 1940.

Hart, Charles Henry and Edward Biddle. *Memoirs of the Life of Jean Antoine Houdon, the Sculptor of Voltaire and of Washington*. Philadelphia: For the Authors, 1911.

Hopkinson, Edward Jr. *Drexel & Co.: Over a Century of History*. New York: Privately printed, 1952.

Hoyt, Edwin P., Jr. *The House of Morgan*. New York: Dodd, Mead, 1966.

Jackson, Stanley. *J. P. Morgan*. New York: Stein and Day, 1983.

Knutson, Lawrence. "Statue Honors Drexel." *Chicago Tribune*, August 5, 1965. DFS/DUM.

Konkle, Burton Alva. "Francis Martin Drexel." *Girard Letter* (Girard Trust Co.) 14, 1 (December 1933): 1.

Lehr, Elizabeth Drexel. *King Lehr and the Gilded Age*. Philadelphia: Lippincott, 1935.

Loderhose, H. O. "History of Morgan, Harjes & Cie. (now Morgan & Cie.), 1872–1932." Typescript, April 1933. At Morgan & Cie., Paris.

Morgan, J. P., Jr. "Reminiscences." Typescript. JPM/NY.

"Mr. Drexel's Friends and Foes." Editorial. *Philadelphia Press*, July 5, 1893. DFS/DUM, vol. 1: 31.

"Norland" (possible pseudonym). "Anthony J. Drexel, the Model Banker and Citizen." *New York Press*, October 30, 1873.

*Penrose, Boies. "Early Life of F. M. Drexel." *Pennsylvania Magazine of History and Biography* 60 (October 1936): 329–57.

"Personal Recollections of Francis M. Drexel" (by "B.S.R."). *Public Ledger*, 1893(?).

"Profile of A. J. Drexel, Jr." *Vanity Fair*, May 1910.

Rottenberg, Dan. "The Drexel Century." *Town and Country* (November 1991): 225–27; 288–90.

Rottenberg, Dan. "Family Tithes." *American Benefactor* (Winter 1998): 64–69.

Satterlee, Herbert L. *J. Pierpont Morgan: An Intimate Portrait 1837–1913*. New York: Macmillan, 1939.

Silver, Joshua. "The Anthony J. Drexel Mansion." Thesis, University of Pennsylvania, 1988–89. Drexel family file, DUM.

Sinclair, Andrew. *Corsair: The Life of J. Pierpont Morgan*. Boston: Little, Brown, 1981.

Staub, Geraldine et al. "Francis Martin Drexel: An Artist Turned Banker." Introduction to Drexel University Museum catalogue, 1976.

*Strouse, Jean. *Morgan: American Financier*. New York: Random House, 1999.

Wright, D. W. "Another Philadelphia Story: The Drexel-Morgan Alliance." Manuscript. JPM/NY and EIA.

Philadelphia Background

Baltzell, E. Digby. *Philadelphia Gentlemen: The Making of a National Upper Class*. 1958; reprint Philadelphia: University of Pennsylvania Press, 1979.

"Big Banker Drexel." *New York World*, April 19, 1885.

Biographical Encyclopedia of Pennsylvania of the Nineteenth Century. Philadelphia: Galaxy Publishing Co., 1874.

Burt, Maxwell Struthers. *Philadelphia: Holy Experiment*. New York: Doubleday, 1945.

*Burt, Nathaniel. *The Perennial Philadelphians*. 1963; reprint Philadelphia: University of Pennsylvania Press, 2000.

Butler, William and William Strode, eds. *Drexel University: A Century of Growth and Challenge*. Louisville, Ky.: Harmony House, 1992.

The Church of the Saviour. 100th anniversary pamphlet. November 1950.

Colonial and Revolutionary Families of Pennsylvania: Genealogical and Personal Memoirs. New York: Lewis Historical Publishing, 1930–.

Connelly, James F., ed. *The History of the Archdiocese of Philadelphia.* Philadelphia: Archdiocese of Philadelphia, 1976.

Fee, Edward M. *The Origin and Growth of Vocational Education in Philadelphia to 1917.* Philadelphia: Westbrook Publishing Co., 1938.

Fisher, Sidney George. *The Diary of Sidney George Fisher, 1834–1871.* Ed. Nicholas B. Wainwright. Philadelphia: Historical Society of Pennsylvania, 1967.

Gallman, J. Matthew. *Mastering Wartime: A Social History of Philadelphia During the Civil War.* 1990; reprint Philadelphia: University of Pennsylvania Press, 2000.

Garvan, Beatrice B. *Federal Philadelphia: Athens of the Western World.* Philadelphia: Philadelphia Museum of Art, 1987.

Genealogies of Pennsylvania Families: From the Pennsylvania Magazine of History and Biography. Baltimore: Genealogical Publishing Co., 1981.

Guinther, John. *Philadelphia: A Dream for the Keeping.* Tulsa, Okla.: Continental Heritage Press, 1982.

Hotchkin, Rev. S. F. *Rural Pennsylvania in the Vicinity of Philadelphia.* Philadelphia: George W. Jacobs, 1897.

Jackson, Joseph. *Encyclopedia of Philadelphia.* Harrisburg, Pa.: National Historical Association, 1931.

Jordan, John W., ed. *Colonial and Revolutionary Families of Pennsylvania.* 1911; reprint Baltimore: Genealogical Publishing Co., 1978.

Jordan, John W., ed. *Encyclopedia of Pennsylvania Biography.* New York: Lewis Historical Publishing Co., 1914–.

Light, Dale B. *Rome and the New Republic: Conflict and Community in Philadelphia Catholicism Between the Revolution and the Civil War.* Notre Dame, Ind.: University of Notre Dame Press, 1996.

Loetscher, Lefferts A. "Presbyterianism and Revivals in Philadelphia Since 1875." *Pennsylvania Magazine of History and Biography* 68 (January 1944): 54–92.

Lukacs, John. *Philadelphia: Patricians and Philistines.* New York: Farrar, Straus and Giroux, 1981.

MacKay, Winnifred K. "Philadelphia During the Civil War." *Pennsylvania Magazine of History and Biography* 70 (January 1946): 3–51.

Mactier, William L. *The Musical Fund Society of Philadelphia.* Philadelphia: Privately printed, 1910.

Mahony, Daniel H. *Historical Sketches of the Catholic Churches and Institutions of Philadelphia.* Philadelphia: Privately printed, 1895. HSP

McDonald, Edward D. and Edward M. Hinton. *Drexel Institute of Technology: A Memorial History, 1891–1941.* Camden, N.J.: Haddon Craftsmen, 1942.

McMichael, Clayton, ed. *Philadelphia and Popular Philadelphians.* Philadelphia: The North American, 1891. DFN/HL.

Meyerson, Martin and Dilys Pegler Winegrad. *Gladly Learn and Gladly Teach: Franklin and His Heirs at the University of Pennsylvania, 1740–1976*. Philadelphia: University of Pennsylvania Press, 1978.

Montgomery, Thomas L., ed. *Encyclopedia of Pennsylvania Biography*. New York: Lewis Historical Publishing Co., 1923, 1937, 1945.

National Cyclopaedia of American Biography. New York, J. T. White, 1926–67.

Oberholtzer, Ellis Paxson. *Philadelphia: A History of the City and Its People*. Philadelphia: J. S. Clarke, 1912.

A Retrospective of Holy Trinity Parish, 125th Anniversary, 1789–1914. Philadelphia: F. Mc-Manus, 1914.

Scharf, J. Thomas and Thompson Westcott. *History of Philadelphia, 1609–1884*. 3 vols. Philadelphia: L.H. Everts, 1884.

Seidensticker, Oswald. *Erster Teil der Geschichte der Deutschen Gesellschaft von Pennsylvanien von der Gruendung im Jahre 1764 bis zur Jubelfeier der Republik 1876*. Philadelphia: German Society of Pennsylvania, 1917.

Stevenson, George. "Looking Back 50 Years on Financial Philadelphia." *Public Ledger*, February 1913. SBS.

Toll, Jean Barth and Mildred S. Gillam. *Invisible Philadelphia: Community Through Voluntary Organizations*. Philadelphia: Atwater Kent Museum, 1995.

Tourscher, Francis E. *The Hogan Schism and Trustee Troubles in St. Mary's Church, Philadelphia, 1820–1829*. Philadelphia: Peter Reilly Co., 1930.

Townsend, John W. *The Old "Main Line"*. Philadelphia: Privately printed, 1922.

Wainwright, Nicholas B. *History of the Philadelphia Electric Co.* Philadelphia: Philadelphia Electric Co., 1961.

Ward, Townsend. "The Germantown Road and Its Associations." *Pennsylvania Magazine of History and Biography* 6 (1882): 1–20.

Weigley, Russell, ed. *Philadelphia: A 300-Year History*. New York: Norton, 1982.

Banking and Finance

Carosso, Vincent P. *Investment Banking in America: A History*. Cambridge, Mass.: Harvard University Press, 1970.

Carosso, Vincent P. *More Than a Century of Investment Banking: The Kidder Peabody & Co. Story*. New York: McGraw-Hill, 1979.

Clews, Henry. *Fifty Years in Wall Street*. New York: Irving, 1908.

Edwards, George W. *The Evolution of Finance Capitalism*. London: Green and Co., 1938.

Ferguson, Niall. *The House of Rothschild: Money's Prophets, 1798–1848*. New York: Viking, 1998.

Fischer, David H. *The Great Wave*. New York: Oxford University Press, 1996.

Geisst, Charles R. *Wall Street: A History*. New York: Oxford University Press, 1997.

Gordon, John Steele. *The Great Game: The Emergence of Wall Street as a World Power, 1653–2000*. New York: Scribner, 1999.

Govan, Thomas P. *Nicholas Biddle: Nationalist and Public Banker, 1786–1844*. Chicago: University of Chicago Press, 1959.

Hidy, Ralph W. *The House of Baring in American Trade and Finance, 1763–1861*. Cambridge, Mass.: Harvard University Press, 1947.

Katz, Irving. "Investment Bankers in American Government and Politics." Dissertation, New York University, 1964.

Kindleberger, Charles P. "Origins of U.S. Direct Investment in France." *Business History Review* 48 (Autumn 1974): 385–86.

Mayer, Martin. *The Bankers*. New York: Weybright and Talley, 1974.

Perkins, Edwin J. *Financing Anglo-American Trade: The House of Brown, 1800–1880*. Cambridge, Mass.: Harvard University Press, 1975.

Redlich, Fritz. *The Molding of American Banking: Men and Ideas*. 2 vols. New York: Hafner, 1947, 1951.

Sobel, Robert. *Panic on Wall Street*. New York: Macmillan, 1968.

Sylla, Richard. "Forgotten Men of Money: Private Bankers in Early United States History." *Journal of Economic History* 36 (March 1976): 173–88.

Temin, Peter. *The Jacksonian Economy*. New York: W.W. Norton, 1969.

Wainwright, Nicholas B. *The Philadelphia National Bank, 1803–1953*. Philadelphia: Wm. F. Fell, 1953.

Wechsberg, Joseph. *The Merchant Bankers*. New York: Pocket Books, 1968.

Railroad Histories

Burgess, G. H. and Miles Kennedy. *Centennial History of the Pennsylvania Railroad Co., 1846–1946*. Philadelphia: Pennsylvania R.R. Co., 1949.

"History of the Reading System." Hagley Museum and Library summary.

Holton, James L. *The Reading Railroad: History of a Coal Age Empire*. Laury's Station, Pa.: Carrigues House, 1989.

Sipes, William B. *The Pennsylvania Railroad*. Philadelphia: The Passenger Dept., 1875.

Ward, James. *J. Edgar Thompson: Master of the Pennsylvania*. Westport, Conn.: Greenwood Press, 1980.

Other Works

Barron, C. W. *More They Told Barron*. New York: Harper & Brothers, 1931.

Barron, C. W. *They Told Barron: Notes of the Late Clarence W. Barron*. New York: Harper & Brothers, 1930.

Birmingham, Stephen. *Our Crowd: The Great Jewish Families of New York*. New York: Harper and Row, 1967.

Bradley, E. Sculley. *Henry Charles Lea*. Philadelphia: University of Pennsylvania Press, 1931.

Calkin, Homer. "The *Public Ledger*: An Independent Newspaper." *Pennsylvania Magazine of History and Biography* 64 (January 1940): 43–55.

Childs, George W. *Recollections*. Philadelphia: Lippincott, 1890.

"Commotion Among the Brokers, or the Shavers Shaving." *Public Ledger*, February 27, 1841, 2, col. 3.

Cooke, Jacob Ernest and Jean Gordon Cooke. "The Philadelphia Biddles." Manuscript.

Cooke, Jay. *Jay Cooke's Memoir*. Manuscript, 1895. Baker Library, Harvard University.

Crafts, Wilbur F. *Successful Men of To-Day: And What They Say of Success*. New York: Arno Press, 1883.

Davis, John H. *The Bouviers*. London: Farrar, Straus & Giroux, 1969.

Easton, Thomas. "Deflationary Winners." *Forbes*, November 16, 1998.

Emery, Edwin and Henry L. Smith. *The Press and America*. Englewood Cliffs, N.J.: Prentice-Hall, 1954.

Grant, Ulysses S. *Personal Memoirs*. Cleveland: World Publishing Co., 1952.

Gras, N. S. B. and Henrietta M. Larsen. *Case Book in American Business History*. New York: F.S. Crofts & Co., 1939.

Groner, Alex. *The American Heritage History of American Business & Industry*. New York: American Heritage, 1972.

Guedalla, Philip. *The Hundred Years*. London: Hodder and Stoughton, 1936.

"Heritage" (quoting reminiscence of J. Peterson Ryder). *Drexel University News*, Summer 1978, 8.

Herold, J. Christopher. *The Age of Napoleon*. New York: American Heritage, 1963.

Holbrook, Stewart. *The Age of the Moguls*. New York: Doubleday, 1954.

Josephson, Matthew. *The Robber Barons*. New York: Harcourt, Brace, 1934.

*Larson, Henrietta M. *Jay Cooke, Private Banker*. Cambridge, Mass.: Harvard University Press, 1936.

*Larson, Henrietta M. "Jay Cooke's Early Work in Transportation, *Pennsylvania Magazine of History and Biography* 59 (October 1935): 362–73.

Liebling, A. J. *Liebling Abroad*. New York: Playboy Press, 1981.

Logan, Sheridan A. *George F. Baker and His Bank, 1840–1955: A Double Biography*. St. Joseph, Mo.: Privately printed, 1981.

McFeely, William S. *Grant: A Biography*. New York: W.W. Norton, 1981.

McPherson, James. "The Unheroic Hero," *New York Review of Books*, February 4, 1999.

Myers, Gustavus. *History of the Great American Fortunes*. New York: Modern Library, 1907, 1936.

*Oberholtzer, Ellis Paxson. *Jay Cooke, Financier of the Civil War*. Philadelphia: George W. Jacobs, 1907.

Rosengarten, J. G. *French Colonists and Exiles to the United States*. Philadelphia: Lippincott, 1907.

Sargent, Charles Sprague and Emma Worcester Sargent. *Epes Sargent of Gloucester and His Descendants.* Boston: Houghton Mifflin, 1923.

Shinn, Earl. *Art Treasures of America, Being the Choicest Works of Art in the Public and Private Collections of North America.* 3 vols. Philadelphia: G. Barrie & Co., 1879.

Spooner, Walter W. *Historic Families of America* . New York: Historic Families Publishing Association, 1907(?).

Stern, Madeleine B. "George W. Childs: Poor Richard the Second." *Publishers Weekly* 150, 25 (December 21, 1946): 3332–40.

Strouse, Jean. "The Brilliant Bailout." *New Yorker*, November 23, 1998.

Vassar, Matthew. *The Autobiography and Letters of Matthew Vassar.* Ed. Elizabeth Hazelton Haight. New York: Oxford University Press, 1916.

Wecter, Dixon. *The Saga of American Society.* New York: Scribner, 1927.

Young, John Russell. *Around the World with General Grant.* New York: American News Co., 1879.

Acknowledgments

More than twenty years have passed since I set out to reconstruct the life of Anthony J. Drexel. Over that period a great many people contributed their time, expertise and moral support toward my efforts. It is a measure of how much time has passed that some of these people have died in the interim and others have retired, including my original agent on this project, Julie Fallowfield. To all who have participated in this project, my appreciation is long overdue.

For much of those years my research took a back seat to my need to earn a living. In the 1990s two magazine assignments concerning the Drexel family substantially increased the time I was able to devote to the project. My thanks, then, to my editors—Frank Zachary at *Town & Country* and Nelson Aldrich and Larkin Warren at *The American Benefactor*—for tuning in to my passion.

Most significantly, this project was permanently rescued from the back burner by the interest of Constantine Papadakis, president of Drexel University. In 1997, shortly after he arrived at that school, Papadakis was heard to wonder why no one had ever written a biography of Anthony Drexel. In short order I was introduced to him and he arranged for a research grant that enabled me, for the first time, to make the life of Anthony Drexel my first priority. The grant came with no strings attached, other than that I produce a finished book. Without that financial boost the book would have taken far longer to complete than it did.

If I was the father of this baby, a small circle of interested parties functioned as its godparents. Philip Terranova and Karen Biddle of Drexel University (she the wife of a Drexel descendant); Drexel family members Mae Cadwalader Hollenback and John R. (Nick) Drexel IV; and D. W. Wright, corporate historian of J. P. Morgan & Co., all responded over the years as if they had a vested interest in my subject, which of course they did. Jean Strouse's fifteen years of research on her biography of Pierpont Morgan occurred concurrently with mine, and during that period she often shared her findings and insights with me by mail, email, and in person. Charles Morscheck, an art history professor at Drexel University, alerted me to the presence of many boxes of uncatalogued material in various campus storage rooms and unstintingly helped me sift through and analyze them. Other Drexel University faculty members who shared valuable insights include Richard Hykes, Robert C. Landsiedel, Ivy Strickler, and Patrice Weiglein.

{ 243 }

I'm especially grateful to Professor Irving Katz of Indiana University, D.W. Wright of J. P. Morgan & Co., and Lou Baldwin, biographer of Saint Katharine Drexel, all of whom read my manuscript and provided valuable critiques.

I'm grateful to similarly selfless scholars and experts elsewhere who permitted me to tap their knowledge in their specialized fields of expertise: Vincent Carosso (concerning J. P. Morgan), Joseph Kern (administrator of the Drexel family office), F. J. Dallett (old Philadelphia families), E. Digby Baltzell and Anne Biddle Mikhalapov (Philadelphia's WASP upper classes), William Brady (the Pennsylvania Railroad), H. Gates Lloyd, 3rd (Drexel & Co.), John J. W. F. McFadden (Anthony Drexel's partner George Thomas), Penny Batcheler, Charles Peterson, and George Thomas (Philadelphia's architectural history), Jefferson Moak of the Philadelphia City Archives (early street locations), and Lee Richards (Philadelphia's Episcopal history).

Almost without exception, descendants of Anthony Drexel whom I approached in the United States, Britain, and France were gracious, generous, and genuinely interested in my project. My deep thanks, then, to Anthony J. Drexel Biddle III, Noreen and John R. Drexel III, Jane Drexel Porteus, Joan and Gouverneur Cadwalader, Jr., Gouverneur Cadwalader III, Paul Ingersoll, Mary Ponsonby, Countess of Bessborough, Christopher Finch-Hatton, Earl of Winchilsea and Nottingham, Michael and Tania Parker, Angier Biddle Duke, Anthony Drexel Duke, Anthony Drexel Duke, Jr., Livingston Biddle, Jr., Lady Daphne Straight, Amanda Straight, Robin Finch-Hatton, Francis Gowen, Anthony Baker, James Paul, David Drexel, Antelo Devereaux, General Nicholas Biddle, Frances and John Train, George F. Baker, IV, Minnie Cassatt Hickman, A. J. Drexel Paul, Jr., Wendy Paul, Anne and Reeve Bright, Katherine Beaumont, and Caspar and Sue Tiarks. The latter two were especially hospitable, inviting me to spend a night at their farm in the English Cotswolds.

For the same reason, my similar thanks to these descendants of Anthony Drexel's brother, Joseph Wilhelm Drexel: Frances Haythe, Ulrica (Patsy) Randolph, Josephine Parker, Charles Van Pelt, Abby Van Pelt Griscom, and Katharine and Martin Beaver.

Librarians and archivists at virtually every institution I visited went out of their way to be helpful. My thanks, then, to Robert Parks, Christine Nelson, Inge DuPont, Sylvie Merian, and Vanessa Pintado at the Pierpont Morgan Library in New York; to Sister Maria McCall, Sister Margaret O'Rourke, Sister Mary Hottenroth, Sister Roselle, and Stephanie Morris at the archives of the Sisters of the Blessed Sacrament in Cornwells Heights, Pennsylvania; to Stephen Freeth, keeper of manuscripts, and Martin Devereux, Elizabeth Gow, Sharon Tuff, and

Charlie Turpie at the Guildhall Library in London; to Richard Tyler and Liz Harvey at the Philadelphia Historical Commission; to Richard Boardman, the map specialist at the Free Library of Philadelphia; to Marge McNinch and Katie Newell at the Hagley Museum and Library in Wilmington, Delaware; to Linda Stanley, Patricia Cossard, and Mariah Hall at the Historical Society of Pennsylvania in Philadelphia; and to Eugene R. Gaddis, Archivist of the Wadsworth Atheneum in Hartford, Connecticut.

Some staff members of historical institutions went out of their way to perform research tasks for me when I could not get to their facilities in person. My special thanks to Kurt Bell, librarian/archivist of the Railroad Museum of Pennsylvania in Stroudsburg; Christine Friend of the Philadelphia Archdiocesan Historical Research Center; and Julie Thomas, research specialist at the Chicago Historical Society.

Several businesses also provided access to their valuable historical holdings. For granting me access I am grateful to W. Thacher Brown and Jackie Scott at 1838 Investment Advisors in Radnor, Pennsylvania and Richard Elliston and Anthony Whitter at Deutsche Morgan Grenfell Bank in London. John Leach, superintendent of Woodlands Cemetery in Philadelphia, provided me with access to the Drexel family vault. Minni Santilli, whose father owns the original Drexel & Co. office on Third Street in Philadelphia, provided useful insights into the evolution of that building.

Finally, this book would not have come to pass without the skill and enthusiasm of Robert Lockhart, Alison Anderson, and Bruce Franklin of the University of Pennsylvania Press, who assiduously shepherded it through to publication. And for the essential service of finding such a well suited-publisher I am grateful to my agent, Louise Quayle of the Ellen Levine Literary Agency in New York.

Index

Where families and companies carry the same name, family members are listed first.

Abell, Arunah S., 74; founder of *Public Ledger*, 73

Academy of Music, 50, 142, 173

Academy of Natural Sciences, 20

Aetna Fire Insurance Company, 91

Allez, Mary Paul Munn, 178–79

Allibone, S. Austin, 54

Altstatten, Switzerland, 12

American Philosophical Society, 20

American Publishers' Circular and Literary Gazette, 73

Amnesty International, 179

Analectic, 20

Anderson, Major Robert, 59

"Another Philadelphia Story" (Wright), xii

Athenaeum, 20

antitrust laws, 82

Appenzell, Switzerland, 12

Arctic Explorations (Kane), 54

Astor family, 177

"Awful Riots," 42, 43, 200

Baltimore and Ohio Railroad, 40, 128. *See also* railroads

Baltzell, E. Digby, 177

Bank of Commerce, run on, 56

Bank of North America, 20

Bank of the United States, 27, 28, 40, 105; Second, 20, 27–29, 33, 39, 40

banks, banking, 27, 28, 29, 56, 68, 81; bills of exchange, 39; correspondents, 48; and Federal Reserve, 29, 68, 175, 176; impact of California Gold Rush, 44, 55; importance of private banking partnerships, 45; and issuing currency, 28; Panic of 1857, 56; post-Civil War expansion of, 79–80; private, 40, 41, 42, 45, 48; and railroad financing, 47–48, 127, 133; secondary market for bank notes, 28–29, 40; state-chartered, 28, 40–41, 200

Baring Brothers, 45, 48, 49, 51, 98, 108; rejects Drexel & Co. as correspondent, 49, 50, 51; and U.S. railroads, 128

Barker, Abraham, 49

Bavaria, 9, 10, 16, 18

Bazeley, Charles, 43

Beebe, James M., 91

Belmont, August, 80, 108, 216; and U.S. Treasury business, 114

Bennett, James Gordon, 73

Bicking family, 34–35

Biddle, Anthony J. Drexel (grandson of AJD), 125, 126, 178, 186; and U.S. Marine Corps, 178

Biddle, Anthony J. Drexel, Jr., 172

Biddle, Craig (grandson of AJD), 125

Biddle, Edward, 104, 105, 106, 123, 141, 177, 185, 186; death of, 177; lack of interest in business, 105, 123, 124; leaves Drexel & Co., 124, 220; relationship with AJD, 123, 124, 125–26; writings of, 177

Biddle, Emilie Taylor Drexel (daughter of AJD), 46, 52, 97, 104, 105, 123, 124, 141, 185, 186; death of, 125, 141; and music, 125, 142; trust funds for sons, 125, 177

Biddle, Livingston (grandson of AJD), 125, 126

Biddle, Livingston, Jr., 179

Biddle, Nicholas, 20, 28, 33, 105, 182; helps stabilize U.S. banking system, 27

Biermann, Peter, 14, 16
bills of exchange, 39
Blaine, James G., 82
Blankenburg, Rudolph, 146
Board of Brokers, Philadelphia, 35
Boker, George, 35
Boker, Julia Riggs, 35
Bolivar, Simon, 196; FMD paints, 23
Bonaparte, Napoleon, 16, 17; invasion of
    Austria, 10; FMD sees, 16
bonds: railroad, 40, 47, 134; Drexel, Mor-
    gan joins syndicate to sell, 109; junk,
    180; Reading Railroad and, 163, 164;
    U.S. Treasury, 61, 108, 113
Bories family, 21, 43
Boston & Maine Railroad, 163. See also
    railroads
Boutwell, George S., 84, 108, 109
Bouvier family, 177
Bouvier, Emma. See Drexel, Emma Bouvier
Bouvier, John, 186, 205
Bouvier, Michel, 34, 53, 198, 205–6
Bowdoin, George S., 131, 186
Brodhead (Broadhead), Antoinette (or
    Elizabeth) Rozet, 190
Brooks, Mr., 37–38
Brown family, 45, 177
Brown, John, 60
Brown, Josephine, 179
Brown, Matilda, 45
Brown Brothers & Co., 71, 104; and Read-
    ing Terminal, 162
Brown, Shipley & Co., 71, 85, 86
Bryn Mawr College, 154
Buchey, Madame Athenaide, 26, 196
Buck, Nicholas, 22
Bull Run, Battle of, 66, 92
Bullitt family, 43
Bullitt, John C.: Philadelphia charter, 146;
    and Reading Railroad reorganization,
    132

Bullitt, Logan, 124
Burk, Addison, 154
Burns, Walter H. (son-in-law of JSM),
    169, 171, 186; partner of JSM, 122, 186;
    and third Reading failure, 163–64, 167,
    168, 228
Burt, Nathaniel, xv

Cadwalader family, 177
Cairo and Vincennes Railroad, 113, 129.
    See also railroads
California: Drexel, Sather & Church in,
    46; gold rush, 44, 46, 47; office closed,
    55, 202, 206
Cameron, James D., 169–70
Carlsbad, 141; AJD's annual trip to, 115,
    143–44, 160, 167, 168
Carnegie, Andrew, 159
Carosso, Vincent, xii
Cassatt family, 177
Cassidy, Mary, 140, 152
Cathedral of St. John the Divine, xii, 158
Catholic Church, 9, 11, 114; Drexel family
    philanthropy, 139, 151, 225; and Hookey
    family, 22; last rites for FMD, 68; and
    Roset family, 35; schools, 149, 151, 225;
    Hoganite rebellion, 42–44, 200; women
    in, 155, 157
Central High School, 150
Chandler, William E., 81
Chase, Salmon P., 61, 63, 65, 66, 67
Chase Manhattan Bank, 175
Chernow, Ron, xiv
Chicago, Drexel role in development of,
    203
Childs, Emma Bouvier Peterson, 186, 206
Childs, George William, xvi, 3, 4, 72, 73,
    81, 86, 106, 107, 113, 126, 153, 154, 157, 165,
    173, 186, 206, 216, 219; AJD names son
    after, 76, 173; co-executor of FAD's es-
    tate, 151; death of, 176; AJD insists on

portrait, 166; and Drexel patronage xii, xiii, 74–75, 77; emulates Benjamin Franklin, 53, 73; establishes Reform Club, 145; establishes suburban community, 142–43; eulogizes AJD, 170; friendship with AJD, 53, 54, 55; friendship with Grant, 69, 116, 117; and Jay Cooke & Co., 77, 82, 83, 176; on Katharine Drexel becoming a nun, 156; marries Emma Bouvier Peterson, 186; negotiates with Great Britain on Civil War claims, 108; ownership of *Public Ledger*, 37, 74, 210; partnership with R. E. Peterson, 54; philanthropy of, 153; purchases *American Publishers' Circular and Literary Gazette*, 73; purchases New York real estate for Drexel, 102–3; supports legislation preventing secret gold sales, 82

Childs & Peterson, 54

"Cholly Knickerbocker." *See* Paul, Maury H. B.

Church of the Saviour, 52, 151, 152, 205

Cisco, Mr., 66

Civil War, xiii, 3, 59, 63, 74; changes in American society and technology, 79; corruption during, 66–67; financing of, xii, 60, 61, 63–68, 71, 79, 107; Hall Carbine Affair, 92–93

Cleveland, Grover, 116, 169, 170

Commercial & Financial Chronicle, 101, 102, 129

Committee of One Hundred to Fight the Gas Trust, 146

Confederacy, 59, 60, 66–69; and postwar claims, 108

Conkling, Roscoe, 82, 84

Constant, Benjamin, 166

Convent della Madonna, 10, 12

Conwell, Henry, Bishop of Philadelphia, 42–43

Cooke, Francis, 62

Cooke, Henry D., 63, 66, 84

Cooke, Jay, xvi, 47, 61–67, 79, 80, 84, 112, 117, 132, 140, 159, 161, 162, 165, 186; appreciation of importance of press, 77; argues with Childs, 77, 176; controls Northern Pacific Railroad, 87, 107; failure, 110, 112, 113, 127, 134; final loan campaign of, 77; and financing Civil War, xii, 4, 62, 65, 66, 70, 71, 80, 107; forms syndicate with AJD, 80; friendship with Grant, 112, 116; letter of condolence to AJD, 160; opens London office, 80; opens Washington, D.C. office, 67; opposes legislation prohibiting secret gold sales, 82–83, 84; and Panic of 1873, 166; and Pennsylvania loan, 64, 65; and political patronage, 82; purchase of Treasury notes, 63, 64; recoups fortune through mining investments, 176; relationship with AJD, xii, xiii, 63, 65, 66, 70, 72; supported by *Public Ledger*, 74; syndicate to sell post-Civil War bonds, 108; and transportation securities, 84; weaknesses in organization, 81, 82

Cooper Union, 154

Cope, Caleb, 39

Corbin, Austin, 132, 162, 163

Coster, Charles H., 131, 167, 186

Crédit Mobilier, 107, 109

Critical Dictionary of English Literature (Allibone), 54

Curtis, Cyrus H. K., 176

currency, currency brokers, 13, 25, 27, 28, 38; and bills of exchange, 39; FMD becomes broker, 29; function of Bank of the United States, 27; and National Banking Act, 68; in Philadelphia, 35, 36; secondary market for bank notes, 28–29; Specie Circular, 28; trading in (money shaving), 27; uncurrent money, 38

Dabney, Charles H., 94–95, 186

Dabney, Morgan & Co., 94, 97, 99, 110

Dahlgren, Eva Drexel, 179

Damrosch, Walter, 142

Delaware & Hudson Canal Co., 128

Denniston, Wood & Co., 96

Depew, Chauncy, 159

Diepoldsau, Switzerland, 12

Dornbirn, Austria, 9, 10–12, 16–18, 67, 194, 195

Drew, Daniel, 81, 112

Drexel, Alice Gordon Troth, 173, 185, 187

Drexel, Anthony Joseph (AJD), xi, xii, xiv, xvii, 23, 26, 50, 53, 56, 61, 62, 81, 84, 133, 139, 157, 177, 185, 186; annual trips to Carlsbad, 115, 143–44, 160, 167, 168; birth of daughters, 52; business practices of, xiii, 70, 86, 121, 122–23, 134; and civic responsibility of banker, 56; and Committee of One Hundred, 146; construction of Reading Terminal, 162, 163; and Cooke failure, 112–13; death of, 170, 174; daughter marries Edward Biddle, 104–5; death of daughter Emilie, 125; death of son, 76; declines post as Secretary of Treasury, 104, 115; detests politics, 64, 116, 145; and Drexel Institute, xiii, 157–59; and Edward Biddle, 123, 124, 125; establishes suburban community, 142–43; and Fairmount Park Art Commission, 145; and Gowen, 130–31, 162; first meeting with Morgan, 1, 2, 3, 51, 96–97; formation of Drexel, Morgan & Co., 97–102; forms new partnership agreement with brothers, 69; founder of J. P. Morgan, xi, xii; and government bonds during Civil War, 61–67; and Grover Cleveland, 116, 169, 170; home in West Philadelphia, 52, 97; illness of, 167–70; income of, 72, 101, 133; interest in education, 150, 153–54; invests in real estate, 142–43; joins FMD's firm, 29, 38, 41; letter of condolence from Jay Cooke, 160; marries Ellen Rosét, 45; McLeod's statements infuriate, 165; meets with JSM, 95, 213; move to Rittenhouse Square, 49, 204; and music, 141–42; names son for Childs, 76; and need for European contacts, 50, 52, 85; and need for new partners, 121–22; negotiates with Great Britain on Civil War claims, 108; opens Drexel, Harjes, 85; and Pennsylvania loan, 64, 65; and Pennsylvania Railroad, 127–28, 133–35, 165; personality and manner, 4, 114, 115, 134, 222; and Philadelphia society, 123–24; philanthropy of, 152, 153; portrait by Constant, 166; privacy, xiv, 5, 117, 133, 145, 170; and *Public Ledger*, 37, 74–75, 76, 77, 142, 210; and Reading Railroad, 130–32, 162–69; reaction to Katharine becoming a nun, 156; records of, xvi; and Reform Club, 145; relationship with children, 172–74; relationship with father, 53, 91; relationship with George W. Childs, 53–55, 77; relationship with grandsons, 126; relationship with JPM, xi, xiv, xv, 4, 97, 104, 109, 110, 128, 129, 217; relationship with Jay Cooke, 63, 65, 67, 70–71, 80, 81–82, 83, 84, 108, 134; relationship with Joseph Drexel, 110–11, 117; relationship with JSM, 131, 135–36; relationship with mother, 26; relationship with nieces, 53, 114, 126, 140, 144, 145, 151; and religion, 35, 43–44, 46, 52, 114; responsibility for bank, 39, 41, 44, 46, 68; returns account to Morgan, 86; role as mentor, xii, xv, 48, 86, 100, 132; and South Mountain

Water Company, 146; split with Joseph Drexel, 118–19, 124–25; supports prohibition of secret gold sales, 82; withdraws account from Morgan firm, 71, 85; youth and education, 26, 35, 39; will and family trusts, 172–73, 180–81

Drexel, Anthony Joseph, Jr. (son of AJD), 141, 172, 173, 181, 185, 186; divorce, 173; leaves firm, 172–73; marriage, 145; serves in World War I, 178

Drexel, Anton (brother of FMD), 67, 185, 186, 194

Drexel, C. Howard, 179

Drexel, Caroline (sister of AJD). See Watmough, Caroline Drexel

Drexel, Catherine Hookey (wife of FMD), 23, 25, 33, 185, 187; birth of children, 22, 23, 25, 26, 196, 197; and catholicism, 46, 53; death of, 139; marries FMD, 22

Drexel, Elizabeth (niece of AJD). See Smith, Elizabeth L. Drexel

Drexel, Ellen Bicking Rosét (wife of AJD), 35, 53, 97, 143, 154, 185, 187, 198, 202; birth of daughters, 53; death of, 159, 198; death of son, 76; hosts reception for Grant, 117, 145, 223; illness of, 158; marries AJD, 45, 184; and religion, 35

Drexel, Emilie Taylor (daughter of AJD). See Biddle, Emilie Taylor Drexel

Drexel, Emma Mary Bouvier (second wife of FAD), 53, 185, 185, 206; and catholicism, 53, 139; death of, 139, 140; philanthropy of, 53, 150

Drexel, Frances Katherine (daughter of AJD). See Paul, Frances Katherine Drexel

Drexel, Francis A. (Frank) (FAD, brother of AJD), 22, 45, 46, 50, 53, 104, 185, 187, 206; and catholicism, 53, 114, 139; death of, 140, 150; education of, 39; forms new partnership agreement with brothers, 69; income of, 72, 101, 133; joins FMD's firm, 38, 41; marries Hannah Langstroth, 35, 185; Morgan on, 217; and music, 141; personality of, 114; philanthropy of, 150, 151, 224; and purchase of Public Ledger, 75; widowed, 53, 126, 140; will, 224; withdraws from Drexel & Co., 140

Drexel, Francis Anthony (son of AJD), 185; death of, 76

Drexel, Francis (or Franz) Joseph (grandfather of Anthony Drexel), 9, 11, 13, 185; participates in Tyrolese revolt, 14, 194; FMD visits, 16–17; death of, 67

Drexel, Francis Martin (FMD, father of Anthony Drexel), 5, 26, 34, 35, 37, 49, 50, 53, 55, 56, 61, 64, 95, 105, 114, 177, 182, 185, 187, 198; apprentices to painter, 10; arrives in United States and settles in Philadelphia, 18, 19, 20, 21; becomes currency broker in Louisville, 29–30, 197; birth of children, 22, 23, 25, 27, 196, 197; death of, 67–68; descendants of, 177–78; devotion to Tyrolese freedom, 10; difficulties with Bernard Gallagher, 22–23; diversification of, 67; Drexel, Sather & Church, 46, 55, 202, 203; education of, 9, 10; elected to German Society of Philadelphia, 21; elected to Musical Fund Society, 21; engaged to Mary Fisher, 22; and European affiliations, 50, 51; exhibits paintings at Pennsylvania Academy of Fine Arts, 21; financial position of, 55; flees draft into Napoleonic army, 11, 12; forms Drexel & Co., 40; gives AJD major responsibility for bank, 41, 44; growth of firm, 39–40; itinerant portrait painter, 18; learns about "portable credit," 13, 25; losses due to New Brunswick Bank

INDEX

notes, 37–38; marries Catherine Hookey, 22, 185; moves to Rittenhouse Square, 49; office in Philadelphia, 33, 35, 36; opens Chicago office, 48, 203; and painting after Battle of Leipzig, 17; real estate lawsuit, 41; and religion, 46; relationship with sons, 26, 53, 91–92; sells railroad bonds, 40; starts businesses in Philadelphia, 25; teaches art at girls' seminary, 21; travels through Europe, 12–18; travels to South America, 23–25, 26; visits Dornbirn, 16–17, 195; visits France, 15–16; withdraws from firm, 55; writes memoirs, 25–26, 196

Drexel, George W. Childs (son of AJD), 76, 97, 141, 185, 185; becomes owner of Public Ledger, 173; donates Alcedo to U.S. Navy in World War I, 178; sells Public Ledger, 173, 176

Drexel, Hannah J. Langstroth (wife of FAD), 35, 53, 140, 185, 187; death of, 53, 126; philanthropy of, 224

Drexel, Heloise (sister of AJD). See Smith, Heloise Drexel

Drexel, J. Armstrong, 178
Drexel, Rev. Jeremias, 194
Drexel, John Rozet (son of AJD), 141, 173, 181, 185, 187
Drexel, Josefa Marlotte, 184
Drexel, Joseph Wilhelm (brother of AJD), xiv, 25, 50, 68, 87, 98, 111, 114, 117, 124, 177, 179, 185, 187, 196, 203; forms new partnership agreement with brothers, 69; founder of New York Philharmonic Orchestra, 141; income of, 72, 101, 133; maintains banking connections in Germany and France, 85, 111; on Morgan calling loans, 112; and purchase of Public Ledger, 75; relationship with Morgan, xiv, 110–11, 117, 118, 217;

philanthropy of, 153, 225; withdraws from Drexel, Morgan, 118, 119, 120, 121, 217

Drexel, Katharine (niece of AJD, daughter of FAD), xiii, xvi, 53, 115, 150, 154, 157, 168, 187, 224, 225; audience with Pope, 155; on Aunt Ellen's death, 159–60; on becoming a nun, 156–57, 226; and Bishop James O'Connor, 155–56; business acumen of, 150, 174; canonization of, 181, 185; courage of, 174; does not attend opening ceremonies of Drexel Institute, 159; education of, 140–41; founds Sisters of the Blessed Sacrament, 156, 157, 159; lives with AJD after father's death, 140; support of Catholic institutions for Indians and blacks, 150–51, 155. See also Sisters of the Blessed Sacrament

Drexel, Louise B.(niece of AJD). See Morrell, Louise B. Drexel
Drexel, Lucy Wharton, 185
Drexel, Mae E. (daughter of AJD). See Stewart, Mae E. Drexel
Drexel, Magdalena Wilhelm (grandmother of AJD), 16, 185
Drexel, Margarita Armstrong, 173, 185, 186
Drexel, Marie Rozet (daughter of AJD), 52, 185, 187; death of, 53
Drexel, Mary Johanna (sister of AJD). See Lankenau, Mary Johanna Drexel
Drexel, Mary S. Irick, 173, 185, 187
Drexel, Sarah (daughter of AJD). See Fell, Sarah Drexel
Drexel, Susanna (sister of FMD), 16, 185, 194
Drexel & Co., 2, 4, 72, 80, 142, 170; acceptance of outside partners, 69; AJD assumes major responsibility for, 45; AJD's sons work at, 141, 150; AJD's will provides for continuity of, 172; be-

{ 252 }

comes private investment bank and brokerage, 180; and Civil War, 68, 79, 108; closes Chicago branch, 68, 69; closes Drexel, Read, 69; construction of new facility, 147–48; and Drexel Building, 181, 182; and Edison Electric Light Co., 127; Edward Biddle and, 105, 106, 124; ends dual partnership, 180; European branch, 48–49, 85; FAD withdraws from, 140; family withdraws from, 172, 173; finances major utility projects, 179; and First National Bank of Philadelphia, 81; formation of, 40; formation of Drexel, Harjes & Co., 85, 86, 95–96; formation of syndicates, 80; George Peabody & Co. affiliation, 50, 51, 52; and gold prices, 71; and government bonds, 41, 48, 61, 63; mergers of, 180; and Mexican War, 41, 48; need for new partners, 121–22; new offices of, 50, 52, 53; New York affiliation, 48, 69; opens Drexel, Winthrop, 69; and Panama Canal syndicate, 127; and Panic of 1873, 111; and Pennsylvania loan, 64, 65; and Pennsylvania Railroad, 80, 134; performance evaluations instituted at, 122–23; and railroad bonds, 47, 127; and Reading Railroad, 162, 163, 164, 166–67; reduced to branch of J. P. Morgan & Co., 179; R. G. Dun report on, 104; "sweat equity," 86, 123; transfers funds from Morgan to Brown, Shipley & Co., 71, 85. *See also* Drexel & Smith; Drexel Burnham Lambert; Drexel, Harjes & Co.; Drexel Harriman Ripley; Drexel, Morgan & Co.; Drexel, Read & Co.; Drexel, Sather and Church; Drexel, Winthrop & Co.

Drexel & Smith (Chicago branch), 48, 203

Drexel Burnham Lambert, 180, 181; and junk bonds, 180

Drexel Firestone, 180

Drexel, Harjes & Co. (Paris branch), 85, 87, 212, 215; becomes Morgan, Harjes & Co., 175; and Franco-Prussian War, 86, 95–96; and U.S. Treasury business, 114

Drexel Harriman Ripley, 180

Drexel Institute of Science and Technology (Drexel University), 157–58, 167, 174, 181, 228; commissions portrait of AJD, 166; memorial service for AJD, 170–71; opening ceremonies, 159, 171

Drexel, Morgan & Co., xi, 118, 120, 193; builds offices in New York, 103, 104, 120; and Delaware and Hudson Canal Co., 128; finances Edison Electric Light Co., 127; formation of, 97–101; J. P. Morgan calls firm's loans, 110–11; Joseph Drexel role at, 111, 112, 119, 120; joins syndicate to sell government bonds, 108; leads Panama Canal syndicate, 127; management of, 101–2; need for new partners, 121, 122; and Panic of 1873, 113; partnership agreement, 101, 102; and Pennsylvania Railroad, 128; and Reading Railroad, 131, 164; renamed J. P. Morgan & Co., 174; and U.S. Treasury business, 114

Drexel, Read & Co. (New York branch), dissolved, 69; purchase of government bonds, 61

Drexel, Sather & Church (California branch), 46, 47, 48, 202, 203; closed, 55, 202, 206

Drexel, Winthrop & Co. (New York branch), 69, 85, 87, 98; Winthrop eased out and replaced by JPM, 96

Duke family, 177

Duke, Angier Biddle, 178, 179

Duke, Anthony Drexel, 178, 179

Dun, R. G. *See* R. G. Dun

Duncan Sherman & Co., 92, 94

Dutch Reformed church, 35, 46

E. W. Clark & Co., 62, 80; and First National Bank of Philadelphia, 81; forms syndicate with Drexel and Cooke, 80; and railroad bonds, 47, 62
Eastman, Arthur, Hall Carbine Affair, 92
Edison, Thomas Alva, 149, 159
Edison Electric Light Co., 127
1858 Investment Advisors, 182
Episcopal church, 43, 44, 114, 151
Equitable Life Insurance Society, 103
Erie Railroad, 107; Fisk and Gould take over, 81; scandal, 109. See also railroads
Evening Public Ledger, 176

Fabbri, Egisto, 122, 133, 186
Fahnestock, Harris, 70, 112
Fairmount Park Art Commission, 145, 152
Federal Reserve Act, 68, 175
Federal Reserve Board, 29, 176
Fee, Ellen, 45
Fell, Sarah Drexel. See Van Rensselaer, Sarah Drexel Fell
Fell, John R., 185
Fels, Samuel, 181
Finch-Hatton, Christopher. See Winchilsea, Christopher, 16th earl of
First National Bank of Philadelphia, 81
First National Bank of Washington, 112
Fisher, Martin, 22
Fisher, Mary, 22
Fisher, Sidney George, 33, 56
Fisk, Jim, xiv, 66, 81, 107
Fitler, Edwin, 159
Forney's War Press, 71
Fort Sumter, 59, 60, 61, 66
France, 10, 12; Drexel relief efforts, 86; FMD travels to, 15–16; Morgan role in Franco-Prussian War, 3, 94. See also Franco-Prussian War

Franciscus, James M., 29, 197
Franco-Prussian War, 3, 86, 95
Franklin, Benjamin, 21–22, 53, 73
Franklin Field. See University of Pennsylvania
Fremont, General John C., 92, 93

Gallagher, Bernard, 22–23, 25
Garrett, John, 128
Gates, Thomas S., 180
Gates, Thomas S., Jr., 180
General Electric, 175
George Peabody & Co., 92; affiliation with Drexel & Co., 50, 51, 52; taken over by JSM, 71, 87
German Society of Philadelphia, 21
Germantown Friends School, 149
Gettysburg, Battle of, 68, 69
Geyelin family, 21
Girard, Stephen, 20, 25; and Girard College, 153, 154
Girard Bank, 20; and railroad bonds, 47
Godfrey, Charles, 120, 123, 188
gold, 28, 29, 44, 46, 47; bill to prevent secret sales of, 82–84; flight from U.S. at beginning of Civil War, 60; impact on banking system, 55; Morgan purchases of, 93–94, 135; prices at Cooke and Drexel houses, 71
Goldman (private bank), 51
Goodwin, James Junius, 93, 94, 95, 99, 188
Gould family, 177
Gould, Jay, xiv, 81, 84, 107
Gowen, Franklin B., 163; attempts to monopolize coal properties, 129–30, 131; president of Reading Railroad, 129; replaced by reorganization syndicate, 132, 162; suicide of, 162, 163
Grand Army of the Republic, 152
Grant, Ulysses S., 69, 70, 78, 82, 104, 115, 117, 152; AJD holds reception for, 117,

145, 223; friendship with AJD, 4, 69, 115–16, 117, 143, 218; friendship with Childs, 69, 116, 117; and Greenback Bill, 116; offers to make AJD Secretary of the Treasury, 104, 115; receives gift of house in Philadelphia, 78, 210; scandals in administration, 112; supports Native American education, 151

Greenback Bill, 116

Grunberger, Dr. A., 167, 169, 223

Grundlock, Gottlieb, 21, 195, 21

Hall Carbine Affair, 92–93

Hambro (private bank), 45, 51

The Happiest Millionaire, 178

Harbor for Boys and Girls, 179

Harjes, Henry, 176–77

Harjes, John H., 4, 85–86, 87, 106, 144, 188; death of, 176; and Drexel, Harjes & Co., 85, 186; and Drexel, Morgan & Co., 100; relief efforts during Franco-Prussian War, 86

Harjes Brothers, 85

Harper's Weekly, 103, 175

Harris, Joseph, 166

Harris and Stotesbury, 190

Haskins, H. C., 169

Haverford College, 149

Hayes, Rutherford B., 82

The Hero in History (Hook), xiii

Hoe, Richard, 74

Hogan, Fr. William, 42–43

Hollenback family, 34

Hollenback, Matthias, 190

Holy Trinity Roman Catholic Church, 22, 43, 196

Hook, Sidney, xiii

Hookey, Anthony: and controversy in Catholic Church, 43; father of Catherine Hookey Drexel, 22, 186; founder of Holy Trinity Church, 22

Hookey, Catherine. *See* Drexel, Catherine Hookey

Hopkinson, Elisa Swain, 35

"The House of Drexel" (Carosso), xii

The House of Morgan (Chernow), xiv

The House of Morgan (Hoyt), xi, xiv

Howe, Mather & Co., 91

Hoyt, Edwin, xi

Hunt's Merchants' Magazine, 41

Huntington, Collis P., 84

Illinois Central Railroad, 81. *See also* railroads

Independence National Bank, 147

Independence National Park, 181

industrial education, 149–50

Ingersoll family, 177

International Harvester, 175

Irving, Washington, 20

J & W Seligman & Co., 51, 80, 98, 108; and U.S. Treasury business, 114

J. M. Beebe, Morgan & Co., 91

J. P. Morgan & Co., xi, xii, xiii, 92, 175; AJD role in formation, xi; and Edison Electric Light Co., 127; ends dual partnership, 180; gold purchases, 93; Hall Carbine Affair, 92–93; merged with Chase Manhattan Bank, 175, 180; and Panama Canal syndicate, 127; and Panic of 1873, 113; and railroads, 127

J. S. Morgan & Co., 95, 102, 171, 215; acquires George Peabody & Co., 87; Drexel affiliation gives superior London position, 128; Drexel moves account from, 71, 85; Drexel returns account to, 86; and Pennsylvania Railroad, 128, 165; and Reading Railroad, 163–64, 167, 228; and U.S. government bonds, 109; and U.S. Treasury business, 114

J. T. Van Vleck, Read & Co. *See* Van Vleck, Read & Drexel

Jackson, Andrew, 27–28, 182

Jackson, Helen Hunt, 155

Jarvis, Russell, 73

Jay Cooke & Co., 71, 79; collapse of, 107–8; forms syndicate with Drexel and E. W. Clarke & Co., 80; general agent for Pennsylvania state loan, 64, 65; and gold prices, 71; and First National Bank of Philadelphia, 81; and Northern Pacific Railroad, 87–88; opens branches, 67, 80; relationship with Drexel, 108, 109; sale of transportation securities, 84; and syndicate to sell government bonds, 109; and Washington and Georgetown Street Railroad Co., 81

Jay Cooke, McCulloch & Co., 80

Jefferson, Thomas, 35, 48

Jefferson Medical College, 116

Jersey Central Railroad, 163

Joffre, General Joseph Jacques, 178

Journal of Commerce, 104

Kane, Elisha Kent, 54

Kennedy, Jacqueline Bouvier, 177

Kenyon, Cox & Co., 112

Ketchum, Edward, 93

Krone, Ludwig, 14, 15

Kuhn family, 51

Kuhn, Loeb & Co., 80, 108

Kyle, Alexander, 55

Langstroth, Hannah. *See* Drexel, Hannah Langstroth

Laning family, 34

Laning, Mary, 190

Laning, "Pretty Polly" Hollenback, 34

Lankenau, John D., 185, 188; co-executor of FAD's estate, 151; German Hospital renamed for, 152

Lankenau, Mary Johanna Drexel (sister of AJD), 22, 185, 188

Lankenau Hospital, 152

Law Dictionary (Bouvier), 184, 205

Latrobe, Benjamin, 20

Lazard Frères (Paris), 85

Lea, Henry Charles, 145, 170

LeBrun, Napoleon, 50

Lee, General Robert E., 68, 69, 78

Lehigh Coal & Navigation Co., 80

Lehigh Valley Railroad, 163. *See also* railroads

Lewis family, 20

Loeb (private bank), 51

London Times, 170

Long Branch, New Jersey, 69

Louisiana Purchase, 48

Louisville, Kentucky, 29, 33

Louisville and Nashville Railroad, 40

Ludlow, John, 188

Ludlow, Dr. John Livingston, 46, 68, 76, 188

Ludlow, Mary Ann Rozet, 46, 190

Lutheran church, 35

Mackay, Alexander, 33

MacManes, James, 145–46

Maidstone, Christopher, 178

Manes, Henry, xii

Manley, Mr., 37

Market Street. *See* Philadelphia, financial district

Markoe family, 20

Marshall, James, 44

Marty, Martin, 43

McAlmont family, 130

McCulloch, Hugh, 70; partner of Jay Cooke, 80, 186; consults with AJD, 116

McKean, William V., 76, 83, 84, 186

McLeod, Archibald A., 110, 216, 222; becomes president of New York & New

England Railroad, 175; becomes president of Reading Railroad, 163, 186; begins extreme expansion of Reading, 163; 166; blames AJD for difficulties, 164–65; third failure of Reading, 164; resigns, 164. *See also* Reading Railroad

McParlan, James, 129–30

Mellon family, 177

Merchants Exchange, 35

Metropolitan Opera, 142

Mexican War, 41, 60, 69

Meyer, John, 12

Milan Academy of Fine Arts, 12

Milken, Michael, 180

Molly Maguires, 129–30

money shaving. *See* currency

Montgomery, Mr., and New Brunswick Bank notes, 37

Montgomery, Alabama, 59

Moore, Henry D., 64, 65

Moorhead, J. B., 47

Moorhead, William, 47

Morgan: American Financier (Strouse), xii

Morgan, George H., 94, 95

Morgan, John, 102

Morgan, J. Pierpont (JPM), xi, xii, xiii, xvi, 4, 29, 87, 88, 106, 107, 102, 109–10, 131, 189, 215, 219, 222; attends opening of Drexel Institute, 159; business practices, 135; calls Drexel, Morgan loans, 110; distraught at AJD's death, 171; education of, 92; first meeting with AJD, 1, 2, 3, 9, 51, 96–97; and formation of Drexel, Morgan & Co., 97–101; and gold purchases, 93; Hall Carbine Affair, 93; health of, 3, 95, 97, 109; on Joseph Drexel, xiv, 111; makes Goodwin partner in firm, 93; net worth, 101, 133, 213; new partners for Drexel, Morgan, 121; and New York Central Railroad,

128–29, 132; R. G. Dun report on, 3, 94, 109; and railroad market, 132–33, 135; and Reading Railroad, 132, 162–64, 166–67, 175; relationship with Cooke, 108, 113; relationship with AJD, xi, xiv, xv, 4, 97, 104, 109, 110, 128, 129, 135–36, 228; relationship with father, 91–92, 94, 110; renames firm J. P. Morgan & Co., 175; split with Joseph Drexel, 117, 118, 124; Seligman's description of, xiv; streamlines American economy, 175; and U.S. Treasury business, 114, 127

Morgan, Joseph (father of JSM), 91; organizes Aetna Fire Insurance Co., 91

Morgan, Junius Spencer (JSM, father of JPM), xi, xii, xvi, 87, 91, 92, 98, 108, 111, 113, 122, 129, 172, 189, 219; affiliation with George Peabody, 51; arranges son's first meeting with AJD, 2, 95, 96; bonds for Franco-Prussian War, 3; death of, 160; formation of Drexel, Morgan & Co., 98, 99, 100; Hall Carbine Affair, 93; knowledge of railroad financing, 127; loans to French government, 94; net worth, 101, 133; partnership with Drexel, 101; and Pennsylvania Railroad, 134; and Reading Railroad, 130; relationship with AJD, 86, 87, 95, 131, 213; relationship with Cooke, 108, 109; relationship with son, xv, 91–92, 94, 110; and South Mountain Water Company, 146; takes over Peabody & Co., 71, 87

Morgan, Harjes & Co., 175

Morgan, Miles, 91

The Morgans (Carosso), xii

Morrell, Edward, 187, 224

Morrell, Louise B. Drexel (niece of AJD), 150, 154, 167, 168, 189, 224; education of, 140–41; lives with AJD after father's death, 140; philanthropy of, 151–52

Morton, Levi P., 108, 109, 114, 189; partner

of JSM, 91; attends opening of Drexel Institute, 159
Morton, Bliss & Co., 108, 109, 114, 120
Munroe & Co., 85
Musical Fund Society, 21

Nalle family, 21
Napoleonic Wars, 10, 11, 12
National Banking Act of 1863, 68, 81
National City Bank, 69, 96, 99
National Cordage Company, 165
national debt. *See* U.S. Treasury
National Endowment for the Arts, 179
National Republican, 104
National Science Foundation, 181
Native American Party, 42
Native Americans, 151, 155, 174, 225, 226
Neubauer, Dr., 167
New Brunswick Bank Notes, 37–38
New Century Guild, 153, 158
New York & Harlem Railroad, 55. *See also* railroads
New York & New England Railroad, 163, 175
New York & New Haven Railroad: Reading encroaches on, 163; stock watering, 55
New York Central Railroad: financing, 128–29; "peace pact" with Pennsylvania Railroad, 132; Reading encroaches on, 131, 163
New York Herald, 73, 76, 117
New York Journal-American, 177
New York Press, 176
New York Stock Exchange, 98, 103; JPM rescues in Panic of 1907, 175; and New York Central financing, 129; Panic of 1873, 113
New York Times, 75, 176
New York Tribune, 112
Newbold family, 21, 195

North Missouri Railroad, 80
Northern Pacific Railroad, 87, 88, 107, 132, 134, 140

Ochs, Adolph, 176
O'Connor, James, Vicar of Nebraska, 150–51, 155, 156, 226
O'Farrell, Noreen Drexel, 179
Ohio Insurance and Trust Company, 55

Panama, 46, 47, 202; Canal, 127
Panic of 1857, 29, 39, 55, 56, 62
Panic of 1873, 113, 114, 118, 164, 166
Panic of 1893, 165, 174
Panic of 1895, 175
Panic of 1907, 175
Paul, Frances Katherine Drexel ("Nanny"), 52, 122, 141, 181, 185, 189; and music, 142; death of, 160–61
Paul, James W., Jr., 185, 189; partner in Drexel & Co., 122, 141; remains at firm after AJD's death, 172, 187
Paul, Maury H. B., 177
"Pauline." *See* Allez, Mary Paul Munn
Peabody, George, xv, 47, 51, 91, 99, 127, 214
Peabody, S. Endicott, 214
Peale, Rembrandt, 20, 21
Peirce College, 150
Penn, William, 20, 42
Pennsylvania: bond issues, 64, 65, 80; Confederate incursions into, 68
Pennsylvania Academy of Fine Arts, 20, 21
Pennsylvania Convention Center, 175
Pennsylvania Railroad, 1, 2, 96, 133, 142; "peace pact" with New York Central Railroad, 132; and Reading Railroad, 131; relationship with Drexel & Co., 80, 127–28, 133–34, 135; relationship with Speyer & Co., 134, 165
Pennsylvania Supreme Court, 41
Pennypacker family, 20

Penrose, Boies, 24, 119

Pepper family, 20

The Perennial Philadelphians (Burt), xv

Peterson, Robert E., 54, 184, 205, 206

Philadelphia, 20, 25, 33; Awful Riots in, 42; City Hall, 146, 148; Civil War unites, 60; cultural and financial development of, 20; educational opportunities in, 149; financial district, 35, 36, 38; FMD arrives at, 18–19; and immigrants, 34; and railroads, 44; and religion, 20, 42–44; social order, 21, 33–34, 123–24

Philadelphia & Erie Railroad. *See* Sunbury and Erie Railroad

Philadelphia & Reading Railroad. *See* Reading Railroad

Philadelphia Bulletin, 75, 159, 170

Philadelphia Centennial Exposition, 158

Philadelphia Electric Company, 179

Philadelphia Inquirer, 74, 176

Philadelphia Gas Trust, 145–46, 147

Philadelphia Orchestra, 173

Philadelphia Public Ledger, xii, 4, 37, 38, 50, 54, 73, 142, 154, 170, 185; AJD ownership, 37, 210; announces establishment of Drexel Institute, 157; Childs purchases, 75, 77; circulation, 75–76; critical of Cooke, 82, 83, 107; editorial policy of, 73, 74; George Drexel becomes proprietor, 173; McLeod on, 165; on New Brunswick Bank Notes manipulation, 38; on Northern Pacific Railroad, 107; openly opposes political patronage, 81; on Reading Railroad, 130; supports legislation prohibiting secret gold sales, 82–83, 84; sale of, 173, 176; technological improvements, 73–74

Philadelphia Stock Exchange, 49, 148

Philadelphia Times, 156

Pierpont Morgan Library, xii

Pinkerton Agency, 129

Port Folio, 20

Potter, Henry Codman, xii, 4, 158, 171

Pratt Institute, 154

Princeton, New Jersey, 25, 26

Protestant Banner, 42

Protestant revivalism, 42

Public Service Electric and Gas Company of New Jersey, 179

Publishers Weekly, 73

Pullman, George, 163

Quakers, 43; influence in Philadelphia, 20; and religious tolerance, 42; opposed to slavery, 60; secondary schools run by, 149

Quay, Matthew, 147

R. G. Dun: report on J. P. Morgan, 3, 94, 110; report on FMD, 68; report on Drexel & Co., 68, 104

railroads, 39, 40, 55, 56, 63, 112, 113, 127–36, 149; and banking houses, 127, 133–34; and European investment, 48; financing, 40, 47, 62, 80, 81, 84, 86, 87, 88; growth of stimulates U.S. economy, 127; and JPM stabilizing influence, 135, 175; and Panic of 1893, 165, 166; stock manipulation, 55. *See also* individual railroads

Reading Railroad, 67, 162, 163–69, 175, 176, 222; coal operations, 129, 130, 163; construction, 131; Drexel, Morgan and reorganization syndicate, 131–32; Gowen removed as president, 132; impact of on U.S. economy, 130; and J. L. Welsh, 132; and McLeod, 163; receivership of, 131, 162; syndicate of investors, 163; third failure, 163–64, 167, 168, 228, 164, 166, 167

Reading Terminal, 162, 163

Reform Club, 145, 170

Rieder (artist), 21
Riggs, Julia. *See* Boker, Julia Riggs
Rittenhouse family, 20
Roberts, George, 134, 165
Robinson, John Norris, 98, 101, 118, 187, 189
Roca, Bernardo, 24
Rogers, Jacob C., 187
Roosevelt family, 177
Rosét, Ellen. *See* Drexel, Ellen Bicking Rosét
Rosét, Jacques Marie, 34, 189; and religion, 35
Rosét (Rozét), John, 34, 35, 189
Rothschild bank, 45, 46, 51, 80, 98, 108, 109, 216; and U.S. Treasury business, 114; and U.S. railroads, 128
Rothschild, Hannah Mayer, 46
Rozet, Antoinette (Elizabeth). *See* Brodhead, Antoinette Rozet
Rozet, George Hollenback, 190
Rozet, Mary Ann. *See* Ludlow, Mary Ann Rozet
Rozet, Sarah. *See* Smith, Sarah Rozet
Runge, Gustavus, 50
Runnemede, 126, 140, 143, 158, 220
Rush, Benjamin, 35
Rutgers family, 177
Ryan, Archbishop Patrick, 151

Sailer, Joseph, 73
St. Francis de Sales Industrial School, 152
St. Joseph's Church, 42, 43
St. Mary's Church, 42, 43
St. Mary's Convent, 156
Saronno, Italy, 10, 12
Sather & Church, 202
Saturday Evening Post, 176
Save the Children, 179
School of Industrial Art, 154
Schuyler, Robert, 55

Seligman family, 51, 79–80
Seligman, Joseph, xiv, 111, 116
Seligman, & Co. *See* J & W Seligman & Co.
Seligman Frères (Paris), 85, 108
silver, 28, 29
Sisters of the Blessed Sacrament, 159, 174, 226
Sloan, Samuel, 52, 205
Smith, Charles M., 190, 203
Smith, Elizabeth L. Drexel (niece of AJD), 53, 115, 141, 143, 150, 154, 190; death of, 160; education of, 140–41; lives with AJD after father's death, 140; philanthropy of, 151–52
Smith, Heloise Drexel (sister of AJD), 27, 185, 190
Smith, James Charles, 185
Smith, Sarah Roset, 190, 203
Smith, Walter G., 190
Snyder, Simon, 22
Society for the Prevention of Cruelty to Animals, 152
South Mountain Water Company, 146
South Sea Bubble, 28, 107
Specie Circular (1856), 28
Speyer & Co., 134, 165
Spring Garden College (Institute), 150, 152, 154
Stebbins, James, 169
Stevens, Simon, 92, 93
Stewart, Charles T., 185
Stewart, Mae E. Drexel, 53, 141, 185, 190;
Stock Board (Philadelphia), 59
Stotesbury, Edward T., 115, 123, 190
Stotesbury, Thomas, 190
Strawbridge, Justus, 146
streetcars, 140
Strickland, William, 20
Strouse, Jean, xii
Stuart, George H., 78

Stuart, Gilbert, 20, 23
Students for a Democratic Society, 179
Sub-Treasury Building, 103
Sully, Thomas, 20, 21
Sunbury and Erie Railroad, 47
Swain, Elisa. *See* Hopkinson, Elisa Swain
Swain, William M., 73, 74, 188
Swarthmore College, 149
Switzerland, 9, 11, 12, 13, 14, 16, 17, 18

Tammany Hall, 66
taxation. *See* U.S. Treasury
Taylor, Moses, 69, 96
Taylor, Zachary, 69, 70
technology, post-Civil War advances in, 70
Third Reformed Dutch Church, 46
Third Street. *See* Philadelphia, financial district
Thomas, George C., 190
Thurnher, Caspar, 11, 12
Tiarks, Caspar, 178
Tiarks, Henrietta Finch-Hatton, 178
Tiarks, Sue, 178
Train, Frances Cheston, 174
Trinity Church, New York, 103
Trumbull, Lyman, 81, 211
Turner, Eliza Sproat, 153, 158
Tweed, William M. ("Boss"), 107
Tyrol, 9, 10, 11, 14, 17, 194

Union Pacific Railroad, 107
United Gas Improvement Company, 179
United States Steel, 175
United States Treasury, 41; and Civil War, 60–61, 63, 64, 67; Drexel expands relationship with, 48; Drexel, Morgan markets securities of, 127; dwindling reserves, 176; and Jay Cooke, 65, 82; and Mexican War, 41, 60; national debt, 60; and secret gold sales, 82, 84; shifts bro-

kers after Cooke's failure, 113–14; taxation, 60
University of Pennsylvania, 46, 149, 152; Drexel & Co. finances Franklin Field, 179; Drexel & Co. rescues from debts, 180; Palestra, 179

Van Rensselaer, Alexander, 173, 185, 190
Van Rensselaer, Sarah Drexel Fell ("Sallie"), 53, 141, 171, 173, 185, 188
Van Vleck, Read & Drexel, 48
Vanderbilt family, 177
Vanderbilt, Cornelius, 66, 84
Vanderbilt, William, 128–29, 131
Vassar, Matthew, 153
Vauclain family, 21
Vermilye & Co., 80
Vermont Central Railroad, 63
Vicksburg, Battle of, 69
Vorarlberg, 10, 11

W. H. Newbold & Son, 21, 195
Wagner, Richard, 142
Walker, Pamela Drexel, 179
Wanamaker, John, 146, 150, 163
Watmough, Caroline Drexel, 27, 55, 185, 190
Watmough, John Goddard, 185, 190
Warburgs (private bank), 45
Ward, Samuel G., 49
Washington and Georgetown Street Railroad Co., 81
Washington Packet and Transportation Company, 62
Wayne, Pennsylvania, 153, 154
Webster, Daniel, 39
Welsh, John Lowber, 121, 132, 166, 188
Wharton family, 177
Wharton, Lucy, 185
Whig, 26
Whitney family, 177

Widener, P. B., 66, 67
William Penn Charter School, 149
Wilson, Joseph M., 158
Wilson, Woodrow, 175
Winchilsea, Countess of, 178
Winchilsea, Christopher Finch-Hatton, 16th earl of, 179
Winthrop, Eugene, 85, 86, 191
Winthrop, Robert, 69, 85, 87, 96, 98, 99, 172, 191

Wistar (Wister) family, 20
Wollstonecraft, Mary, 12
Wright, D. W., xii, xiii–xiv
Wright, J. Hood, 101, 118, 120, 122, 133, 191, 214
Wyeth family, 177

Xavier University, 174